LAW FIRM MANAGEMENT

WOMEN OF
THE WOMAN'S GUIDE TO
POWER IN LAW

MW00861788

2010 Edition

Ida O. Abbott, J.D.

WEST.

A Thomson Reuters business

For Customer Assistance Call 1-800-328-4880

Mat #40887613

About the Association of Legal Administrators

Association of Legal Administrators (ALA), *Your connection to knowledge, resources and networking*, is the premier management resource for the legal profession. Founded in 1971, it is the largest international association providing support to professionals involved in the management of law firms, corporate legal departments, and governmental agencies. ALA represents legal management professionals who are thought leaders and industry experts on legal management issues such as finance, human resources, systems and technology, facilities, marketing, and practice management. ALA provides high-quality educational opportunities and services to more than 10,000 members in 30 countries. ALA also operates the Legal Management Resource Center (LMRC), *http://thesource.alanet.org*, an online resource that answers legal management questions. To learn more about ALA visit *www.alanet.org* or call 847. 267.1252.

Association of Legal Administrators

75 Tri-State International
Suite 222
Lincolnshire, IL 60069-4435
Phone 847.267.1252
Web site: *www.alanet.org*

In Memoriam

D.J. Lantonio

Whose efforts on behalf of this series have been invaluable

About the Author

Ida O. Abbott, J.D., President of Ida Abbott Consulting LLC, is an internationally recognized leader in the field of lawyers' professional development. Her firm specializes in helping employers develop, retain, and advance talented lawyers, and in helping talented lawyers achieve career success. She has more than 30 years of experience as a practicing lawyer and consultant to law firms, and is an elected Fellow of the College of Law Practice Management. Ida is co-founder and Director of the Hastings Leadership Academy for Women at the University of California Hastings College of the Law, where she is also a Faculty Fellow. She serves as co-Chair of the Women in Law Empowerment Forum, sits on the Advisory Board of the New York Women's Bar Association Foundation, and leads the Women Managing Partners Roundtable. Her company, Ida Abbott Consulting LLC, works with law firms of all sizes, and with individual lawyers and leaders, throughout the world. www.IdaAbbott.com

DEDICATION:

To my parents, Genia and Rubin Offenbach, for their boundless love, extraordinary resilience, and inspiring example.

INTRODUCTION: Women in law firm leadership: Why it matters

There is not a single statistic or survey that says women lawyers have achieved equality in terms of pay, position, power, or opportunity.

—Diane Yu, 2008

This book is for women who want to be leaders in their firms — or think they might — and want some guidance to help them achieve their aspirations. It is for women who hope to be in charge or find themselves in charge and want to be the best leaders possible. It explains how women can make the most of their personal strengths, build critical alliances, and overcome the obstacles in their way to achieve their leadership goals. While the focus is on women, this book is not just for women. By explaining the dynamics of leadership in the unique setting of a law firm, it shows all lawyers how to become effective law firm leaders. It opens the door into law firm leadership so that highly motivated women and men can walk through.

Why do we need a book on leadership for women in law firms? There are thousands of books on leadership, and many of them focus on women. But none of them tell women who aspire to leadership how to overcome the unique challenges they will confront along the way. This book is intended to provide insights, information, and tools to help women in law firms create the strategies they need to become the successful leaders they want to be. It tells women what to do now to become leaders without waiting for law firms to change, and how to be more effective in carrying out their responsibilities and change agendas when they are leaders.

Law firms are harsh work environments. For women in particular, they are among the most difficult professional settings in which to achieve success.[1] In a large national study of women in 10 professional fields, "the line tracking women's share of leadership roles follows a straighter downward path as the potential to assume a leadership role rises, than in any other professional

---

[1]*The White House Project report: Benchmarking women's leadership* (Nov. 2009), http://benchmarks.thewhitehouseproject.org; US Equal Employment Opportunity Commission [EEOC] (2003), *EEOC diversity in law firms study.*

sector."[2] In order to break into the inner circles of law firm power, women need to understand what leadership means in a law firm and how to operate effectively within that context. Rather than wait for the playing field to be truly equal, women need to be able to play the game on the field as it is. As they succeed, they can—and will—change the rules of the game.

Law firms hire women and men with similar levels of intelligence, education, skills, talents, and commitment. None of these attributes are gender-based. When women start their careers as associates in law firms, they possess these traits to the same degree as male associates. But something happens along the way that discourages them from becoming law firm partners and leaders. Unlike male associates, whose interest in partnership grows with their years in private practice, women lose interest in partnership the longer they work in a firm.[3] Even women who do become partners frequently leave for other types of jobs or remain in the firm but do not become the law firm leaders they could be.[4]

The virtual absence of women at the top underscores the institutional and professional factors that favor men and disadvantage women in law firms. Women have been at least 40% of law school graduates for more than a generation. During that time, women and men have been entering private practice in law firms in about equal numbers, and in firms of 100 lawyers or more, women have started at a higher rate than men.[5] Given the number of women who have begun their careers in private law firms over nearly three decades, we would expect to see them well represented in upper law firm ranks. But numerical parity at the entry level has not translated into equality at upper levels. In 2010, though women constitute more than one-third of lawyers, they remain appallingly underrepresented in every position of leadership and influence in law firms. While men's representation increases at every level of seniority and leadership,

---

[2]*The White House Project report* (Nov. 2009).

[3]Hildebrandt International (2007), *Understanding associates: new perspectives on associate satisfaction and morale.*

[4]One 2007 study by the MIT Workplace Center found that 15% of women partners, vs. one percent of men, leave their firms. Harrington, M., & Hsi, H. (2007). *Women lawyers and obstacles to leadership: a report of MIT Workplace Center surveys on comparative career decisions and attrition rates of women and men in Massachusetts law firms*, MIT Workplace Center.

[5]NALP (Aug. 2003), Employment patterns — 20 year trends — 1982 — 2002, *NALP Bulletin.*

women's representation declines sharply.[6]

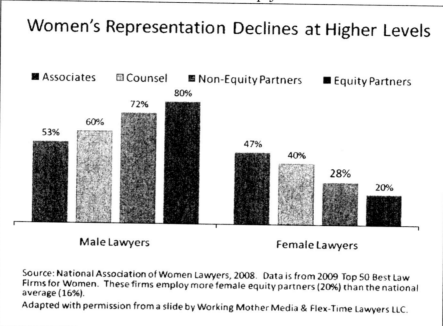

Women's Representation Declines at Higher Levels

■ Associates   ▦ Counsel   ■ Non-Equity Partners   ■ Equity Partners

Male Lawyers: 53%, 60%, 72%, 80%

Female Lawyers: 47%, 40%, 28%, 20%

Source: National Association of Women Lawyers, 2008. Data is from 2009 Top 50 Best Law Firms for Women. These firms employ more female equity partners (20%) than the national average (16%).

Adapted with permission from a slide by Working Mother Media & Flex-Time Lawyers LLC.

The higher up you look at every level of leadership, the smaller percentage of women you find. Women represent only 19.21% of all partners and 16% of equity partners; they hold only six percent of top leadership positions; and they are less than one percent of the most highly compensated lawyers in law firms. Catalyst estimates that at the current rate of advancement, women will not achieve parity with men in law firm partnerships until 2086.[7]

While individual women have achieved prominence in law firms, attained highly respected leadership positions, made great sums of money, and exerted considerable influence, they did so by overcoming pervasive bias and daunting obstacles that men did not have to face.

Today's women lawyers are not as willing to tolerate this situation. They are better informed and have more choices than they ever had in the past. Women with the intelligence, education, and drive that have led them to pursue legal careers also

---

[6]Working Mother Magazine & Flex-Time Lawyers LLC (Sept. 2009), *Best law firms for women — executive summary*, http://www.flextimelawyers.com/best/press20.pdf.

[7]Catalyst (2009), *Women in law: quick takes.*

have the wherewithal to seek and create opportunities for success in other practice settings. They are sought by business, government, and other employers that offer attractive career opportunities in less constricting work environments. Women take advantage of these opportunities because they are impatient with the lack of change in their firms and reluctant to keep fighting for change when past struggles have borne little fruit. They are more likely to leave, and to leave more quickly, for work environments where they believe professional advancement and recognition are more open to them and where they can find greater career flexibility. It is not that women are unable to become partners or leaders in law firms; it is that the law firm workplace is so unwelcoming that they become discouraged and move to places where they can apply their talents and achieve success with fewer impediments.

We have known of this situation for years. Dozens of books and published reports probe why women leave firms and analyze why those who stay do not achieve leadership roles.[8] Most of this literature reaches similar conclusions as to the primary reason for women's absence from the highest levels of law firms: persistent bias that translates into barriers to advancement. This bias, whether overt or unconscious, leads to harmful assumptions about women's competence and commitment to practice; fewer mentors and developmental work assignments; inadequate support for practice and business development; and inflexible career expectations that penalize women for having responsibilities and priorities outside of work. One especially problematic manifestation is law firms' insistence on an outdated "one size fits all" career model that is inherently unsuitable for most women lawyers, especially those with children. This entrenched and narrow view prevents the career and schedule flexibility that women need, and it causes women to leave law firms prematurely when they cannot resolve work-life conflicts.

Numerous publications also prescribe concrete steps, programs and policies to eliminate the biases, destroy the barriers, and help women become leaders.[9] Any firm that wants to keep and advance women into leadership can find many excellent resources

---

[8]See, e.g., Epstein, C.F. (1993), *Women in law* (2d Ed.) (Urbana: University of Illinois Press); Rhode, D.L. (2001), *The unfinished agenda: women and the legal profession*, ABA Commission on Women in the Legal Profession; English, H. (2003), *Gender on trial: sexual stereotypes and work/life balance in the legal workplace* (New York: ALM Publishing). Many other references are cited throughout this book.

[9]See, e.g., ABA Commission on Women in the Profession (2008). *From visible invisibility to visibly successful*, American Bar Association; Catalyst (2001), *Making change: advancing women in law firms*; Harrington, M., Williams, J.C.,

and examples to guide them. But law firms are extremely slow to change, especially when they do not feel an urgent need to do so, and very few firms have made the commitment and exerted the effort to implement the recommended changes in a comprehensive way.

Because the barriers remain firmly in place for women after all these years, they deter many highly talented and motivated women, with and without children, from trying to become leaders or even partners in their firms. When there are few women with respect, recognition, and influence equal to their male peers, many women lawyers conclude that they cannot succeed in the firm, so they leave. This becomes a chronic problem, because it deprives firms of a possible cure: women leaders, role models, and mentors who might inspire other women to stay and advance into leadership.

The situation is not entirely bleak and we are starting to see progress. Some law firms have begun to realize that retaining and advancing women lawyers is vital to their business survival. Enlightened firms also recognize that having women in leadership gives them an edge in recruiting and hiring, makes them more attractive to many clients, and gives them a competitive advantage in the marketplace. These firms have taken steps in the right direction by codifying policies and adopting programs that address women's concerns. They sponsor firm wide women's initiatives, offer training for women in business development and opportunities for leadership development, and adopt parenting leave, reduced-hour policies, and extended leave with re-entry options.

As beneficial as these measures are, however, most of them are programmatic, not transformational. Many of these initiatives are designed to help women operate better in a man's world, which is essential but not enough. They fail to confront the real problem, which is the underlying assumption that the world will remain as it is, dominated by men and based on a man-centered economic and leadership model.

That assumption is wrong. Women are in the legal profession to

---

Calvert, C.T., & English, H. (2007), *Advancing women in the profession: action plans for women's bar associations*, Report on the conference; National Association of Women Lawyers (2008), *Actions for advancing women in law firm leadership*; The Opt-In-Project (2007), Heller Ehrman LLP, http://sites.google.com/a/optinproject.org/www/; Women's Bar Association of the District of Columbia (2006), *Creating pathways to success*; New York City Bar Association (2006), *Best practices for the hiring, training, retention & advancement of women attorneys*; Rikleen, L.S. (2006), *Ending the gauntlet: removing barriers to women's success in the law*.

stay and their sizeable presence will ineluctably change law firm norms and culture. The process has been painfully slow, but as more women move into leadership, the changes will speed up. In order to retain the enormous pool of leadership talent that women represent, firms will have to tear down the fundamental cultural and structural barriers that continue to exclude women from leadership even when they have the skills and put in the effort required for success. They will have to change their work culture and power structure to embrace women, valuing their differences from as well as their similarities to men. To do that will take education to eliminate bias; better work and talent management systems; acceptance of leadership approaches and styles to which firms are not now accustomed; and a different economic model that values more than billable hours and rewards all contributions to the health, stature, and profitability of the firm. This amounts to a cultural and systemic revolution and it will face stiff resistance and require passionate and determined women leaders. It will happen; the question is not whether but how soon.

All of the developments we have been seeing herald an opportune moment for women to take the controls and propel this burgeoning change movement forward. The current recession is accelerating the momentum for change and women leaders need to be actively involved in order to steer their firms in the right direction. Without women leaders engaged in the change process, the progress that has been made to date could be erased and conditions for women could get worse instead of better.

Women must exploit the incipient willingness of firms to consider new economic models, family-friendly policies, and flexible career paths, and expand that willing attitude into a genuine and broad-based commitment to institutional change. After decades of slow and incremental progress, women cannot wait any longer for law firms to drive the initiative. Too much time has passed with few tangible results. Women must stand up and take charge. Women who have earned the right to sit at the table of power are ready to claim their seats, and they need not wait to be invited.

Individually and collectively, women possess considerable power that can be brought to bear to help law firms become places where women can have the same good work, rewards, and career satisfaction that men have always enjoyed. Women represent 31.6% of all lawyers nationwide[10] and in many firms they make up half or more of the associates. They have skills, experience and client

---

[10]ABA Commission on Women in the Profession (2008), *A current glance at women in the law 2008*, American Bar Association. http://www.abanet.org/women/CurrentGlanceStatistics2008.pdf.

relationships that firms rely on, and some women partners control a substantial amount of business. If women harnessed and exerted their power, firms would be shocked at how much they depend on women lawyers because firms take their women lawyers for granted. They mistakenly assume that the pipeline of women associates will continue to supply their needs so they can afford to let individual women remain frustrated and leave.

Considering the force women represent in the profession, they have been surprisingly meek in gathering and asserting their collective power. Women will only be able to achieve their personal goals and implement their vision for a better law firm if they are able to turn this potential clout into a base of real and effective power in their firms. So women need to understand more fully where power comes from in a law firm and how they can get it. They need to recognize the power they have and use it to accomplish the things that are important to them. As Stanford Business School professor Jeffrey Pfeffer points out in his book, Managing with Power, "Knowledge without power is of remarkably little use. And power without the skill to employ it effectively is likely to be wasted."[11]

Women who want to succeed on their own terms and create better career conditions for the women who follow them need to set their sights high and make the right moves to get where they want to go. Whether a firm actively supports women's advancement or the management team still doesn't get it, women must take the lead. Those women already in or poised for leadership roles can show the way. You can implore other women to stay at the firm, support each other's dreams of success, and invite them to join you on the journey to the summit. This book can serve as your guide.

Why should women become law firm leaders?

Being a leader takes a great deal of time and energy. It is filled with responsibilities and fraught with risk, is often contentious, and does not bring glory or even gratitude from those who are led. So why should women bother with leadership? Because it is good for women individually, for women lawyers collectively, and for the firms in which they practice.

Leadership gives you control over your career. There is little secu-

---

[11]Pfeffer, J. (1994), *Managing with power* (Boston: Harvard Business School Press).

rity for anyone in private practice today. Women who want control over their careers must establish their own sources of career security. In law firms, those sources are a book of business, strong client relationships, and close connections to other lawyers in the firm who respect you. These factors are also the bases for law firm leadership.

Being a leader makes it possible for you to protect your interests and your future. Leadership enables you to get things done, shape the direction of your career, and influence the firm's business strategy. Leadership gives you access to information and resources that support your practice; it expands your network and builds your reputation inside and outside the firm; and it helps you engage other people to help you achieve your goals for yourself, your clients, and the firm.

If you do not become a leader, you cede control over much of your career to those who do. You let others set the work conditions, policies, strategic direction, and support for your practice. You have less input into decisions about your status and compensation. In short, if you are not a leader, you give up a great deal of autonomy and self-determination.

Leadership gives you new ways to excel. Many women who go into law practice enjoy being in charge, helping others, and making a difference in the world. They are internally driven to become leaders; they like being leaders and are good at it. Before they ever join a law firm they have been leaders in school, community activities, social and political causes, and previous careers. If you are highly motivated to lead, law firms offer many kinds of leadership opportunities. You can take leadership positions on committees and task forces, as head of a department or practice group, as managing partner of an office or the firm, and as leader of a client team or client relationship. In all of these roles, you can demonstrate and perfect your leadership skills, acquire valuable leadership experience, and feel a sense of great accomplishment.

Leadership can also reinvigorate your career. Many women find that when they achieve mastery in one area, they look around for new challenges. Being a law firm leader requires learning and exercising new skills that are very different from your legal skills and expertise as a practicing lawyer. Leadership gives you a chance to operate in a new arena and master new skills without leaving your firm. You get to work closely with, and learn from, colleagues who have different abilities and perspectives, including executive level managers in the firm. As a leader, you will expand your thinking by spending more time looking outside the firm to track trends in the marketplace and follow new developments in the business of law. As a representative of your firm, you will have the opportunity to interact with other leaders from other firms and industries.

Creating a new leadership persona can be exhilarating. If you enjoy constantly learning new things and desire variation in your career, then leadership will stimulate your mind and satisfy your craving. If you like to push beyond your comfort level, to test yourself in new ways, and to forge new paths, then leadership may be just what you need.

Being a leader means you can be a change agent. Leadership is about dealing with change. Whether creating your own vision of where the firm should go or responding to external forces, leadership involves producing and coping with change. As a leader, you can set and implement agendas for change. You can create a vision and enlist others to carry it out. You can work with like-minded women and men who have the desire and the will to tear down barriers, eliminate biases, and change the dynamics of power relationships in order to build new models of law practice. You can move toward a culture that is supportive and humane, not solely profit-driven and hours-based. Law firm leadership is the "critical foundation on which a positive culture can be built."[12] You can only make that happen if you take the lead.

The absence of women from law firm leadership has resulted in law firms whose culture, power structure, and leadership look much the same today as they have for generations. It is widely acknowledged that this law firm model is broken,[13] but the people who benefit from the model are in no hurry to change it. It is women, minorities, and other disempowered lawyers who will benefit the most from change. Women cannot overcome powerlessness or unfair expectations unless they actively lead efforts to abolish these conditions. They cannot effectively fight institutional bias unless they become leaders in sufficient numbers to overturn the perceptions that allow bias to continue. They cannot control their own careers in law firms unless they participate in setting the standards and redesigning the systems that determine career success. If women shun leadership roles, they allow current

---

[12]Rikleen, L.S. (2006), *Ending the gauntlet: removing barriers to women's success in the law* (Thomson/Legalworks), 289.

[13]Ribstein, L E., (Sept. 2009), The death of big law, University of Illinois Law & Economics Research Paper No. LE09-025; Rikleen, (2006), *Ending the gauntlet;* Chesler, "E.R. (Dec. 2008), Kill the billable hour," *Forbes Magazine,* http://www.forbes.com/forbes/2009/0112/026.html; Chandler, M., Cisco General Counsel on state of technology in the law, Jan. 25, 2007, http://blogs.cisco.com/news/comments/cisco_general_counsel_on_state_of_technology_in_the_law/.

inequities to continue.

In a seminal paper on women lawyers in 1987, law professor Carrie Menkel-Meadow contemplated "whether women who enter the profession will conform to a 'male' model of what it means to be a legal professional or whether the profession will innovate and adapt to new, previously excluded, entrants who may have new perspectives to offer on how the practice of law can be conducted."[14] Until now, most women who aspired to reach the top have adapted to the male model of law practice. To succeed in their firms, they played by the boys' rules. Sometimes the boys bent the rules to accommodate them but the rules remained intact. Now women have started to push back. They are insisting that their different needs, styles, and career patterns be accepted – not just accommodated – and that the prevailing male model of practice must be recast. Being a leader allows you to influence that change and make it happen faster.

Leadership provides an outlet for your creativity. Leaders look beyond the horizon to find better ways to operate law firms, provide services to clients, and serve the public. Most lawyers spend their days handling the legal work in front of them. While that work can involve fashioning creative arguments and agreements, being in a position to think about what law practice could look like tomorrow – and to make it happen – can unleash your creative energies on a much larger scale. It can energize you, feed your need for personal achievement, and increase your professional satisfaction. Especially at this moment in time, when the fundamental model of private practice is evolving, women who have big ideas should seize the opportunities for innovation that leadership offers.

Leadership means power to achieve desired results. Leadership gives you the power to make things happen and have an impact. Understood in this sense, power is positive, desirable, and essential. No matter how brilliant your vision is, you cannot implement it unless you have the power to make it happen. Power provides access to information, resources, and other influential people; it enables you to demand fair treatment and compensation; it gives you the ability to accomplish the things that are important to you; it allows you to hold others accountable for their promises and responsibilities; and it enables you to empower other women and help them also become leaders. One woman I

---

[14]Menkel-Meadow, C. (May 1987), The comparative sociology of women lawyers: the "feminization" of the legal profession, in *Institute for Social Science Research, Volume III. 1986-87 – Women at Work: The Conference Papers*, UCLA Law School.

interviewed who has been both a prominent law firm leader and general counsel of a large public company viewed leadership as *"a means to create a culture that is more hospitable, less bureaucratic and complex, where you have a voice and the ability to get things done."*

Lawyers are generally suspicious of other lawyers who are ambitious for leadership and they have particular trepidation about women who want power. But women do not need to apologize for their ambitions. Indeed, it is existing law firm leaders who should be on the defensive. How can they justify the failure to retain and promote half of their talent pool? Considering the high number of extremely capable women they have hired over decades, firms should be ashamed to have so few women in power. In an environment where women have historically been excluded from power, and where capable leaders are acutely needed, law firms should be assiduously enlisting and supporting women who aspire to leadership roles.

For their part, women must become comfortable in seeking and wielding power rather than shying away from it. A 2005 study by the Center for Work-Life Policy found that only 15% of highly qualified female lawyers singled out "a powerful position" as a very important career goal.[15] In fact, that goal ranked lowest in their priorities. Why is this? One explanation might be that women view power negatively because they associate it with an autocratic model of leadership which exerts power over others. Another reason might be that women disdain as unprofessional and "unfeminine" individuals who acquire and use power in a deliberate and manipulative way. United States Solicitor General Elena Kagan offered a different explanation when she was Dean of Harvard Law School. She surmised that women's experience in law practice has left them feeling both unfulfilled and powerless to create the kinds of meaningful work lives they desire.[16] Whatever the reasons, women who fail to appreciate that they need power for career success face a major roadblock to leadership. In contrast, women who reframe their thinking and embrace power as an instrument of responsible change can be highly effective and productive leaders.

Being a leader makes your work more meaningful. Many women find fulfillment at work when they feel that what they are doing

---

[15]Hewlett, S.A., & Luce, C.B. (Mar. 2005), Off-ramps and on-ramps, *Harvard Business Review*.

[16]Remarks by Dean Kagan on the status of women in law, Harvard Law School, Nov. 17, 2005, http://www.law.harvard.edu/about/dean/women-in-law.html.

makes a difference. Law firms offer many opportunities to take the lead on critical legal, economic, and social issues of the day, not just for business clients but also for pro bono clients, communities, non-profits and individuals. When you are in law firm leadership, you are better able to choose and address the issues and causes that are important to you.

Leadership also enables you to have a positive impact on the careers of others, which is an important motivator for many women. In particular, as mentors and role models, women leaders can guide and inspire other women to follow them into leadership. Having a critical mass of women in leadership who display different styles, attributes, and career paths, can help keep the pipeline of future women leaders full. As more women move into leadership, it becomes more likely that the women behind them will advance more readily. They will be more confident and able to overcome gender-related obstacles. Even if they cannot eliminate bias entirely, with enough different women in leadership roles, "bias would simply slip by without hampering us."[17] Many women would find this result a profoundly meaningful accomplishment.

Leadership brings financial rewards. For some women, as for many men, making a lot of money is a primary motivator. The financial rewards of law firm leadership can be significant, as lawyers are among the highest paid professionals. At present, men hold most of the power in law firms and their compensation reflects it. Male lawyers make significantly more than women do at every level of seniority and experience. In fact, women lawyers in 2008 earned only 80.5% as much as their male counterparts,[18] and women equity partners in 2009 earned only 88% as much as male equity partners, a difference of $66,000.[19]

Leadership, especially through rainmaking power, can open paths for women to greater financial rewards. Being respected as a leader and rainmaker gives you leverage when you negotiate for appropriate credit and payment for the work you do. Sitting on the management, executive, or compensation committee gives you the ability to participate in or at least influence compensa-

---

[17]Rhode, D.L., (Ed.) (2003), *The difference difference makes* (Stanford: University Press), 178.

[18]Catalyst (2009), *Women in law: quick takes*; According to the U.S. Census Bureau (August 2008), the legal profession overall had the lowest ratio of women's earnings to men's earnings (51.1 percent) of all the 26 occupation groups studied. Men in legal occupations earned the most ($105,233).

[19]The National Association of Women Lawyers [NAWL] (Oct. 2009). *Report of the fourth annual national survey on retention and promotion of women in law firms*, The NAWL Foundation.

tion decisions. Being a leader also enables you to help set the criteria for compensation. You can press for financial recognition for the aspects of practice in which women excel but which are not valued as greatly under existing schemes, such as recruiting and committee participation.

The legal marketplace needs fresh approaches to leadership. The business world in which law firms operate today demands a new style of leadership. Firms are facing a turbulent, unpredictable economy and they are being challenged in every direction and on a global basis. Clients are demanding limits on fees, more efficient delivery of legal services, and greater diversity. Many legal processes are being unbundled, systematized and outsourced, and new law firm business models are emerging that transform the way legal services are delivered and paid for. Some areas of practice are disappearing while others are being created. The challenges that will confront law firms in the future will become even greater and more complex, and firm leaders will require many new skills and diverse perspectives. To find leaders able to handle these challenges, firms that have a deep and expansive pool of leadership talent will have a competitive advantage. Firms that fail to bring women into that pool will be at a serious loss.

Women lawyers are well suited to meet the challenges of the new legal marketplace. At a time when change is constant, women who have less vested in the old ways of doing business and managing law firms may be in the best positions to take the helm. They are not as tied to the way things have always been done, and they can bring fresh perspectives and modern ideas to improve law firm practice, structure, and management.

Women can also bring more relevant approaches to law firm leadership. Business theorists and consultants now emphasize that in the changing business world, the individualistic, directive and authoritarian traits that have traditionally been associated with leadership (and masculinity) are giving way to more collaborative, empowering, relational, and supportive qualities. These modern leadership characteristics, which are aligned with women's natural styles, are more suitable for a fast-moving world in which organizations are more diverse and team-oriented, and where workers expect to have a voice and be well-treated. In law firms, where leadership efficacy is based in large part on high quality interpersonal relationships, these leadership traits should be extremely beneficial, and women with strengths in these areas will be able to use them with good results.

More importantly, women do not need to choose between

masculine or feminine styles because effective leaders use aspects of both. They adapt their styles to fit the circumstances they face. There are times when leaders must be assertive and forceful, and other times when being empathetic and caring is a more suitable technique. By learning what works best for her, each woman can develop her own individual style, with variations for different situations. And when more women are in leadership roles and exhibit a greater variety of styles, the stereotypes that impede women today will give way to an acceptance of greater diversity in defining effective leadership for everyone.

Your law firm needs you. This is a good time to be a woman with leadership aspirations. Law firms need women leaders. The paucity of women in leadership has ominous implications for firms. In spite of the large number of women entering law firm practice, men become equity partners at a rate four times greater than women and hardly any women move into top leadership. While firms might have been able to ignore this extreme imbalance in the past, they can no longer afford to do so. Leadership talent is scarce and firms urgently need the perspectives, talents, and skills of women who are among their best lawyers and most promising leaders. The challenge for law firms is to persuade women to stay and become the leaders that these firms need. Firms must convince women that remaining in a law firm and moving into leadership there is desirable. Until now, that has not been an easy sell, and law firms have not tried very hard because they have not felt a sense of urgency. Now time may be running out.

The recession has led law firms to reduce their legal workforce, but they are still in a tight market for good leaders and the competition for leadership talent will only increase in the future. As a result of layoffs, deferrals, and turnover, many firms have reduced the number of potential leaders in the pipeline at the very time they expect 70% of law firm partners to retire over the next few years. It is estimated that more partners will retire from law firms in the next 10-15 years than the total number who retired in the past 30 years. Firms will need to replace these retiring lawyers who constitute most of the firm's current leadership. Considering how many women enter private practice, they could be natural replacements for those leaders – if only firms groomed them for leadership. As law firms begin to address these alarming demographic trends, smart firms will soon realize that they are wasting precious resources when they discourage women from becoming leaders.

Having more women in leadership is also vital for law firm economics. Gender diversity in leadership is good for law firms financially, while its absence may lead to a loss of business.

Research in the corporate sector over many years consistently shows a positive correlation between high numbers of women senior executives and stronger financial performance.[20] Much of the research suggests that more female representation in the senior ranks leads to better firm quality and performance.[21] The more women there are in senior positions, the stronger the correlation becomes.

Law firms without women in leadership may pay a penalty for their absence. Increasingly, clients are expecting firms to have women in leadership roles. When almost half of all new lawyers, 46% of associates, and 33% of all law firm lawyers are women,[22] law firms cannot argue that there is an insufficient supply of capable women lawyers. In addition, "[w]omen now drive the world economy,"[23] and women lawyers should be available to serve them. The number of women who are potential purchasers of legal services is growing. Many companies are now owned or run by women and the number is rising rapidly. According to the Center for Women's Business Research, women majority-owned companies account for 40% of all privately-held firms in the U.S., and their growth rate is twice the rate of U.S. firms as a whole.[24] In 2008, approximately 10.1 million privately-held women-owned companies employed more than 13 million people and generated $1.9 trillion in sales.[25] Moreover, 18.4% of Fortune 500 General Counsel are women[26] and women comprise 40% of in-house lawyers.[27] Not all of these women insist on giving their business to other women, but they may distrust a firm where there are no

---

[20]Adler, R.D., & Conlin, R. (Fed. 2009), *Profit, thy name is ... woman?*, http://www.miller-mccune.com/business__economics/profit-thy-name-is-woman-1007; Catalyst (2007), *The bottom line: corporate performance and women's representation on boards*; Catalyst (2004), *The bottom line: connecting corporate performance and gender diversity*; Desvaux, G., Devillard-Hoellinger, S., & Meaney, M.C. (Oct. 2008), A business case for women, *McKinsey Quarterly*.

[21]McKinsey & Company (2007), *Women matter*; Catalyst, *The Bottom Line*, 2004 and 2007.

[22]NALP (Oct. 2009), Law firm diversity demographics show little change, despite economic downturn.

[23]Silverstein M.J., & Sayre, K. (Sept. 2009), The female economy, *Harvard Business Review*.

[24]Silverstein & Sayre (Sept. 2009), The female economy; Boushey, H. & O'Leary, A. (Eds.) (2009), *The Shriver report: a woman's nation changes everything,* A study by Maria Shriver and the Center for American Progress.

[25]Center for Women's Business Research, *Key facts about women-owned businesses, 2008-2009 update.*

[26]*Diversity & The Bar Magazine,* Minority Corporate Counsel Association, July-Aug. 2008.

[27]Zabcik, B. (June 2009), Measuring diversity: what's good enough?, *Corporate Counsel.*

prominent women for them to consider.

In fact, many clients are insisting on diversity, including gender diversity, in their outside law firms. Clients are requiring law firms to demonstrate measurable results in retaining and advancing women, and they are demanding that women be placed in leadership roles on their cases and deals, and in managing client relationships. More than 100 General Counsel have signed The Call to Action,[28] making a personal commitment to increasing diversity in the legal profession by making a law firm's progress on diversity, including gender diversity, a significant factor in deciding whether to hire or continue working with a firm. The signatories' companies have begun to withhold or withdraw millions of dollars of legal business from firms that cannot demonstrate a commitment to diversity. Many of the corporate clients active in the Call to Action are also working with law firms to promote workplace flexibility, recognizing that firms cannot achieve true diversity without enabling lawyers to reconcile work with personal demands.[29]

The business case for gender balance in law firm leadership is well established and compelling. Women who take advantage of the demographic and economic forces behind it will find many opportunities for productive and meaningful leadership roles.

About this book

A great deal of data has been published about women in law firms, and there are many conferences every year about how to advance women lawyers in the legal profession. Most of the written materials and conferences focus on what law firms and other legal employers should do to retain and advance women. This book is different. It is directed to women, not firms. It is intended to help women understand what they are up against and give them the tools, confidence, and inspiration to take their careers into their own hands. Women who read this book will better understand how law firms work and how to apply that knowledge to their advantage. They will learn how to become leaders and then as leaders, how to use their power to build a better, more inclusive law firm. But men who lead law firms should also read this book. They will learn why women leave their firms and what they can do to stop the exodus and retain the capable women leaders they need.

---

[28]http://www.clocalltoaction.com/.

[29]One example is The Project for Attorney Retention's Diversity and Flexibility Connection, an initiative in which corporate general counsel and law firm leaders are highlighting the connection between work-life strategies and diversity objectives. http://pardc.org/.

This book does not present a template for leadership, nor does it lay out a formula with step by step instructions for success. Instead, it explains how each woman can find and use the leadership strategies and styles that work best for her. It tells you how to approach your leadership development strategically, navigate around the barriers you will face, and use the political dynamics of the law firm to your benefit. It examines subjects that women rarely discuss but are vital to successful leadership, such as politics, power, and money, and how to acquire and use all three to your advantage. It urges you to find out how your firm really operates and how decisions really get made, as well as the unwritten rules that control both. This book gives readers many answers, but it also gives you the questions to ask so that you can make informed and astute career decisions whether or not law firm leadership is your goal.

I have drawn on several sources for the information presented in the pages that follow. In addition to relying on publicly available research data, I conducted confidential interviews with 60 women leaders from law firms in cities throughout the United States, as well as women who work for U.S.-based firms from offices in London, Sydney, and Hong Kong. These women were all partners in law firms that ranged in size from one-office firms of 15 lawyers to global giants of more than two thousand lawyers. They have held a broad range of leadership roles and positions. Several of them are highly successful rainmakers with substantial books of business and others are relationship partners for major firm clients. Many women are in, or have held, positions as managing partners, practice group leaders and department chairs. Three are, or have been, heads of large global law firms and many have served on their firms' highest governance committees as well as on compensation, policy, finance and partner elevation committees. A sizeable number of the women have been the partners in charge of recruiting, professional development, and diversity in their firms.

The youngest leader I interviewed started law practice in 1999; the most senior in 1971. Five leaders self-identified as lesbians, eight are African American, three are Asian American, two are Latinas and one is Chinese. They practice in a wide variety of legal specialties and have worked in numerous private law firms. Many of the women have practiced in corporate legal departments, government agencies or their own firms before going to their current firms. One has been a judge. Two women are in-house, one the General Counsel of a Fortune 50 company, the other the Deputy General Counsel of one of the world's largest management consulting firms. Throughout the book, when I refer or attribute comments to a "leader" or "woman leader," I am referring to one of the women I interviewed. Unidentified quotes in italics also come from those women.

The Hastings Leadership Academy for Women, a leadership development program for women law firm partners, has been another valuable source of information and insight. As Director of the Leadership Academy, which I co-founded with Professor Joan Williams at Hastings College of the Law in San Francisco, I have had the unique opportunity to work with highly talented and motivated women partners and to learn about their aspirations and concerns, the factors that drive them, and those that thwart their progress.

My own experience as a practicing lawyer, adviser to law firms, and coach and mentor to lawyers for 35 years naturally forms a large part of my thinking on the subject of women in leadership. Throughout my career I have been involved in efforts to retain, promote, and advance the gifted women lawyers who practice in law firms. I have observed and been part of a great deal of the progress that has brought more women into law firm partnership and leadership. But I also feel frustrated that women's advancement into partnership and leadership has been so slow. The societal and institutional impediments to women's success are so firmly entrenched that tens of thousands of women lawyers butting their heads against the glass ceiling for more than three decades have opened just a small passageway that allows only a few women to get through and reach the top. This book is my attempt to accelerate the process and get rid of the glass ceiling completely.

How this book is structured

The challenges that women must overcome to become law firm leaders stem from societal, institutional, and personal constraints. This book is divided into three sections, each of which emphasizes one of these constraints but also explains how all three interrelate. Practical suggestions for dealing with these challenges are presented throughout the book.

Part 1 looks at the unique leadership challenges that women face and men do not. It examines the stereotypes, biases, and other factors that create obstacles for women and make their experience different from that of their male colleagues. Most of these obstacles result from societal pressures and have a profound influence on how women think about their careers and the choices and trade-offs they have to make in order to become leaders in their firms.

Part 2 studies leadership within the context of law firms and discusses how law firm structure, culture and politics, as well as lawyers' personalities and attitudes create special challenges for law firm leaders. Most of these challenges are not unique to women at all, but they do have implications that affect women differently than they do men. This section looks at how the dominant law firm culture, unwritten rules and prevailing economic model have been detrimental to women and how women can succeed in spite of them.

Part 3 deals with the personal aspects of leadership and gives women a framework for becoming successful leaders. It describes how women can achieve their career aspirations and find meaning and satisfaction as law firm leaders. This section begins by asking readers to come to terms with their career ambitions. For those who want to be a leader now or in the future, it explains what they need to know and do in order to achieve that end. Throughout, it offers guidance for executing leadership responsibilities effectively and responsibly and it concludes with advice for empowering the next generation of women leaders.

To help provide a framework for the process, I coined the acronym **ASPIRE.** The letters stand for six elements essential for women's leadership success:

- **A**mbition
- **S**trategy
- **P**ersonal Power
- **I**nterpersonal Dynamics
- **R**esilience
- **E**mpowerment

Each of these elements has a chapter devoted to it. In *Ambition,* we look at why it is important for women to be ambitious and to be honest with themselves about what they really want in their life and career. Having a clear vision of who you are, what you want, and where you want to go is the first step toward becoming a successful leader. When you are aware of your personal strengths, values, and drives, you can determine what is most important to you and build your career around your priorities.

The chapter on *Strategy* emphasizes the importance of thinking strategically about your career. It describes how to develop and execute a strategic long-term plan to become the leader you want to be. It examines the two principal paths to leadership in a law firm, rainmaking and management, and because so much leadership development occurs in committee work, it gives special attention to choosing committee activities strategically. This chapter also discusses self-management, particularly time management, setting priorities, and delegation. The last part of the chapter presents issues to consider and strategies to use when trying to be a leader and have a family.

The *Personal power* chapter explains how to be an effective advocate for yourself. It shows you how to recognize your personal power, use it in order to be taken seriously as a leader, and reap the rewards you deserve for your contributions to the firm. To help you avoid being undervalued and undercompensated, it helps you determine what you are worth and advises you how to ensure that you get the credit and compensation you deserve. The chapter also describes different kinds of compensation systems and offers advice on how to reframe your expectations and present your case to maximize your rewards under any system. One key aspect of personal power is the ability to project the image of a credible and confident leader, and the chapter also presents advice on how to do that.

Because most of a leader's work involves other people, the chapter on *Interpersonal dynamics* discusses how to develop techniques to build trusting relationships, communicate effectively, and get buy-in from the people you lead so that they work together productively to advance the firm's and their own shared interests. It also presents suggestions for managing conflict between individuals and groups and for dealing with difficult partners.

Resilience is the set of attitudes and attributes that make it possible for women leaders to withstand the difficulties of leadership and still succeed in the role. This chapter explains how to maintain the self-confidence, thick skin, and mental and emotional health you need to survive and thrive in a very tough job.

One of the responsibilities of a leader is the *Empowerment* of others who also have the desire to become law firm leaders. This chapter describes why and how to develop, promote and advocate for women leaders who will continue and expand efforts to create a better law firm. It also explains how to reframe discussions, challenge assumptions, and create new metaphors to change the way we think about women and leadership.

It is my hope that the women and men who read this book will come away with a better appreciation of the complexities of law firm leadership, especially for women, and that the information and encouragement you find in these pages will help you become supremely effective law firm leaders. Many readers may find the job of law firm leader to be daunting. But lawyers enjoy thorny problems and tough challenges, so rather than view the realities of leadership as discouraging, I hope you will find them enticing and exciting.

We are on the brink of a revolution in the way law firms operate and profit. Where these transformational changes will take us is an open question. The uncertainty of the outcome is a compelling reason for women to step forward and assert their leadership. Partners with a stake in maintaining the status quo will resist the kinds of structural and cultural changes that will lead to greater gender balance, so women and like-minded men must take the initiative. Now is the time to seize the opportunities that uncertainty presents. Now is the time to underscore the confluence between what women offer and what law firms need to succeed in the new business environment. Now is the time to assert new approaches to governance, operations, attitudes, and practices that will make your law firm better for yourself, your colleagues, and those who follow you. Now is the time to start creating the future.

Table of Contents

CHAPTER 14. INTERPERSONAL DYNAMICS

CHAPTER 15. RESILIENCE

CHAPTER 16. EMPOWERMENT

Index

Part I

UNIQUE CHALLENGES FOR WOMEN LEADERS

Chapter 1

Barriers to Women's Leadership

§ 1:1   Introduction

> **KeyCite®:** Cases and other legal materials listed in KeyCite Scope can be researched through the KeyCite service on Westlaw®. Use KeyCite to check citations for form, parallel references, prior and later history, and comprehensive citator information, including citations to other decisions and secondary materials.

---

§ 1:1   Introduction

Women face barriers to leadership that do not affect men. Most of the obstacles derive from stereotyping that leads to bias against women as leaders. It has been said that "only women have gender" because a male leader's gender attracts no attention or comment; it is indistinguishable from his role as a leader. Leadership is strongly associated with masculine behavior stereotypes, so a man is judged on his effectiveness as a *leader*, but a woman is judged on both her leadership effectiveness and her behavior as a *woman*.

We have come a long way from the late 19th century when educated women were demonized as unnatural monsters "whose vital energies were being diverted from their wombs to their brains."[1] However, we have not come far enough. As a society, we continue to ascribe certain gender roles to men and women. Roles for men tend to center on work, while those for women are oriented toward home and family. Expectations that men and

---

[Section 1:1]

[1]Warner, J. (July 2009), Dangerous resentment, New York Times,, http://opinionator.blogs.nytimes.com/2009/07/09/dont-hate-her-because-shes-educated/.

1

women will act according to those gender roles lead to bias against individuals who do not conform to them. Gender bias remains alive and prevalent, especially in law firms.

We start Part I by examining the most common forms of stereotyping and bias that prevent women from moving up to leadership: double binds, racial bias, sexual orientation bias, maternal wall bias, and bias against lawyers who work part-time or in other flexible arrangements. The subsequent chapter addresses the challenges that women face in trying to be authentic leaders and how you can develop an authentic leadership style in spite of them. We then explore some common traps that women leaders fall into and how to avoid them. Lastly, we look at some of the unique issues that women leaders often confront when they work with other women in the firm.

Chapter 2

Stereotyping and Gender Bias

KeyCiteʀ: Cases and other legal materials listed in KeyCite Scope can be researched through the KeyCite service on Westlawʀ. Use KeyCite to check citations for form, parallel references, prior and later history, and comprehensive citator information, including citations to other decisions and secondary materials.

---

§ 2:1   Confronting a multilayered glass ceiling

Many young women lawyers fail to appreciate the negative impact of stereotyping and gender bias on women's careers. Young women who have grown up without experiencing overt bias enter the workplace believing that gender is no longer a disadvantage for women and that gender bias is no longer an issue which they need to worry about. Women lawyers have definitely made steady progress over the years and the barriers created by gender bias are not as impenetrable as in the past. But bias is still very present in the legal workplace. Women lawyers who feel no gender-based constraints throughout the early years of their career are frequently caught by surprise when they experience bias for the first time. One leader stated, *"I experienced more sexism when I was managing partner than in my whole career."*

Women who work long and hard to become partners are often disheartened to discover that the glass ceiling in law firms is multilayered. Women break through to partnership only to face another layer when they aspire to leadership. A woman who has excelled and achieved professional success up to the point of partnership finds her progress blocked, often for the first time in her life. Having proven that she is smart enough to be a fine lawyer, she still has to prove that she is dedicated and tough enough to be a good leader.

This second glass ceiling has a serious psychological impact on women partners. Many women who find themselves in this predicament fight back. They catch on to what is happening and do whatever they need to do to break through that next layer. In contrast, other women start to question their abilities and scale back their ambitions. Rather than see it for what it is—institutionalized bias—these women feel demoralized and blame themselves. One leader described how her early experience in a law firm eroded her confidence: *"My first firm was not good for women, and I did not feel I fit in. When I left, I wondered if the problem was me: did I have the skills to be a private practice lawyer?"*

When talented women see few advancement opportunities ahead, they leave their firms for other jobs just at the point where they should be moving into partnership or leadership. While leaving may be the best option for some women, it is not always the most desirable one. Many women would rather stay but know that they are better—and deserve to be treated better—than the firm acknowledges.

If you want to become a leader, either in your current firm or your next one, it is important to understand how gender stereotyping and bias may affect you and the other women in the firm. Whether or not you personally experience bias, you need to know what it is so that you can recognize it, fight it, and eliminate it.

§ 2:2 Gender stereotypes, bias, and double binds

Remember, Ginger Rogers did everything Fred Astaire did, but she did it backwards and in high heels.

—Faith Whittlesey

Whether you are conscious of it or not, as a woman leader you are subject to stereotyping and bias. Gender stereotyping refers to generalizations and preconceived notions about how men and women differ. These views are widely held by both men and women because they are the result of socialization in the families and cultural environments in which we live, as well as in the law firms and profession in which we work. Stereotypes may be "descriptive," creating assumptions about the natural characteristics of men and women, or "prescriptive," leading to assumptions about how men and women should behave. The notion that men are naturally autonomous and that women are communal is descriptive; that men should work and that women should be mothers is prescriptive.

We use stereotypes to help us categorize people into groups, and then we immediately make mental associations that unconsciously affect our thoughts, actions, and decisions about people in those groups. That way we can relate to people automatically, without having to figure them out individually each time we encounter them. While stereotypes make our initial encounters efficient, they affect how we perceive, interpret, and remember events. When we interact with someone, these stereotypes influence what we pay attention to or ignore, how we interpret what the person does or says, and what we recall about the person after we part. Stereotyping does not mean that we dislike a particular person and/or group but simply that we make automatic assumptions about them.

Numerous studies show that gender stereotyping influences perceptions of women's competence and that these perceptions disadvantage women leaders.[1] For a man, gender is unacknowledged; he fits seamlessly into the leadership role because leadership is presumed to be masculine. In contrast, a woman leader's gender is a salient factor and perceived as an obstacle to her being a leader. In one study of executives' performance evaluations of male and female leaders, comments about gender were 25 times more prevalent in the evaluations of women than in those of men.[2] No matter how she behaves, a woman leader's gender makes her stand out as "different." It puts her at odds with prevailing leadership norms and may thwart her success. She is evaluated negatively because she does not fit into a category people are accustomed to, and is, therefore, less likely to be recommended for a leadership role.

Bias occurs when stereotypes sway our thoughts and ideas about people, even people we know well. Gender bias refers to preferences or favoritism toward one sex over the other.[3] Gender bias in favor of men and against women is pervasive throughout organizations, leading people to view and treat men more charitably than women.[4] For instance, if two parents arrive late for a morning meeting, people may not even notice that the man was late, but they will notice that the woman was. They will as-

---

[Section 2:2]

[1]See, e.g., Warren, A.K. (Feb. 2009), *Cascading gender biases, compounding effects: an assessment of talent management systems*, Catalyst.

[2]Lyons, D., & McArthur, C. (Sept. 2007), Gender's unspoken role in leadership evaluations, *Entrepreneur*, http://www.entrepreneur.com/tradejournals/article/169413774__5.html.

[3]Warren (Feb. 2009), *Cascading gender biases, compounding effects.*

[4]Eagly, A.H., & Carli, L.L. (Sept. 2007), Women and the labyrinth of leadership, *Harvard Business Review*.

sume that the women had child care problems and question her priorities or abilities to be a leader.[5] In law firms, associating male stereotypes with leadership is not surprising since 81% of law firm partners and 95% of leaders and top rainmakers are men.

The solution is not as simple as treating male and female lawyers equally. A firm may apply the same norms but they are masculine norms and have a differential impact when applied to women. Diversity consultant Arin Reeves notes that it is one thing to treat all people equally by giving everyone a pair of shoes, but the impact differs when all the shoes are size 11. For women who wear a size 7 the shoes are not much help. An African American leader I interviewed spoke of her firm which prides itself on treating every lawyer the same. They mean well, but they fail to realize that not every lawyer fits the common mold:

> *My firm treats people equally. That's good except there's no recognition that my issues are different than the white guys'. I'm the first in my family to go to college, much less law school. There are no CEOs in my family who can send me business. I live in a different part of town from them. They don't recognize the differences in my life so they treat me under the same standard as the old white guy when it comes to business generation.*

As a consequence, these standards work against her. They may be equal but they are not equitable.

One of the most blatant illustrations of how the same behavior deemed positive in men is judged negatively in women is shown in a Harvard Business School case study. Many prominent business schools use a case study involving Heidi Roizen, a highly successful venture capitalist and veteran of the high-tech industry in Silicon Valley. It describes her as hard-driving with an outgoing personality, a vast personal and professional network, and a stellar reputation for professional excellence and outstanding results. Several of the business schools ran an experiment that determined that gender bias makes a significant difference in the way that people perceive the same behavior in men and women. They used two sets of the case study that were identical except in one regard: in half of the copies distributed to students the subject was named Heidi and in the other half the subject was called Howard. Except for pronouns and Heidi having been a high school cheerleader while Howard was a football player the text of the case studies was exactly the same.

Business school students uniformly rated both Heidi and How-

---

[5]McCracken, D.M. (Nov.-Dec. 2000), Winning the talent war for women: sometimes it takes a revolution, *Harvard Business Review*.

ard as highly effective and competent. However, while students liked Howard and viewed him admirably as a go-getter, they rated Heidi as overly aggressive, not likeable, and someone they would not want to hire or work with.[6] The more assertive they thought Heidi was the more severely they judged her. (Notably, male students judged Heidi more harshly than female students did.). We like to think that there is less stereotyping among the younger generation but these results show how pervasive it still is, even among highly educated business school students. Heidi did not conform to their notion of accepted gender roles, so they disapproved of her while praising exactly the same behavior in her male counterpart.

In the past, gender bias was overt and unabashed. Many of us who entered law practice in the late 1970s were told directly that we could not be lawyers because "women are too emotional/too pretty/not smart enough" or a hundred other foolish reasons. Today most bias is unspoken, although comments on legal blogs can be a shocking reminder of just how much overt bias still exists. Bias today is also subconscious, hidden, or implicit. People do not necessarily intend to favor men over women and most people would deny that they do. Nonetheless, studies have shown that bias creeps into women's lives and impacts their ability to be leaders in many ways:

- Women must work harder to prove their competence. In evaluations, women are judged on their performance ("she hasn't shown that she can do it"), while men are assessed on their potential ("he just needs some time"). When women succeed, their success is attributed to external factors ("she got the business because the client is her friend"), while it is assumed that men succeeded on their merit ("he landed that client because he worked hard"). Conversely, women's failings are attributed to their own inadequacies ("she is disorganized"), but when men fail external factors are blamed ("he has too much work"). These nuances are subtle but critical; they mean that women have to work harder to prove that they are as competent as their male colleagues for whom competence is presumed.

- Assignments reinforce stereotypes. Projects and positions that are assigned to women tend to reinforce the stereotype of women as more people-oriented rather than business-focused. So, for instance, women are expected to keep the team together while men are asked to do strategic planning.

---

[6]Flynn, F., Anderson, C., & Brion, S., *Too tough, too soon: familiarity and the backlash effect* (working paper), Stanford University.

A common example is when firms appoint female and male co-managing partners. The woman is usually given personnel and office administration responsibilities while the man is given a more business- and client-centered portfolio. Even at this executive level, women with financial acumen are relegated to less business-focused positions. One leader I interviewed said that partners labeled her as good with "soft" issues and she saw that as a trap: *"I can't be seen as dealing just with issues they see as soft; I have to prove I'm economically driven."*

- Women are expected to have—but are not rewarded for—good interpersonal skills. Because stereotypes lead to expectations that women have superior interpersonal skills a woman gets no special recognition as a leader for having that ability. For women, good people skills are not valued as strengths but rather as "what women do." However, women whose interpersonal skills are less polished are seen as deficient. In contrast, there is no similar expectation for men, so men suffer no penalty if they lack people skills. In fact, when a man is collaborative and empathetic, he is seen as more qualified for leadership because of this "special talent."

- Women leaders are not given the same respect as men. Lawyers and staff do not treat requests and assignments from women partners with the same sense of urgency and seriousness that they give to those from men. For instance, associates will make excuses to women partners and refuse to take certain assignments when they would never behave the same way to a man. Similarly, women leaders are not acknowledged for their leadership. One woman leader who shares the managing partner role with a more senior male partner and is being groomed to take over the full position when he steps down has heard men and women in the firm say, "I don't know if we're ready for a female to lead the firm." Although partners selected her to be the co-managing partner of the firm, they perceive the man, but not her, to be a leader.

- Behaviors of some women are attributed to all women. One woman's behavior is sometimes attributed to all women. This is especially problematic when there are few women leaders to begin with because without many others to compare her to, a woman leader's comments and actions are easily exaggerated. In one example, a male office managing partner announced that the office would no longer sponsor women's events. He had concluded that women were not invested in the firm because "women partners never attend partnership meetings." The office had four women partners out of 30. Far more men than women skipped partner meetings, but when one or two women did not attend, their absence seemed more significant than the actual numbers warranted.

- **Stereotypes negatively impact women's compensation.** Women lawyers make less money than men do even when they put in the same time and have the same experience and client base. Many people assume that women do not need or want as much money as men because they have husbands who can support them. In one egregious example, a woman partner learned that she was paid less than a male colleague solely because the compensation committee felt that he needed more in order to support his family. To add to the insult, members of the committee knew, but evidently ignored, that she was the sole breadwinner in her family. In fact, many women lawyers, including 70% of women lawyers of color, are the sole or primary wage earner for their families.[7] Such assumptions about "needs" based on gender or family status are based on outdated stereotypes. They are damaging and wrong and should not be a factor in calculating a partner's compensation.[8]

One manifestation of stereotyping and bias is the double bind. Double binds are situations where you cannot win no matter what you do. Women face a classic double bind when they try to be leaders. If they exhibit behaviors traditionally considered feminine they are seen as "too soft" to be leaders and thus are not respected. In contrast, if their behavior is highly businesslike they are perceived as "too tough," which makes them unlikable. As a result, they are perceived in a negative light either way. Women leaders receive many contradictory messages about how they should behave that put them in no-win situations. Some of the contradictory messages that women confront are presented in Table 2.1.

Stereotypes about proper gender roles create a false dichotomy about women's and men's leadership characteristics, which are in fact not mutually exclusive. Research has found that according to stereotypes, the defining qualities of women leaders are "taking care" behaviors and the defining qualities of male leaders are

---

[7]ABA Commission on Women in the Profession (2006), *Visible invisibility: women of color in law firms*, American Bar Association.

[8]ABA Commission on Women in the Profession (2006), *Visible invisibility*.

"taking charge" behaviors.[9] "Taking care" involves being friendly, sensitive, and compassionate, as well as having strong interpersonal skills. "Taking charge" characteristics include being ambitious, assertive, competitive, and action-oriented. These "taking charge" traits also happen to be the characteristics typically associated with leadership. Thus, men are perceived as "natural" leaders but women who demonstrate the same behaviors are not seen as leaders because they contradict people's expectations of how women should behave. Instead, women who take charge are judged as harsh, aggressive, or uncaring.

Table 2.1: Contradictory Messages That Create Double Binds for Women	
Masculine Behaviors	Feminine Behaviors
Take risks	Be deliberative
Be tough	Be supportive
Ask for what you want	Do not be pushy
Expect excellence	Give people a chance
Take more work	Model work-life balance
Promote yourself	Be modest
Be decisive	Be collaborative

Stereotypes perpetuate the myth that men are superior leaders, but there is "no defensible argument that men are naturally, inherently, or actually better suited to leadership than women are."[10] In fact, gender differences in leadership are almost nonexistent. Research "consistently finds that women compare favorably to men as leaders. Women might show advantages in some areas and men in others, but the differences are usually small and the bottom-line results the same."[11] Studies do find that women and men have somewhat different leadership styles and that women's styles, which are more collaborative and participative, tend to be more generally effective.[12] But analyses of more than 40 studies of leadership, spanning more than 15

---

[9]Catalyst (2005), *Women "take care," men "take charge": stereotyping of U.S. business leaders exposed.*

[10]Eagly, A. & Carli, L. (2007), *Through the labyrinth: the truth about how women become leaders* (Boston: Harvard Business School Press).

[11]Howard, A., & Wellins, R.S. (2009), Holding women back: troubling discoveries and best practices for helping women succeed, Development Dimensions International, Inc.

[12]Eagly & Carli (Sept. 2007), Women and the labyrinth of leadership; Caliper (2005), *The qualities that distinguish women leaders.*

years, fail to support the perception that gender is a reliable predictor of how a person will lead.[13] Yet gender stereotypes hold women to higher standards and force them to work twice as hard as men to be accepted as leaders.[14] Whereas men may be presumed capable of leading, women must prove over and over again that they can be effective leaders. They remain in the spotlight and attract higher scrutiny. Their mistakes are overblown and their successes are underplayed.

When there are not a lot of women in leadership, those who achieve it are often "superstars." They have worked incredibly hard to break through glass ceilings and maternal walls and to prove that they can beat the boys at their own game. They seem to be superior at everything they do and they possess enormous reservoirs of stamina and resilience. The problem is that they set the standard so high that other women must continue to work twice as hard to measure up even when the bar for men is much lower. Someone once remarked that, "Women will know we have achieved success when there are as many average women in positions of power as there are average men."

§ 2:3   Bias against women of color

Fewer than two percent of law firm partners are women of color. To make it into partnership, women of color have to overcome tremendous odds and demonstrate enormous strength and perseverance. To become law firm leaders they have to develop strategies for dealing with the usual obstacles, which are compounded by belonging to two minority groups. Even as leaders, many women of color feel like outsiders, never fully included in the mainstream of the law firm. They experience what Supreme Court Justice Sonia Sotomayor described about her own career: "I have spent my years since Princeton, while at law school and in my various professional jobs, not feeling completely a part of the worlds I inhabit . . . [Despite my accomplishments],

---

[13]Catalyst (2005), *Women "take care," men "take charge."*

[14]Eagly & Carli (Sept. 2007), Women and the labyrinth of leadership; Ely, R.J., & Rhode, D.L. (2010), Women and leadership: defining the challenges, in N. Nohria & R. Khurana (Eds.), *Handbook of leadership theory and practice* (Boston: Harvard Business School Press).

I am always looking over my shoulder wondering if I measure up."[1]

Within law firms women of color are more committed to diversity and inclusion efforts than any other demographic group.[2] They are active in, and often lead, their firm's diversity initiatives and women's initiatives, which puts them in a bind. Firms pressure them to do it, but it takes time away from what the firm values more: billing and business generation. They face a second dilemma in firms with separate diversity and women's initiatives. They must choose either to be active in only one initiative or the other, or to devote twice as much nonbillable time if they actively participate in both.

A third problem is that neither diversity initiatives nor women's initiatives fully address the multifaceted issues that women of color have to deal with. These women report experiencing more bias, discrimination, and negative experiences in every aspect of work and advancement than white women or all men.[3] They must contend with "intersectionality," which refers to experiences that result from having multiple identities (e.g., race, gender, ethnicity, immigration status, class) and cannot be explained by any one identity alone.[4] That they have endured and succeeded in this environment is a testament to their talent, creativity, and resilience. It is no wonder that research by Catalyst and the Minority Corporate Counsel Association (MCCA) has concluded that the issues women of color deal with must be addressed separately, not as subsets of gender or race issues.

Almost 100% of women of color leave their original law firms within eight years. Whatever stereotypes, biases, and adverse conditions may exist for white women and minority men, women of color bear "the burdens of both, the privileges of neither."[5] The experiences they face as their careers progress differ significantly from those of men and white women. Many have come from and

---

[Section 2:3]

[1]Lewis, N.A. (May 2009), On a Supreme Court prospect's résumé: 'baseball savior,' *New York Times*, http://www.nytimes.com/2009/05/15/us/15sotomayor.html?_r=2.

[2]Minority Corporate Counsel Association (2009), *Sustaining pathways to diversity: the next steps in understanding & increasing diversity and inclusion in large firms.*

[3]Minority Corporate Counsel Association (2009), *Sustaining pathways to diversity.*

[4]Bagati, D. (2009), *Women of color in U.S. law firms*, Catalyst.

[5]ABA Commission on Racial and Ethnic Diversity in the Profession (1994), *The burdens of both, the privileges of neither*, American Bar Association.

been shaped by vastly different economic, immigrant, and cultural circumstances than the majority of lawyers. As reported in several recent studies, women of color experience more demeaning comments and harassment, find their accomplishments ignored and their mistakes exaggerated, have to overcome negative assumptions about their legal abilities, are denied desirable assignments, and are deprived of access to clients and client development opportunities. They receive evaluations that avoid performance issues and do not give them the information or work experience which they need to correct any deficits. They are excluded from informal networks in the firm and marginalized in firm-sponsored formal networks.

Other burdens come from being the only woman or one of a small group of women of their race or ethnic background in the office or the firm. A particularly vexing problem is the feeling of isolation when there are no people in the firm to whom you can fully relate. An African American woman spoke of the challenges she experienced as a junior partner in charge of a team: "*I was the senior lawyer to some white male associates. I had to correct the client as to who was more senior and in charge.*" She had difficulty finding someone to talk with who understood what she was dealing with as she tried to establish her authority with the client and the team. She spoke with a black male partner and senior white women for advice on how to handle the situation. She had no women partners of color in her firm to talk with.

Being part of a small group also sets you up to be exploited. Firms want to show their commitment to diversity, so from the outset, they ask women of color to spend a lot of nonbillable time representing the firm at hiring activities and diversity events, in client pitches, community activities, and on firm committees. Women of color want to help the firm attract and retain other women and other lawyers of color, so they are motivated to do this work. However, firms usually introduce them to clients or invite them to participate in pitches and activities when it is advantageous to the firm. Firms make no effort to use those events to advance the woman's career.

As a consequence of all these insults, women of color in law firms feel isolated, alienated, and second class. Many of the stresses that white women feel are doubled for women of color. They have to reconcile the physical differences of their gender and race so that they can be accepted within the firm and at the same time remain true to the communities they come from. In addition, they need not just prove their ability and career commitment as a woman but must also overcome negative assumptions about their ability as a racial minority. When an African

American woman was made practice group leader in a global firm, some partners asked, "Why was she given that position? Was it because of affirmative action?" Her retort was that law firms *entrust leadership to people who can produce. After all, this firm is a business. My leadership is about results.*"

Similarly, when women of color are asked to take positions of authority, especially if the position is related to diversity, they often wonder, as one woman did, *"Was I offered this position because I am qualified or because of my race? I don't want to be chosen just because of race. I want to make the choice for myself. I don't want someone else to put me in a slot because of my race or gender."*

Women of color frequently have to prove themselves in ways that other lawyers do not. When an African American woman, an income partner, was asked to become her firm's Diversity Director, she insisted on waiting until she became an equity partner. She explained, *"I didn't want others to think I was doing it out of tokenism or because I couldn't be a successful lawyer. I needed the credibility that comes with proving my value as a lawyer first."*

Women of color whom I interviewed feel that there is growing acceptance of minority lawyers, and they attribute much of this to the increasing emphasis on diversity by law firms and especially by clients. One leader said, *"A big factor has been corporations emphasizing diversity. That has had a profound effect on how law firms—men—look at leadership circles. They have to put women into leadership positions, and then they have these "aha" moments when they realize women can do it."* But these women still question the sincerity of firms' and clients' commitment to diversity. One leader of color said, *"Companies talk about diversity but don't mean it. New work still goes to the old white guys."* She described how she and one of her white male partners jointly pitched their services to a company. The General Counsel, who publicly advocated diversity, sent the work to her male partner. Another leader of color had a white woman mentor who freely gave her career advice but never invited her along on a pitch or to meet clients. As both cases demonstrate, lawyers talk a good game about diversity, but their actions often fall short.

Among the women of color I interviewed, all but the youngest women leaders had felt the pain of bias and barriers related to gender and/or race, yet they did not complain that race or gender were obstacles to their advancement. It was there and they dealt with it. They used race and gender as opportunities rather than handicaps and did not let bias stop them from getting to where they wanted to be. These women set clear goals, employed self-confidence and perseverance, built a strong client base, and found multiple mentors. They are supremely resilient. These strategies and attributes are vital for all women who aspire to leadership, but they are career-savers for women of color because the hazards they face are so much greater. As one woman of color said, *"The world is a tough place. I won't let it or anyone stop me. I need to let things roll off and use humor to get me through. As a successful person, you always have to deal with tough things."*

The women of color who were interviewed also held a strong belief in their ability to succeed and were determined to achieve their dreams. They spoke of growing up strong and confident, of being competitive, hard driving, and determined to win. An Asian American leader spoke for many when she said, *"I always intended to be a great lawyer."* An African American leader spoke of her difficult childhood and how it drove her to become a leader: *"I came from extreme poverty. Being a leader is my responsibility. When you come from poverty, you have no options but to lead. If you were successful enough to get out of poverty, you have to be a leader."*

§ 2:4 Sexual orientation bias

People have become increasingly aware and accepting of sexual diversity in the workplace. Still, stereotypes based on sexual orientation sometimes affect lawyers' and clients' perceptions about who is well-suited for leadership. While gender and race are usually apparent to others, sexual orientation is not. Unlike heterosexuals, lesbians need to choose whether to be open about their sexual orientation at work or remain closeted. Some are very forthright and secure in discussing their sexuality. Others choose to stay quiet or to let only select people know. Those who are out to some but not to others find it difficult to remember who knows and who doesn't and to manage the situation without confusion. The fact that lesbians have to decide whether to be open or silent about their sexual preference creates extra stress that straight leaders do not have to contend with.

Lesbians have to be on their guard during conversations about what to reveal without causing a negative reaction in others. It can be highly problematic and stressful when socializing with heterosexual partners or clients and their spouses, and it often has a chilling effect on social interactions. One leader I interviewed believed that most young women today are comfortable with both their sexuality and being identified as lesbians. However, she was still concerned about being active in the firm's LGBT affinity group. In a previous job she had been known as a lesbian first and a lawyer second. She wanted to avoid being known in her current firm primarily as a "lesbian lawyer."

In many firms, being openly gay would be detrimental to a woman's leadership prospects, so lesbians tend to keep secret many aspects of their lives that are essential to their identity. This frequently creates serious dilemmas. If they have not revealed their sexuality, they fear that someone else will or that they will inadvertently "out" a friend or partner who is still in the closet. They cannot talk about their personal lives in ways that heterosexuals take for granted. If they have same-sex partners they are unable to discuss them or bring them to firm functions, and they may be denied benefits and policies that heterosexual couples enjoy. Whether they are open about their sexuality or not, they may be subjected to derogatory comments, attitudes, and jokes about homosexuals.

If lesbians are open about their sexual orientation, they need to consider whether they appear to others as too stereotypically gay and whether that affects their effectiveness as leaders. Women who are openly gay in the office may nonetheless conceal their sexual preference in other settings, such as when dealing with clients. If, for example, they work in a firm or industry where people are provincial, they try to "play to the audience." They may let their hair grow to look more feminine or wear skirts to trial or to client meetings so as not to make their sexual orientation a distraction.

I interviewed several women leaders who openly self-identify as gay. If they were out at work to begin with, they experienced no negative repercussions. In fact, one woman found that being out when she arrived at her firm was an advantage: *"People trust you and do not think you are hiding anything. Then you can be yourself and focus on your work."* Those who came out after they started working at their firms felt great relief and were surprised at how little it mattered to their colleagues and clients. They found that being honest with people saved a lot of energy because they no longer had to worry about concealment and that it had little, if any, impact on their relationships with people, including clients. One leader found herself in an uncomfortable situation with a very conservative client. When he asked her about her personal life, she began to talk about her three children. He then asked what her husband did for a living. She decided not to lie and explained that her husband was a woman. The man responded without hesitation, "Who takes care of the kids?" Her sexual orientation turned out not to be a concern for him.

Not every lesbian leader has had such positive experiences.

One leader, formerly an office managing partner, believes that being outspoken about her sexual orientation slowed her advancement up the leadership ranks. A private person who had neither hidden her sexual orientation nor publicized it, she was asked to lead the new LGBT affinity group being started in her firm. At first she resisted but ultimately said yes. She knew that it was important for the firm and felt that she could do a good job in directing the initiative. At the time she was on a high-speed leadership track and was being groomed for one of the firm's top leadership roles. Then things quickly went sideways. She continued in a leadership role in her office but her ascent on a firm-wide level was stalled. Now she wonders if heading up the affinity group was "leadership suicide."

The lesbian leaders whom I interviewed report encountering awkwardness more often than discrimination. Other people sometimes do not know how to react when they realize that the woman they are dealing with is a lesbian. One leader commented, *"Some people, especially male litigators, do not know how to relate to me or if they should do anything different. Most people try to look for common ground, and I try to help them out. I love sports. I can make some men more comfortable by talking about sports."* One woman explained that she is worried about finding herself in a position where someone reacts in a hostile or discriminatory manner. She does not look for this kind of situation but wants to be ready if it happens. *"I am conscious of what a client might expect. You have to be prepared for negative reactions and think about how you might deal with them."*

While negative attitudes might adversely affect their career progression, stereotypes about lesbians may actually have a positive impact on a woman's career. Many law firms value lesbians more than straight women because they assume that lesbians will not get married or have children. Without the family commitments that cause straight women to cut back or drop out of practice, law firm partners who think this way believe that lesbians will be willing to work and follow career paths just like men. A study in the U.K. by the Centre for Economic Performance found that this kind of thinking led to lesbians having 12% higher employment, and 11% higher compensation, than their heterosexual female counterparts.[1]

Similarly, in research by the Minority Corporate Counsel As-

[Section 2:4]

[1]Chong, R. (Feb. 14), UK report: sexual orientation discrimination at work, *The Glass Hammer*, http://www.theglasshammer.com/news/2008/02/14/uk-report-sexual-orientation-discrimination-at-work/.

sociation,[2] women lawyers reported that bias against them as women was a bigger problem than bias based on sexual orientation, a finding supported by the women leaders interviewed for this book. One gay African American leader I interviewed was very clear about the distinction and its effect on her: *"Being gay makes no difference in my firm. I face more issues being black than gay. I have to avoid the "angry black woman" stereotype so I need to be careful about my style for that reason."* The MCCA study also found that more male lawyers than female believed that their sexual orientation was a barrier to advancement.

§ 2:5 Maternal wall bias

Biology has a singular impact on women. Women lawyers must choose whether and when to have children. If they do not have children, whether by choice or circumstance, they are judged in ways that men are not. They are criticized or pitied for "sacrificing" motherhood for a career. If they do have children, they are criticized for spending too much or too little time with their family. In either case, their leadership qualifications are called into question. When one leader was a senior associate, she adopted a baby at the same time she was being considered for partnership. A partner told her, "I guess you've made your choice," and said that she would not be made a partner. She could have sued the firm, but she left instead and is now the general counsel of an international consulting firm.

This dilemma is unique to women, not just because of biology but also because societal norms are far more fluid and slippery about women with careers than they are for men. Far more than men, women need to figure out how to combine professional and family life. Even with men taking more active roles in family and home life, women still bear a far greater share of responsibility. As psychiatrist Anna Fels has pointed out, women must repeatedly make choices and negotiate at various stages of professional life.[1] Should they have children? When should they have children, before or after partnership? When they have children, how much time should they devote to work and how much to family? Should they "off-ramp" for a while, and if so, for how long? There are trade-offs and risks in each of these choices. One leader who

---

[2]Minority Corporate Counsel Association (2009), *Sustaining pathways to diversity*, 33.

[Section 2:5]

[1]Fels, A. (2004), *Necessary dreams: ambition in women's changing lives* (New York: Anchor Books).

found out too late that she could not have children lamented, *"I made the mistake of waiting until I was a partner to start trying to have a baby. I sacrificed my fertility for my career."*

When women do become mothers, they are subject to stereotyping that is far more insidious and has greater adverse impact on their careers than other forms of bias. This bias arises from the stereotypes that create conflicting expectations for mothers and career women: good mothers should always be available to their children, while good lawyers should always be available to their clients. Therefore, women can't win: they cannot be both good mothers and good lawyers. This "maternal wall bias" subjects pregnant women and mothers to unfavorable treatment at work and interferes with their career advancement.[2] There is a definite softening in societal views toward working mothers; three-quarters of the American workforce now believe that women can work and be good mothers. However, the reality for mothers practicing in law firms has not caught up with this shift in attitudes elsewhere, and bias against mothers is pervasive.[3] One woman of color who holds leadership positions in both her firm and a national women's professional association told me that she had experienced no serious race or gender bias in her firm but was amazed at the bias she encountered at work when she became a mother.

Maternal wall bias starts when women become pregnant. Partners often assume that pregnant women will not come back from maternity leave and will be unreliable if they do. When assigning matters, they think: "She probably won't come back. If she does, she'll want to work part-time. If she goes part-time, I'm better off with John because I can count on him being there for my client." This conclusion is often borne out by the partners' own experience with women who take time off for maternity leave and decide to stay out for longer periods or for good. However, it does a severe disservice to the women who do intend to return to work. In fact, this kind of thinking creates self-fulfilling prophecies. Women who believe they will be marginalized when they return to the firm are more likely to seek work alternatives elsewhere.

Studies have found that mothers are chronically stereotyped as less competent than other workers. They are seen as less capable and less worthy of an employer's investment than women without

---

[2]Swiss, D., & Walker, J. (1994), *Women and the work/family dilemma* (New York: John Wiley & Sons).

[3]ABA Commission on Women in the Profession (2008), *Fair Measure*, American Bar Association.

children and men with or without children; they are also seen as less competent than they were before they had children.[4] Whether or not people question a mother's intellectual abilities, they assume that she is working less and has reduced her commitment to the firm. Women who return to work full time after having children are invariably asked by some partners when they plan to return to a full-time schedule; it is simply assumed that they are working part-time. The assumption that mothers have lost their talent and motivation makes law firms view them as less promising prospects for leadership. They are given fewer assignments and business opportunities that would help them become leaders. Consequently, mothers are frequently underpromoted and underpaid.

The experiences of women who become mothers and men who become fathers are drastically different. People assume that mothers are less competent and less committed even if they were stars before they gave birth or are the primary wage earner in the family. Not only do women lawyers generally earn less than men but mothers earn less than women without children. This is referred to as a "mommy penalty."[5] In contrast, new fathers are seen as more stable and committed to their work because of their family responsibilities and tend to receive higher salaries than men who are not fathers. Unlike mothers, who are penalized for having children, fathers receive a "daddy bonus."[6]

When it comes to work distribution, law firms make many stereotypical assumptions about new mothers without trying to find out what a mother wants to do. When people assume that women with young children are not suitable for leadership or are too distracted to handle it, mothers are denied leadership roles for which they are ready and to which they aspire. They are disregarded for certain job opportunities that they might want because people assume that the increased work requirements would adversely affect their families. This is often the case where relocation and travel are involved. Firms assume that they know what all mothers' preferences are when they should be asking each mother what assignments and responsibilities she wants to accept.

---

[4]Cuddy, A.J.C. (Feb. 2009), Just because I'm nice, don't assume I'm dumb, *Harvard Business Review*; Williams, J.C., Manvell, J., & Bornstein, S. (2006), *Opt-out or pushed out: the untold story of why women leave the workforce*, The Center for WorkLife Law, University of California, Hastings College of the Law.

[5]Buchanan, N.H. (Oct. 2008), *Why do women lawyers earn less than men? Parenthood and gender in a survey of law school graduates* (GWU Legal Studies Research Paper No. 449), The George Washington University Law School.

[6]Buchanan (Oct. 2008), *Why do women lawyers earn less than men?*

In business, stereotyping prevents women with children from being offered expatriate assignments which are considered important for aspiring leaders. Catalyst has found that only 13% of corporate managers who are sent to jobs abroad are women although 80% of women are more likely to accept a position abroad when offered than men are.[7] Companies erroneously assume that women with children will not want to relocate and will have a more difficult time if they do. But women expatriates report no more work-family conflict than men do and 76% of expatriate women said that being a woman had a positive or neutral impact on their effectiveness overseas.[8] In law firms, the problem comes up frequently in matters involving travel. New mothers are not asked or even considered for out-of-town work because it is assumed that a woman would not want to be away from her baby. However, some women would eagerly accept the assignment and would find ways to make it work. A woman's husband might be a stay-at-home dad, she may be comfortable leaving the child with a caretaker, or she might take the baby and a nanny with her when she travels.

Stereotypes also subject women leaders—but not men—to unfair judgments about their work and family choices, and judgmental co-workers can imperil a mother's chances for leadership. A common example is the highly successful woman partner who is accused of being too extreme in her devotion to work. Men are rarely faulted as women are for having no family or for working too hard. If a woman has no spouse or children, people assume her life lacks a greater meaning beyond work and they tsk-tsk that she has made too many sacrifices for her career. If she does have children, works until the moment of delivery, edits documents during labor, takes off very little time after delivery, and spends a great deal of time on the road, they disapprove of that behavior, too. Much of this disapproval is voiced by other women who have their own vision of the ideal working mother—and it does not look like these women. Some of the leaders I spoke with told of lawyers who worked to defeat such "extremely devoted" women in firm elections or to prevent their appointment to positions of leadership because their example might alienate younger women.

Most women lawyers tend to define their success in terms of both career and family. They want to practice law and care for their children, and they want to do their best as lawyers, leaders, and mothers. They do not want to be forced to choose career or

---

[7]Catalyst (2000), *Passport to opportunity: U.S. women in global business.*

[8]Catalyst (2000), *Passport to opportunity.*

family but worry that they cannot excel at both. One leader expressed the constant conflict she feels because work demands leave her so little time for anything else: *"If you have to bill 2200 hours, plus find new clients, plus lead an office or practice group, when do you have time to fit in a child or a spouse?"* When they try to make it work, they usually have to make compromises at the office and at home. Jack Welch, the former CEO of General Electric, once answered when asked about work-life balance that there was no such thing: "There are work-life choices, and you make them, and they have consequences." He added that women who choose to work less than full-time-all-the-time have few prospects for leadership. He was unduly negative about the leadership possibilities for women who choose other paths but he was right about choices and consequences. One of the career choices women often make is to compromise their ambitions by foregoing leadership positions in order to have a family.

The desire for both a career filled with a rewarding professional life and a satisfying home life is not limited to women. Men also make these choices, and the career penalties for them are also severe. Recent research shows both women and men who interrupted their legal careers to stay home with children or to work part-time earn less and are less likely to make partner.[9] (That study also showed that women who interrupted their careers were the most satisfied of all of the lawyers studied with both their personal and professional lives.). However, women are more acutely affected. During the period of layoffs in 2008 and 2009, virtually 100% of the part-time lawyers who were laid off were women.[10] Moreover, as Anna Fels notes, men do not go through the constant renegotiation required of women because there is more cultural consensus about the roles men play at work and at home. Men define their identities and self-worth in large part by their jobs and paychecks; they play lesser roles in child care and their priorities are more predictable and less conflicted. In contrast, women define themselves in many ways besides work and money, and women's roles are still unsettled and rife with conflict. It is true that more men are choosing to work less or off-ramp for a period to stay home.[11] However, they make these choices without the same frequency, urgency, or inevitability that women do.

---

[9]Buchanan (Oct. 2008), *Why do women lawyers earn less than men?*

[10]The National Association of Women Lawyers [NAWL] (Oct. 2009), Report of the fourth annual national survey on retention and promotion of women in law firms.

[11]See, e.g., Chen, V. (Oct. 2009), Paradigm shift: power-lawyer mom, stay-at-home dad, *The American Lawyer*.

One of the byproducts of this stereotyping and unfair judgment is guilt. Guilt is especially pronounced in mothers who want both great careers and happy families. Women with children often feel that if they are leaders and mothers, they cannot do either as well as they would like. They fret that they are shortchanging either the firm or their family and that whatever they are doing they should be doing something else. One management committee member in a large international firm felt, "*I could be so much better if I spent more time at client work or with my family. I feel tension between looking for balance and being great at what I do. There is an honor that comes with leadership, but I'm not sure if it's worth the sacrifices.*"

Some women manage guilt better than others because they have clear goals and priorities, an accommodating work environment, and support at home. Women who lack these things have a harder time dealing with their guilt. Some women leaders who look back on their lives are disappointed and feel career success came at too great a cost to their personal lives. However, many women leaders feel that they succeeded in both aspects of their lives and are very proud of their accomplishments. One managing partner of a small firm was pleased with both her grown children and her professional accomplishments: "*I felt a great deal of guilt when my kids were little. Now I take great pride in knowing that I built all of this—my family, my practice, and the work I am doing at the firm.*"

§ 2:6 Bias against part-time lawyers and resistance to flexibility

Most women lawyers find it imperative to work part-time at various points in their careers. Although a significant number of women lawyers do work part-time successfully, the bias against part-time law practice still limits the opportunities for aspiring women leaders. Part-time lawyers are stigmatized because they are seen as less committed to their careers, clients, and the firm. Most law firms (including 98% of large firms) have instituted reduced-hour policies for lawyers, but hard-driving lawyers reject part-time work because it is viewed as a career killer. So it comes as no surprise that while 14% of the U.S. workforce, including professionals in other fields like medicine, architecture, and engineering, work part-time, just 5.8% of lawyers in major law firms work part-time, and three-quarters of them are women.[1] While the bias against part-time law practice is lessening across the profession, it nonetheless remains strong. This is especially true for women partners, and many law firms that have excellent part-time policies for associates are not receptive to similar flexibility for partners.

Some people argue that women willingly opt out of partnership and leadership when they have children. We know, however, that women who would prefer to maintain their careers and families often feel that they are pushed out because the firm's career structure and time norms do not allow them to do both.[2] Part-time lawyers do not fit the "ideal worker" model, which expects that lawyers will devote themselves fully and without interruption to their work.[3] It presumes that all successful lawyers engage in full-time practice and disfavors lawyers who work less than full time.

The ideal worker model was established by and for men and reflects men's life and work experience. It assumes that lawyers have a wife at home to care for the house and family—but 93% of married women lawyers have spouses with full-time jobs.[4] It glorifies the lawyer who works nonstop and takes little time for anything else and assumes that the only way to become successful, especially as a leader, is by embracing highly individualistic and competitive masculine behaviors which many women and men find unacceptable. This kind of culture ignores the experiences and life patterns of women, especially those with children. It is extremely hard for most mothers to be ideal workers, yet many women work full time at great physical and emotional cost rather than risk having other lawyers withhold good work and leadership opportunities from them. Stanford law professor Deborah Rhode has pointed out the irony of negative attitudes toward part-time lawyers. Far from part-time work showing less commitment, ". . . it generally takes exceptional career commit-

---

[Section 2:6]

[1]NALP (2009), *Most lawyers working part-time are women—Overall number of lawyers working part-time remains small.*

[2]Williams, Manvell, & Bornstein (2006), *Opt Out or Pushed Out?*

[3]Williams, J. (2000), *Unbending gender: why family and work conflict and what to do about it* (New York: Oxford University Press).

[4]Williams (2000), *Unbending gender.*

ment to juggle competing work and family responsibilities in an unsupportive work environment."[5]

In addition to the biased notions about ideal workers, law firm economics and financial management often generate opposition to part-time partners. Some partners resent what they believe are special concessions to reduced-hour lawyers and the extra burdens which they must bear to cover for those lawyers when they are not at work. Others doubt that partners can serve clients competently if they reduce their hours. Many also decry lower revenues; they believe that part-time partners cannot be profitable. Having all partners work full time maximizes firm revenues; when some partners work part-time, the firm sees less total revenue, which means less income for everyone.

The way that firms treat partners' responsibility for overhead expenses also creates tension between full-time and part-time partners. If part-time partners pay the same overhead as full-time partners, they feel it is unfair because by working less, they use fewer resources and so should pay less. But if part-time partners pay proportionately less for overhead, full-time partners complain that the situation is unfair to them since they have to pay full overhead for themselves plus some overhead expenses of partners who work less. It takes considerable leadership effort to persuade law firm partnerships that partners who work part-time can provide sufficient value to the firm, and in most firms it is decided on a case-by-case basis.

Research shows that reducing your hours does not have to limit your success and that part-time partners can indeed be profitable. A 2009 study by The Project for Attorney Retention (PAR) concludes that partners with part-time schedules are able to have personally satisfying careers and make significant financial and leadership contributions that benefit their firms.[6] According to this study, 12% of women law firm partners and three percent of all partners in the United States work part-time. The part-time partners in the PAR study had sizeable books of business, spent considerable time in business development, generated significant revenue through their own work and the work they distributed to other lawyers, and held leadership positions in their firms, including managing partner, executive committee member, practice group head, and members of high-level committees. Because they served their clients seamlessly, most

---

[5]Rhode, D.L. (Ed.) (2003), *The difference "difference" makes* (Stanford: Stanford University Press).

[6]Calvert, C.T., Chanow, L.B., & Marks, L. (Sept. 2009), *Reduced hours, full success*, The Project for Attorney Retention.

clients did not know they were part-time, and those who did know were supportive. One of the PAR findings is especially striking. Of the 109 part-time partners interviewed for this study

> The vast majority of partners stated that they would likely have left their firms if they could not have worked flexibly. Their career decisions bear this out: more than three-fourths (76%) of the partners interviewed began working reduced hours at their current firms, and the average tenure of those partners is 12 years (ranging from 4 to 37). Given that more than half of women lawyers leave their law firms by their 7th year, this longevity is noteworthy.[7]

The experience of the women leaders I interviewed is in line with PAR's findings. Many of these leaders negotiated part-time or flex-time arrangements at different points in their careers and some of them had reduced-hour schedules as partners. Several of the women who were interviewed became partners while working part-time, were part-time when they were elected or appointed to leadership posts, or worked part-time while they held leadership positions. A few women worked full time but negotiated conditions that limited or gave them greater control over their work schedules. For example, several women with children (from babies to teenagers) limited their travel obligations when they became managing partners or practice group leaders. They still had to travel but they could decide when and how often.

These leaders were able to work this way because first and foremost they were highly respected as lawyers and had skills or traits which the firm deemed very important. Firms agreed to the arrangements because these women had proven their excellence as lawyers, commitment to the firm, and leadership ability. Based on that history, they earned the continuing respect and trust of their partners. Their firms gave them latitude in designing flexible schedules and limiting their obligations even though some partners questioned whether the firm should permit them to work less than full time.

One of the points women leaders raised in negotiating reduced-time schedules was the fact that many full-time partners actually worked part-time. Because of commitments to bar activities, corporate boards, or leadership positions in national organizations, they billed less than full-time lawyers. (Author Lauren Rikleen has noted wryly that most managing partners maintain only a part-time practice.[8]). These leaders persuaded their firms

---

[7]Calvert, Chanow, & Marks (Sept. 2009), *Reduced hours, full success*, 11.

[8]Rikleen, L.S. (2006), *Ending the gauntlet: removing the barriers to women's success in the law* (Thomson Legalworks).

that time for child rearing was just as valuable and worthy of respect.

While they worked part-time, these women remained flexible, available, and visible. Their clients' interests remained foremost and regardless of their work schedules, these leaders were always responsive to their clients' needs. To make sure that they had reliable lawyers and teams to support their clients, they invested the time to supervise and train people and to keep communication channels open. Notably, these women did not limit their activities to client work. They remained active in their firms and participated in leadership roles, recruiting, and other activities that were important to them and valued by the firm.

The women I interviewed had mixed feelings about the advisability of part-time work for women who strive to become leaders. All were sympathetic to women's needs for greater flexibility, but several disfavored women taking part-time status except for a brief period while they have young children. One woman who has a family and is a major rainmaker in her firm believed that, *"You can't be as good a lawyer part-time. You're running a business."* She felt that this was especially true for women who want to be taken seriously as leaders. The critics of part-time schedules for partners reflect the prevalent attitude among partners, including many women, and the concerns that they raise are valid. In small firms and practice groups especially, there may be real staffing constraints that make it impossible for partners to work a reduced schedule. However, the experience and example of many leaders who profitably and successfully work part-time in all types of firms and practice areas shows that most objections can be addressed and overcome.

A related issue involving the desire for flexibility deals with career patterns. Law firms' ideal workers have careers that progress steadily upward throughout their lives. European gender consultants Avivah Wittenberg-Cox and Alison Maitland explain that unlike the uninterrupted and linear upward trajectory of men's careers, women, especially mothers, have an "M-shaped" career curve.[9] In their 20s women start their careers moving upward the same way as men do, but at some point, often in their 30s or early 40s, their career progress dips or plateaus for a period when they have children, then picks up again later.

Some of those dips involve "off-ramping," i.e., taking some period of time away from your career, especially when you have

---

[9]Wittenberg-Cox, A., & Maitland, A. (2008), *Why women mean business: understanding the emergence of our next economic revolution* (San Francisco: Jossey-Bass).

young children. More than 42% of women lawyers off-ramp.[10] Some leave for a few months while others may take years off, especially if they have two or more children. The average time that women lawyers off-ramp is three years. The great majority of women who off-ramp want to return to work, but they have to overcome the negative assumptions about their dedication to their careers. In fact, many women who return to practice after off-ramping for a while are more ready than ever to move ahead, build their client base, and become leaders.

None of the law firm leaders I interviewed dropped out of the workforce completely, but several left private practice for periods of time and then returned, although not necessarily to the same firms. They worked in government agencies, corporate legal departments, business, or the judiciary. Many of these women wanted more flexibility and those other jobs provided it. When the time was right for them, they returned to law firm practice and resumed or stepped into leadership roles. They never questioned the business imperative and competitive nature of law firm life, but they found ways to advance their careers without succumbing to the rigidity of law firm career expectations.

The stigma against part-time work is diminishing. Generation Y lawyers adamantly favor more workplace and career flexibility, and they have substantial support from older lawyers on these issues.[11] The workplace preferences of younger lawyers are shifting to concerns, styles, and values that are stereotypically feminine: they are highly collaborative and team-oriented, and workplace flexibility is as much a concern to them as the size of their paycheck.[11] These younger lawyers—men as well as women—are vocal about their need for time away from work, whether for family or other personal interests. Firms are beginning to appreciate the economic benefit of keeping talented and productive lawyers who have these attitudes and are adopting policies that endorse greater schedule and career flexibility. Women who hope to become leaders on a part-time basis still face an uphill battle but this is an area where progress is being made.

The leaders I interviewed shared many perspectives about flexible work arrangements. Here are some of them:

---

[10]Hewlett, S.A., Luce, C.B., Shiller, P., & Southwell, S. (2005), *The hidden brain drain: off-ramps and on-ramps in women's careers*, Center for Work-Life Policy.

[11]Hewlett, S.A., Sherbin, L., & Sumberg, K. (July-Aug. 2009), How GenY & Boomers will reshape your agenda, *Harvard Business Review*.

[11]Hewlett, Sherbin, & Sumberg (July-Aug. 2009), How GenY & Boomers will reshape your agenda.

- *I am a workaholic. I need to pull myself back. So I take time off between deals. I became partner at [a top NY firm] while working flextime. I had shown them how committed and good a lawyer I was. I took time between deals then, too.*
- *I have been part-time seven years now, billing 2/3 of full-time partner expectations. I spend lots of time on nonbillables too. I just want the flexibility to take time if I need it. My kids are getting older and I want to be with them. Clients don't know I'm part-time because I'm always available, even on some vacations. It took me two years to figure out how to make it work.*
- *I was single and other women with children expected me to pick up the slack for them. Now I have kids and am careful about what I expect of single women.*
- *Now that I have a big book of business, I have much more flexibility. I have more time. I have a good rich work and family life.*
- *I have no kids—that helps my career. But if a part-time person can't do something and expects me to do it, I resent it. Law is a service business; the client keeps calling. It's unfair to ask me to subsidize your choices. Also, I don't favor part-time just for kids. We should allow it for everyone. I would like to teach part time if I could work less, or do legal clinic work or work in a nonprofit. That's just as important as kids. But now I need to spend my spare time doing things that will bring in business.*

Chapter 3

Authenticity and Leadership Styles

§ 3:1   The importance of authenticity

> **KeyCite®:** Cases and other legal materials listed in KeyCite Scope can be researched through the KeyCite service on Westlaw®. Use KeyCite to check citations for form, parallel references, prior and later history, and comprehensive citator information, including citations to other decisions and secondary materials.

---

§ 3:1   The importance of authenticity

Be yourself. Everyone else is already taken.

—Anonymous

Women place a high value on authenticity.[1] Being authentic means leading in a way that feels natural to you. Successful leaders find ways to lead authentically. They realize that they have to be who they are, not who others want them to be. They recognize and build on their unique talents and qualities. They step back and ask: Is this really me? Then they listen to and trust their internal voice.

Women leaders have an easier time being authentic when they establish their credentials first. Once people know that you know your stuff, they give you more respect and latitude. You can be flashy without detracting from your professionalism and authority. Kathi Lutton, an intellectual property lawyer and head of the global litigation practice at Fish & Richardson, loves to wear fancy shoes:

> *You need to dig deep. You need to dig deeper than anyone and understand your field as well if not better than anyone else. You need to do this not because you are a woman but because you care and want to be good. The better you are substantively, the more you*

[Section 3:1]

[1]Wittenberg-Cox, A., & Maitland, A. (2008), *Why women mean business: understanding the emergence of our next economic revolution* (San Francisco: Jossey Bass); Center for Creative Leadership (May 2008), No more glass ceiling: new thinking on women in leadership, *Leading Effectively.*

can express yourself as you are without losing credibility. When I walk into a client event wearing my jeweled manolos, not one client questions whether I understand the use of epitaxial layers in semiconductors or the difference between the network and transport layers in the OSI model.

Authentic leaders know who they are and do not need to adopt another's persona. Many women leaders I interviewed have played competitively in sports or other arenas, succeeding in areas outside of law practice. Some held their own in previous positions in companies, the military, and other fields that were predominantly male. When pressured to behave differently in order to fit in, they might accommodate or adapt, but they did not try to behave in a way that made them uncomfortable. As one leader pondered, *"It's hard enough to be yourself. I can't imagine trying to be someone else."*

"Being yourself" sounds pretty straightforward but it is not always easy to do. The nature of law practice embodies masculine traits; it is adversarial, directive, autonomous, hierarchical, and aggressive. In that environment, women are pressured to demonstrate those behaviors, and many women adapt by employing a masculine style in their law practice. Believing that they cannot be themselves (i.e., display feminine characteristics) if they hope to advance in a male environment, they create "strategies of gender management" that enable them to blend into the established order.[2] They either emulate a masculine image or play down their femininity.

Women today feel less compelled than they did in the past to act "manly." The leaders I interviewed were able to develop more balanced styles that incorporated traits considered both masculine (e.g., being direct and decisive) and feminine (e.g., being supportive and cooperative). You, too, can develop a style that combines the traits that you need to be effective as a leader without worrying about whether they are stereotypically masculine or feminine.

Some male leaders struggle with the desire for authenticity, but women walk a more treacherous path than men. When women try to become leaders in a man's world, they are "damned if they do, damned if they don't." As noted earlier, women are held to higher, conflicting standards and face greater constraints than their male peers. Because people associate leadership traits with men, women face what has been called a "fundamental

---

[2]Oakley, J.G. (Oct. 2000), Gender-based barriers to senior management positions: understanding the scarcity of female CEOs, *Journal of Business Ethics* 27, no. 4, pt. 2.

incongruity"[3] and "an inherent contradiction"[4] between women's female identity and the masculine traits associated with leadership. Because the cultural norms of the law firm are masculine, women lawyers face conflicting expectations for their gender and their job, a classic catch-22. They are denigrated as inauthentic if they adopt "masculine" styles that are believed to be necessary for leadership. If they act in stereotypically feminine ways, however, they do not fit into the masculine norms of the workplace. In either case, the same behavior by a man and a woman is interpreted differently. The attributes and behaviors that are positively linked to leadership in men are deemed unnatural and unattractive in women. A man who is assertive and takes control is admired; a woman who acts the same way is called a bitch. This presents women with impossible choices.

It is important to understand stereotypes about feminine and masculine styles, but it would be a mistake to accept them as true for all women and men. It would also be incorrect to suggest that any leader has only one leadership style. Effective leaders employ a variety of approaches, fitting the particular style they use to the situation at hand. Some women's styles fit comfortably and naturally at the "masculine" end of the spectrum, and there are many men who have a softer, more collaborative and "feminine" style. Most successful leaders combine masculine and feminine styles. While that is usually very effective, women in traditionally male roles sometimes puzzle people when they do not conform to expectations. One successful trial lawyer mused that her style is "gender confused." People have told her, "You think like a man," calculating and intimidating, but they also tell her, "You try cases like a girl," always being polite. Another leader recalled how her gender confounded others about her leadership potential: *"When I was being considered for firm-wide managing partner, some people thought I could do it better because I was a woman; others thought I could do it in spite of being a woman."* It can also be confusing for women. In her book describing the lives and careers of five women physicians who went through medical school together, Dr. Toni Martin describes

---

[3]Eagley, A.H., & Karau, S.J. (2002), Role congruity theory of prejudice toward female leaders, *Psychological Review* 109.

[4]Ely, R. J., & Rhode, D.L. (2010), Women and leadership: defining the challenges, in N. Nohria & R. Khurana (Eds.), *Handbook of leadership theory and practice* (Boston: Harvard Business School Press), ch. 14.

that she felt like she belonged to a "third gender," with a woman's body and a man's job.[5] Many women lawyers can relate to that.

INSEAD professor Herminia Ibarra has studied how people develop a professional identity when they transition into leadership. Her research shows that as men move into leadership, they adopt and imitate various strategies from a broad assortment of role models. Women, on the other hand, prefer to remain "true-to-self" and hold tighter to their natural styles than men do.[6] Women assume that the persona most natural to them is the most effective for being a leader. They continue to transfer to their new roles as leaders the same strategies, traits, and behaviors that have worked for them in the past. This may feel safer and allow women to take pride in being authentic, but it limits their versatility and narrows the foundation upon which to build a leadership identity.

Being authentic is not just about being natural. Your propensity to be authoritarian, indecisive, or unable to say no to anyone may be natural to you, but it will not serve you well as a leader. These behaviors may have worked for you in your past positions, but as a leader, you may need to adopt new ways of dealing with people and circumstances. "Being yourself" as a leader is further complicated because it may be different than "being yourself" as a lawyer. The style that made you a successful lawyer may not be as effective for the situations that a leader has to handle.

One important difference when you become a leader is that you are now leading partners, and you cannot lead them the same way that you lead a team of associates and staff. One new managing partner who is naturally very detail-oriented was criticized for micromanaging people. Her attention to detail served her well when she was reviewing contracts, but partners got angry when she constantly looked over their shoulders on the projects that they were running for the firm. Worried about becoming an ineffective leader, she changed her approach and stopped asking partners for detailed reports about the status of their ongoing projects. She found that by giving up control over the details and focusing on the results, she became more accepted and effective as a leader.

As this example illustrates, leadership is dynamic and requires adaptability. Authenticity does not mean standing still or never

---

[5]Martin, T. (2008), *When the personal was political: five women doctors look back* (New York: iUniverse, Inc).

[6]Ibarra, H., & Petriglieri, J. (Nov. 2007), *Impossible selves: image strategies and identity threat in professional women's career transitions*, INSEAD Faculty and Research Working Paper.

changing. To be authentic, you must remain true to your values; but to get results as a leader, you also have to adapt your style to different people and situations. When partners ask you for favors, if you always play hardball or are viewed as a pushover, your predictability either way leaves you little room to negotiate. You need to know when to push hard or back off and when to press them about current needs or trade short-term outcomes for a long-term goal. You may need to be direct and authoritarian when you must force a decision, democratic and inclusive when trying to build consensus, or supportive when helping a partner who is facing a career crisis. The important thing is to find a range of styles that feel right for you and that also help you to get your job done. If one approach is not working, step back and try to understand why. If another style might work better, give it a try. As you expand your range of leadership styles, your greater versatility will help you to deal with different situations.

This process is not intended to turn you into someone else but rather to help you become a more effective "you." You can maintain your sense of self and at the same time use your social skills to adapt to new conditions. This enables you to extend your range and increase your impact as a leader. One of the women I interviewed recounts how this process worked for her. She left a law firm for a stint in the State Attorney's office and found the experience liberating. She was able to be more creative, take risks, and loosen up in ways that were hard to do in the more rigid culture of her law firm. In the process, she developed a style that was more comfortable, casual, and confident, and ultimately more successful for her when she returned to private practice.

It feels risky and strange when you first "try on" different styles and tactics. You can reduce your discomfort by being methodical about it.

- Observe a leader you admire and find a style or approach that leader uses that seems to be effective for him or her.
- Try it out when an opportunity comes up where it might be useful. When you are doing it, note how you feel, how others react to you, and how effective it is.
- Assess the experience against your personal values and standards to see whether you feel that it is an acceptable approach for you to use in the future.
- Seek feedback from others about how you came across and how effective you were. You can tell someone in advance of a meeting or event that you would like them to observe you and give you feedback about how you do.
- If the new technique does not seem right for you, discard it

from your repertoire. But if it does seem acceptable, consider how and when you might use it again or adapt it in some way.

Trying out different strategies and styles is easier when you can observe a variety of role models and choose the behaviors that seem the most promising for you to emulate. Men have a distinct advantage over women because they have so many more models to observe. Until recently, the only leadership role models available to most women were men because there were so few women who were law firm leaders—and many of those women had developed masculine styles in order to become leaders. Over the years, however, as the number of women lawyers in law firms has steadily increased, women partners started to embrace rather than hide their femininity. As more of them now move into leadership positions, they are finding ways to project authority without using masculine styles that they find uncomfortable and others find unsettling. As author Deborah Blum puts it, "The most heartening part of seeing women rise in the power structure is not seeing them perform like powerful men, but like powerful women."[7]

That is exactly what we are starting to see, especially with women like those I interviewed. For example, many women leaders described themselves as very direct, a quality not usually associated with femininity. They give clear messages, and while they try to be diplomatic, they stay focused on the message. One of those leaders, the managing partner of an intellectual property firm, related that she has been complimented for being nicer than her male predecessor even though she "tells it like it is." He would tiptoe around the issues, trying to be kind and avoid hurting people's feelings, even when he had to fire someone. This created ambiguity that left people nervous and uncomfortable, while with her, everyone knows exactly where they stand—a state which they prefer.

Today's women leaders are creating new styles of leadership. They are both tough and feminine. They are using their femininity to their advantage rather than seeing it as a problem. They are open, collegial, and inclusive, but also assertive, persuasive, and willing to take risks.[8] This gives today's emerging women leaders a wider variety of role models and styles to choose from, and still more will become available as the number of women leaders continues to grow. We can hope that as more people

---

[7]Blum, D. (1997), *Sex on the brain* (New York: Penguin Books).

[8]Caliper Corporation (2005), *The qualities that distinguish women leaders*, http://www.caliperonline.com/brochures/WomenLeaderWhitePaper.pdf.

encounter diversity among women leaders, the range of expected and acceptable styles for leaders—women and men—will expand and the disconnect between "woman" and "leader" will disappear.

One of the important benefits to the profession from having more women in leadership is a greater diversity of leadership styles. Research shows that the more styles a leader can use the more effective that leader can be.[9] A Hay Group study of law firm partners found that partners' ability to utilize a variety of leadership styles resulted in stronger professional performance and higher firm revenues. The Hay Group identified six principal styles of leadership (See Table 3.1):[10]

- The *Directive* style focuses the team's attention on achieving immediate compliance and task completion. It ensures that urgent issues are quickly and effectively addressed.
- The *Visionary* style gives people clear direction, perspective, and context for their work. It inspires people to act independently but in alignment with the goals of the firm.
- The *Pacesetting* style involves leading by example. It gets people to accomplish tasks according to high standards of excellence set by the leader.
- The *Participative* style stimulates creativity and a sense of involvement among team members. It results in widespread commitment to innovation and improvement.
- The *Coaching* style is used to mentor and develop junior professionals. It focuses on long-term professional development and improving the return on the firm's investment in people.
- The *Affiliative* style focuses on team members' personal and professional needs. It creates harmony and connection within the leader's team.

Studying these six leadership styles among lawyers, the Hay Group compared "best" leaders with "average" leaders. They found that the best leaders used a broader range of styles than average leaders. Almost 70% of the best leaders used four or more of the six styles, compared to only 40% of the average group. Moreover, the best leaders used Visionary, Participative, Coaching, and Affiliative styles, which encourage dialogue among group

---

[9]Snyder, S., & Littauer, S. (2005), Leadership flexibility: how outstanding partners get results, *The Journal of Legal Marketing. Also see* Spreier, W., Fontaine, M.H., & Malloy, R.L. (June 2006), Leadership run amok: destructive potential of overachievers, *Harvard Business Review.*

[10]Based on "Leadership flexibility: how outstanding partners get results" and "Leadership run amok: destructive potential of overachievers."

members, more often than Directive or Pacesetting styles, which curtail it.

The best leaders matched their styles to their objectives. When trying to develop strategy or generate ideas, they used the participative style to engage team members and unleash creativity. But in times of crisis or chaos, a directive style was more effective because it focused people's attention and spurred them into action quickly. The best leaders did not overuse the directive style; they used it judiciously and only when appropriate.

Table 3.1: The Hay Group's Six Leadership Styles
Directive: Do what I tell you
Visionary: Come with me
Pacesetting: Do as I do
Participative: What do you think?
Coaching: Try this
Affiliative: People come first

Chapter 4

Traps That Women Should Avoid

KeyCiteʀ: Cases and other legal materials listed in KeyCite Scope can be researched through the KeyCite service on Westlawʀ. Use KeyCite to check citations for form, parallel references, prior and later history, and comprehensive citator information, including citations to other decisions and secondary materials.

---

§ 4:1   The need for strategic awareness

Women have to watch out for "traps" that can derail their careers and prevent them from becoming effective leaders. You may be lured into believing a particular career move will help you, when in fact it may hold you back or pull you off the leadership track. If you are aware of these traps, you can avoid them; if you are caught in one of them you can get out. The key is to recognize them and approach them strategically. Here are three of the most common traps:

- *Tokenism*. Firms sometimes give women "token" leadership roles that sound impressive but advance the firm's, not the woman's, interests.
- *Saying yes*. Women believe that they have to accept any assignments or responsibilities they are offered and end up doing unnecessary and undervalued work.
- *Being a service partner*. Women stay in the shadows of other partners and put their careers in those partners' hands.

§ 4:2   Tokenism

Women are sometimes placed into leadership roles that give them little or no respect, influence, or power. They are simply "token" women who enable the firm to show that its women lawyers hold leadership positions. Firms give these women titles but no clout. Some firms have one or more "women's seats" on their top committees or appoint women to management positions that sound good but carry no weight. Holding these spots for women is often unspoken, not overt, and it benefits the firm's public image because it can point to its women leaders. Firms also use women to attract business when they need to show clients that they are diverse. Partners bring women along on pitches when they think that the potential client expects women on the team. However, they do not engage the women during the pitch meeting, and when the work comes in, they do not make women part of the client team. One leader who objected to being placed on "soft" committees told her managing partner, *"Put me in charge of business functions instead. Don't use me to advertise women in management unless we're really in management."*

Tokenism should be exposed for what it is: an exploitation of women for the firm's advantage. Nonetheless, savvy women who think strategically can take these token positions and turn them to their own advantage. They can do this by taking the "woman's seat" and going on client pitches but refusing to behave like tokens. That is what many of the leaders I interviewed did. They had been placed in roles because the firm needed a woman in leadership. They used their positions to build relationships that helped them acquire mentors, champions, and clients. They learned the firm's business, gained visibility, built and joined informal networks, and acted like leaders. They set themselves up for weightier future leadership positions by developing leadership skills and producing good results.

Tokenism is a special dilemma for women of color. When the leaders of color I interviewed saw a benefit to being a minority, they used it. When an in-house lawyer advised one African American woman, *"Be sure you send your picture in with your proposal,"* she was not offended; her picture got her in the door and her ability got her the business. Here are some other examples of how women of color see themselves and convert their token status to their benefit:

- An Asian American woman leader feels that she brings something unique to the table: *"I use it to my advantage. It never holds me back. It puts me in the spotlight, so I use that by doing a really great job."*
- Another Asian American woman served on numerous committees and task forces. A self-described skeptic, she always raised a lot of questions. *"I looked different anyway, so it wasn't a surprise to people that I would question and speak up."* Because of that, she had more impact.
- An African American woman who chaired her firm's hiring

committee felt that *"People take me at my word on some subjects, because I have credibility . . . . My opinion on women, especially women of color, is often treated as 'super-equal' in hiring decisions."*

- A Latina leader has intentionally made diversity the heart of her leadership advancement strategy. *"I try to become indispensable as a firm resource. I am involved outside the firm. I mentor summer associates and associates. I am known nationally as an advocate for diversity. I am also a working mother and a lesbian. When the firm needs someone in any of several categories I get tapped."*

§ 4:3 Always saying "yes"

When something needs to be done and volunteers are sought, women raise their hands more frequently than men. Women leaders are more likely than men to be asked for favors, more likely to do them, and less likely to be appreciated for the effort.[1] Many women are flattered when asked to take on management responsibilities and feel obligated to say yes. They believe that by working hard for the firm they will be appreciated and valued. They want to be good citizens and believe that requires agreeing to do whatever the firm asks of them. One leader explained why, as a lateral associate, she always agreed to what was asked of her: *"When I started at the firm, I felt insecure. I said yes to everything they asked me to do. I figured it must be a good sign that they asked me to do it. They wouldn't give me this kind of responsibility if they weren't going to make me a partner."* She did become a partner but only by doing far more extra work than her peers did. As another leader cautioned, *"Citizenship and servitude are very different things."*

Women say yes to too many things. They are super-responsible good girls; they do their own work plus whatever else needs to be done that others have neglected. They value other people's time more than their own. While they are reluctant to "impose" on others, they find it hard to say no when asked to give their time. All of this makes them good team players—but at their own expense.

Several women leaders who were interviewed said that they and other women partners in their firms unofficially take on extra leadership roles by doing the job of some other leader, e.g., their

---

[Section 4:3]

[1]Meers, S., & Strober, J. (2009), *Getting to 50/50: how working couples can have it all by sharing it all* (New York: Bantam Books).

practice group leader or co-managing partner. One woman explained, *"The head of my practice group is a great trial lawyer but a terrible manager. He doesn't like to do what he isn't good at, so I basically run the group—in addition to all my other practice and management responsibilities!"* Another woman said that her firm's managing partner has delegated most management responsibilities to another woman partner so that he can spend most of his time doing what he likes to do—practice law.

The women who took on these extra responsibilities chose to do so, but you do not have to. Always saying yes can be dangerous to your career success. Why should you do extra work that someone else could or should be doing? If you have demonstrated a propensity to say yes, people will offer you more time-consuming positions or projects, many of which will be unimportant and they will expect you to keep saying yes. It's like winning the pie-eating contest where the prize is more pie.

This is one area where women can learn a lot from men. Your male colleagues are pickier about the management responsibilities which they undertake and not as compulsive about completing them; they may let things slide or simply neglect to do them. Men more readily delegate tasks to others, spreading the responsibility around and receiving the credit while others do the actual work. Here is how one leader described what she witnessed in her firm:

> *Men who take management positions want the title, the "prestige," but not the work, so they do not spend the time and don't do as good a job but get the credit. They might have an administrative co-chair or someone they delegate the work to—and it's usually a woman, so they get credit for the position (which is sometimes reflected in their compensation), but don't do that much. Meanwhile, the women who do the work get praise for a good job but no compensation or time credit.*

Another leader made this observation:

> *Younger women partners are willing to do the work they're asked to do no matter how unappealing, detail-oriented, or boring. Men would say, "I don't do that anymore. I'm a big picture person," and delegate it to someone else or just turn it down. They cherry pick assignments, the people they work with, etc. They have a greater sense of entitlement.*

All effective leaders need other people to help them carry out their responsibilities. Men in leadership roles are shrewd to enlist other people to do a lot of their management tasks. Those people—often women partners—who do the work for them should make sure that they either get appropriate credit for it or refuse to do it. When you are the leader in charge, you should also delegate much of your day-to-day work so that you can attend to your client relationships and leadership responsibilities. If you give credit to the people who do the work for you, you will have no trouble finding willing helpers.

Similarly, women frequently agree to take on administrative projects and committee assignments without regard to whether the activity will help their careers. You do not need to accept every position or project which you are offered. Before you say yes, consider that many administrative tasks, committee jobs, and management assignments are unimportant to the firm and useless for your career advancement. Even if you feel grateful for the firm's recognition, be selective and protect your time and effort. If planning a firm retreat will get you closer to the key players in the firm, it is a smart thing to do. Say yes. In contrast, if you are asked because no one else wants to do it—by all means, say no. Likewise, women are usually asked to be on less important committees and rarely asked to sit on the more prestigious ones. They tend to say yes to either kind, which is a mistake. You want to say yes only to committees whose members or mission will advance your career.

When you are asked to take a significant project or leadership role, keep two things in mind: you do not have to answer immediately, and "yes" or "no" are not your only choices. Take time to think about what you want to do and then consider your options. In contrast to women who say yes too easily, some women turn down valuable opportunities because they do not think strategically. Often they worry that it will take too much time or that they lack certain skills, or they determine that they want to focus on client development instead. The more appropriate concern should be: how will this assignment advance my career?

To help you determine whether a leadership appointment will benefit your career, ask yourself:

- How does this position advance my career goals?
- Is this the right time and the right position?
- Is this a stepping-stone to another position I want?
- Is there any other compelling reason to say yes?

The choices you make will depend on your personal situation; different women will see different possibilities. If a leadership position fits your career ambitions or interests at the time it is offered, you might jump at the chance to accept it, even though it adds another burden to your life. Another woman might find the same appointment undesirable because of practice, family or other priorities that are more important for her. The position is tempting but the timing is wrong.

Sometimes you face a risk if you turn down an appointment even though you don't want to do it. There may be a cogent reason to say yes. One leader in the New York office of a global firm turned down an appointment as head of the hiring committee because she thought the committee was too time-consuming and did not interest her. However, the Managing Partner considered it one of the most vital positions in the firm. When he asked her again the following year, she knew this would be the last time he would ask her and that if she said no this time, no other committee appointments would be forthcoming.

If you determine that a committee assignment is a good strategic move for you, then find a way to make it work by negotiating terms that address your concerns. You usually have some room to bargain. Table 4.1 lists some questions to help you determine your negotiating position. What would make it easier for you to say yes? Ask for it! Many of the women I interviewed had persuaded their firms to set boundaries around their responsibilities, e.g., through limits on travel, on the number of years or terms they would remain on a committee, or on the kind of administrative support that they needed. When one woman was asked to be managing partner of a global firm, one of the conditions which she negotiated was to travel only on day trips during the summer when her son was home from college. Another woman reluctantly agreed to serve on her firm's management committee for only one five-year term. She told the firm, *"If I'm on the committee, I want no more than one five-year 'sentence.'"*

Table 4.1. Consider your negotiating position

Why do they need you in the position?

What leverage do you have?

What will you bring to the position?

What power and authority will you have? (Go behind what they tell you; find out what really happens. Talk to people who previously held the position.)

What will be the impact on your practice if you take the position?

What resources and support will you need? Do you have a person or team to whom you can delegate day-to-day responsibilities?

It is safe to assume that whatever terms are set, even if in writing, the firm will expect more from you than you agree to. This may affect your compensation, or if you move into a full-time management job, your return to practice when you finish. It is, therefore, critical to have written guidelines about the job expectations as well as objectives and metrics on which you will be evaluated. Negotiate these guidelines to your satisfaction. Spell out the amount of your compensation and what it will be based on. Bargain from strength. In a negotiation, women sometimes get discouraged or give up when their proposals are rejected. But "no" in a negotiation does not necessarily mean "no," especially in the first rounds. Having clarity about your values and career goals should help you decide what you will fight for and how hard. Think through what the job will entail from the time you accept it to the time you transition out at its conclusion, and address issues sooner rather than later.

§ 4:4 Being a service partner

The most highly valued and compensated partners in a law firm are those who bring in new business that keeps other partners, associates, and paralegals busy, often in more than one practice area. Many partners are not major rainmakers, but they have enough of their own business to be self-sufficient, give some work to others, and stay profitable for the firm. Business-generating and self-sufficient partners have the greatest degree of career control and the most possibilities for leadership. Service partners have the least.

Service partners do not bring in their own clients. They manage the clients that rainmakers bring in but do not assume the primary relationship with those clients. Sometimes women fall into a service role because the powerful partner they work for controls the work they get. But some women choose to remain in the background and forego leadership prospects. By serving other partners' clients and avoiding the extra time and responsibilities involved in business development, they deliberately shy away from the risks and pressures of leadership. While this may make sense as a career choice at certain points in a woman's career, it is a risky long-term strategy because it places control over your career in other people's hands.

Because service partners work on other partners' business, they cannot support themselves. Their career status is vulnerable and their opportunities for leadership are slim. The association with rainmakers may bring with it a certain degree of prestige and status if the rainmaker and clients are important enough to the firm. The rainmaker may also be a strong mentor who gives you a steady stream of excellent work and watches out for you. While it sounds appealing, tying your fate to another partner affords you little control or protection, even if that partner is a strong mentor. The relationship may lead to a false sense of security because a rainmaker who relies on you may protect you only so long as you are needed to do their clients' work. When that day ends, you realize that your comfort came at a steep cost: It deprived you of control over your career.

As a service partner, you have very little security, autonomy, or mobility. The rainmaker has you to do the work, but he or she gets to keep the credit, compensation, and client. If the rainmaker leaves and takes the client, you have no guarantee that you can go along. If the rainmaker loses a key client or falls out of favor in the firm, you are stuck. If you want to leave the firm, you have a harder time finding another job because you have no book of business and are too experienced to be a desirable job candidate without one.

Servicing other partners' clients can be a good choice for many women, especially at certain points in their lives. Many women who have young children or are trying to build up specialized technical expertise can benefit from feeling less pressure to bring in their own business. Being a service partner gives you the chance to do what you love best—practice law—without worrying about business development. It can be a great job so long as times are good and you are happy being second chair. But if your ambitions are greater and you want to become a leader, then being a service partner is best as a temporizing or transitional stage.

The trap is that some ambitious women become service partners and never get out. If you see it as a temporary position, you have to be sure that you have an exit strategy. However, because you are at the mercy of a powerful partner, you are never sure that you will be able to execute your strategy. The co-managing partner in a California firm describes how she began as a service partner to a powerful partner and mentor and then eventually became a leader in her own right. Her mentor, who was the head of her practice group, was very controlling and promoted her only when the move was compatible with his needs. He knew that she aspired to higher leadership but needed her to do his client work, so he withheld his support for her appointment to key positions. When the department had grown larger and he no longer needed her as much, he helped her become managing partner. She was smart to voice her leadership goal and lucky that he was, eventually, willing to support it.

To move yourself from the role of service partner into a stronger position you need more than luck. People need to start seeing you as someone who has her own solid client relationships and business. Make sure that people know you desire to move beyond being a service partner and start laying the foundation for your transition by developing your own business, bringing in your own clients, and strengthening your personal relationship with the clients you serve. With regard to current client relationships, clients who see you as the "go-to" partner may start to send business directly to you. When clients want you to run their cases or deals, or they seek advice from you directly, you have more leverage to assert your independence. However, you have to be careful. You may not intend to undermine the existing relationship partner, but that partner may start to view you as a threat and take measures against you, such as directing that client's work to someone else. You do not want to go behind the partner's back, but you do need to be prudent about when and how much to tell the partner about your plan to step out from the shadows and into the limelight.

Chapter 5

Women-to-Women Relationships

KeyCite⁶: Cases and other legal materials listed in KeyCite Scope can be researched through the KeyCite service on Westlaw⁶. Use KeyCite to check citations for form, parallel references, prior and later history, and comprehensive citator information, including citations to other decisions and secondary materials.

---

§ 5:1   Women's expectations of women leaders

Relationships between women raise a separate set of complications for women in leadership positions. There is often talk of "gender wars" and suggestions that women leaders are at odds with other women in the workplace. Whether women are really harder on each other is hard to determine; much of the evidence for it is anecdotal. Some women do try to undermine other women; antagonism sometimes surfaces between women with children and those without; and many younger and older women reject each other's attitudes about work and career. However, law firms are not rife with women-to-women conflict. To the contrary, the leaders I interviewed uniformly seek to foster mutual support among women in their firms, as do the women's initiatives in law firms all over the country. This is consistent with research showing that women on corporate boards and in top executive roles serve as positive role models and mentors who encourage other women to stay and succeed.[1]

In law firms, too, research confirms that having more women

[Section 5:1]

[1]*See, e.g.*, Joy, L. (July 2008), *Advancing women leaders: the connection between women board directors and women corporate officers*, Catalyst; The Lehman Brothers Centre for Women in Business (2007), *Inspiring women: corporate best practice in Europe*, London Business School.

in leadership creates better relations among women, as well as better work conditions and more opportunities for women's advancement.[2] Women associates are more serious about their work, more satisfied with their firm, more self-confident, and more interested in promotion when there are a substantial number of women in senior leadership positions. Gender roles are less stereotypical and less problematic, and significantly, the quality of relationships among women is better. In contrast, the scarcity of women in senior leadership negatively influences women associates. In firms with few senior women leaders, women associates are less likely to perceive gender as a positive basis for identification, less likely to perceive senior women as role models with legitimate authority, more likely to experience competition in relationships with other women, and less likely to find support in those relationships. Overall, they see few role models with whom they can relate, and they have difficulty finding ways to feel personally satisfied and professionally valued as women.

As a woman leader, you need to be able to handle the special expectations and frustrations of the women you lead. You do not want to get caught up in personal struggles over relationships and biased or unrealistic expectations of "niceness," friendship, shared intent, and support for women's concerns. In most cases, treating other women respectfully, setting clear boundaries, and staying focused on the work you are there to do are techniques to help you maneuver through these relationships at the outset and if difficulties arise. By modeling positive behaviors and advising other women how to do the same, you can put to rest the myths and stereotypes that breed distrust and frustrate women's shared concerns. That will help eliminate damaging behaviors like the Queen Bee syndrome and foster cooperation and mutual support among women.

§ 5:2 Expectation of "niceness"

One persistent stereotype facing women is the expectation to be nice. Women in particular expect other women to be nice. This expectation does not apply to men. Because it is expected of women, those who are warm and considerate are denied the "extra credit" that men enjoy when they act that way. Being nice

---

[2]Ely, R. (1994), The effects of organizational demographics and social identity on relationships among professional women, *Administrative Science Quarterly* 39, 203–238; Ely, R. (1995), The power in demography: women's social constructions of gender identity at work, *Academy of Management Journal* 38, 589–634.

is an admirable trait in anyone, but being "too nice" or being expected to be nice under all circumstances can have many negative consequences for women leaders. To begin with, it reinforces and perpetuates the stereotype that women are pleasing and unassertive. It narrows your repertoire of leadership styles because any time you deviate from being nice you will dash someone's expectations. It also thwarts your effectiveness as a leader. People may interpret your niceness as weakness or lack of importance; they may neglect your work, give it lower priority, or put less effort into it because they assume you will be understanding and put up with it.

Women who are not considerate or who are exacting and directive are perceived as bitchy and autocratic. There are some women whose behavior is extreme; they are rude, bullying, obstructionist, and mean. These women seem to believe that in order to show their strength and power they must induce fear in others. These behaviors are unacceptable for women or men, but for women the threshold is lower. Men who instruct their secretary to get them coffee may be excused, while women who do it are met with indignation.

The key is not to worry about being nice but rather what leadership styles are most effective for you to accomplish your job. As noted in Chapter 3, effective leaders adapt to different situations. When you interact with people socially and there is no immediate need to be work-focused, being casual, warm, and friendly is fine. But when you are dealing with work and leadership issues, it is appropriate to be more professional, analytical, and serious. When there is work to be done and you are giving directions, reviewing work product, or running a business meeting, concentrate on the work at hand.

§ 5:3 Expectation of friendship

Many women expect women leaders to be their friends. These expectations are held not just by women lawyers but by female secretaries, staff, and administrators as well. Men do not face the same dilemma. No one expects a male boss to be their friend or ask about their personal life.

Women place great value on connecting and relating with other women. This does not mean that all women are nurturing and friendly; nor does it mean that women leaders must accept other women's assumptions that all women have equal status in the firm. As a woman leader, you need to be able to assert your authority and be respected for it. You should not become imperious, lose your personal interest in the women you work with, or turn into a cold and impersonal manager. However, some distance is advisable. You can be friends outside of the office and in social settings; you can be supportive and friendly in the office; and you should continue to let people know how much you like and value them. However, the fact is that you do not have equal status with subordinates at work, and that needs to be acknowledged.

The reason is that as a leader—or whenever another woman reports to you—your principal obligation is to your clients and the firm. Sometimes you have to criticize the other woman's performance, push her to work harder or stay later, promote someone else to a position that she wants, or even let her go. As a leader, you have to stay aligned with the firm's strategy and interests even when many of the people affected are your friends and what you decide will be problematic for them —or worse. Several women who were interviewed spoke of losing friends because of the decisions they had to make or the actions they had to take as leaders.

It is hard to juggle personal relations and business interests. For many women leaders, this means less time for socializing, personal chit chat, or "hanging out." One way to deal with this is to remain sociable with the women around you but explain the time constraints and pressures that limit your ability to be as involved with them socially as you would like. Let them see that when you succeed as a leader you make it possible to help more of them to be successful.

§ 5:4   Expectation of support for women's issues

Because there are so few women in leadership, women leaders are often seen as representing all women in the firm. As a result, women expect women leaders to agree with, support, and advocate for all "women's" issues, such as part-time practice and parenting leave. They believe that all women share a common bond as outsiders in a masculine organization and assume women leaders will promote these issues whether or not they fit the leader's agenda. For many women, a sense of shared outsider status holds true, but not all women leaders see themselves as outsiders, nor do they share the same concerns, views or priorities as all other women in their firms.

Women leaders who do not make such issues their priorities may be judged severely. When a woman leader disappoints women's expectations on any of these issues, some women become angry and resentful ("Who does she think she is?") or try to reduce her power by criticizing or blaming her ("She has no life outside the office, so she takes it out on us"). By saying they dislike her, they reject her as a leader. In some cases, the rejection is more concrete. One leader I interviewed opposed long-term part-time work options. She was a vocal and effective advocate for women in most areas but did not go as far as the women in her firm wanted on their part-time policy. The reason for her stance was that she believed it hurt women's advancement in the firm to remain part-time over an extended period: *"I want more women to be partners and leaders but am worried that if they stay part-time that will not happen. That's a practical issue and deprives me of other women partners."* This issue was important enough to the other women in the firm that they blocked her appointment to the management committee, where she might have been a powerful voice for women on other issues they cared about.

The issues labeled "women's issues" are political. When you become a leader you walk right into the middle of law firm politics. On issues that have special importance to women, the political process intersects with women's expectations that you will represent and protect their interests. Later chapters explain the political dynamics of law firms and how to maneuver through and around them. In particular, effective communication and trust-building measures are essential to explain the reasoning behind your positions, generate respect for different points of view, and reduce the fallout when your political decisions are unpopular among women in the firm.

§ 5:5 Queen Bees

Queen Bees see other women as rivals and try to protect their status by blocking those women from becoming leaders. Some firms limit the opportunities for women to become leaders and foment competition among women for the few spots open to them. When women believe that there is little room at the top, that competition fosters the emergence of Queen Bees: self-centered women who resist attempts to share the limelight or are threatened by other women who aspire to leadership. Rather than help younger women they try to stop them. Women who engage in this sort of behavior are their own worst enemies. They isolate themselves unnecessarily by cutting off women who could be helpful sources of support to them. They also stir up feelings among women of distrust, alienation, and powerlessness that harm not just those women but the firm as a whole.

The reasons that led women to act this way were understandable in the past when it was very rare for women to reach partnership, much less leadership. The few women who made it often felt a need to protect their turf because they had to fight hard, all alone, to achieve success. Bearing emotional scars and calluses, they found it hard to be sympathetic to other women.

The co-chair of a national practice group who is based in Silicon Valley personally experienced women like this when she started her career: *"In the old days, when I was starting out, other women saw me as competition. Their attitude was you have to do it on your own and not expect anyone's help."*

An office managing partner of a global firm also noted that Queen Bees were common when she went into practice almost 20 years ago: *"Before there was only one spot for a woman, so women had to compete against each other for it."* She added that *"men benefited when women fought each other because it took women out of the group they had to compete against."* Today men and women partners compete against each other for business, resources, and income. In the course of that competition, women and men may try to advance or protect their own interests at the expense of other partners. Women, however, feel more betrayed and disappointed when a woman partner fails to support, or worse, tries to thwart, another woman's success. Whereas a man might act in exactly the same way only a woman partner will be the subject of epithets.

True Queen Bees may still exist but they are becoming anachronisms. Today no firm can afford a partner, female or male, who deliberately prevents the success of top law firm talent. It is more likely today to find women leaders actively trying to help younger women succeed. The women I interviewed felt that there is much less sniping and backbiting among women in firms now than in the past. They believe that women lawyers appreciate the value of supporting each other and these leaders routinely do that. Until there are far more women in law firm leadership, however, conditions will remain ripe for stirring up competition instead of solidarity among women.

Part II

LEADERSHIP IN A LAW FIRM: THE IMPORTANCE OF CONTEXT

Chapter 6

What Is Leadership in a Law Firm?

KeyCiteᴿ: Cases and other legal materials listed in KeyCite Scope can be researched through the KeyCite service on Westlawᴿ. Use KeyCite to check citations for form, parallel references, prior and later history, and comprehensive citator information, including citations to other decisions and secondary materials.

---

§ 6:1   Leadership as process

Leadership is defined by results, not attributes.

—Peter Drucker

There is no single definition or explanation of what leadership is or how it works, nor is there one "best" model of a law firm leader. The only agreement among scholars is that leadership is situational, requiring different qualities and abilities in different situations.[1] For our purposes in this book, I am defining leadership in a law firm as *a process of influencing people to produce positive outcomes for the firm*. This form of leadership requires the ability to envision and articulate a better future or a desired outcome and then to persuade people to help you achieve it. What distinguishes leaders from other partners in a law firm is that their vision, intent, and accomplishments reach beyond their own interests. Leaders serve as catalysts who make things happen by inspiring people to move forward together in a common cause.

Successful leaders come with every type of personality and countless variations of attitudes, capabilities, values, styles, strengths, and weaknesses. They are extroverted and introverted, controlling and hands-off, detail oriented and big-picture thinkers. But effective leaders all focus on the same things: ensuring the competitive advantage and success of the firm, attracting and developing talent, and maximizing the contributions of others in the firm to these endeavors. They do this by concentrating on business strategy and people. Running the business of the firm involves developing and achieving strategic goals that will promote the financial security and success of the firm. Because this can only be accomplished through people, leaders must also ensure that the firm has highly competent, engaged, and productive lawyers and staff who will work together toward a shared vision.

When you become a leader, the people you lead have certain expectations of you. Those expectations are driven by what they personally want and need. As leadership expert Warren Bennis explains, "Every new leader faces the misgivings, misperceptions, and the personal needs and agendas of those who are to be led."[2] People also want to be confident that you know where you are leading them, which they hope is to a better future. To address their concerns, you must be forward thinking, looking across the horizon, and helping followers to envision the exciting possibilities that exist for them in the future that you see. This requires optimism that what will come can be better than the present, whether things are going well or the firm is experiencing hard times. However, creating visions and inspiring hope are not

---

[Section 6:1]

[1]McCall, M.W., Lombardo, M.M., & Morrison, A.M. (1988), *The lessons of experience: how successful executives develop on the job* (New York: Lexington Books).

[2]Bennis, W.G. (Jan. 2004), The seven ages of a leader, *Harvard Business Review*.

enough. Leadership requires that you produce positive results. Leaders must deliver.

§ 6:2 Leadership is based on trust

At its core, law firm leadership is based on trusting relationships. It requires that the people you hope to lead trust and respect you. Leadership is not automatically conferred by the title or position which you hold, the resources which you control, or your personal charm and appeal. Unlike a judge, you cannot order partners to act or unilaterally impose sanctions if they refuse. People only follow you when they believe that it is in their self-interest to do so. When their personal interests diverge from those of the firm as a whole, leaders have to find ways to align or reconcile those interests through persuasion, tradeoffs, incentives, and other strategies. This requires considerable finesse because you have to protect the firm's interests at the same time that each individual whom you lead believes that you are protecting his or hers.

Although your partners may be motivated by self-interest, they must believe that you will act for the good of the firm as a whole and trust you to protect the firm's interests as well as their own. The degree of trust which they place in you is a measure of the quality of your relationships with them. The relationships that facilitate your ability to persuade people to work together for the common good constitute your *social capital*. Leaders with high social capital can draw on their relationships to get things done for themselves and the firm. This is especially important in a law firm because you have very little authority to act on your own, and the less authority you have over the people you lead, the more you depend on their trust.[1]

Trust builds over time so long as people know by your communications and actions that you know what you are doing, that what you are doing makes sense, and that you will do what you say. In situations that are totally predictable, they usually extend trust easily. People know what should be done and what will likely happen as a result. However, in times of rapid change or uncertainty, people are frightened and unsure of what tomorrow will bring. They do not know what should be done or what may happen. As a leader, you ask them to place their future in your hands at the very time when they are feeling most vulnerable.

[Section 6:2]

[1]Salacuse, J.W. (2006), *Leading leaders: how to manage smart, talented, rich, and powerful people* (New York: AMACOM), 192.

Every decision and action you ask of them contains both a potential for benefit and a risk of harm, so people measure the possible risks against what they expect in the future if they follow you. The more confidence they have that you will protect their interests, the more they allow themselves to be exposed to a risk of harm. If you have earned their trust, the risk appears more tolerable.[2]

One of the great challenges for law firm leaders is that law firms are "low-trust environments."[3] Lawyers place little value on developing the personal relationships that build trust or the interpersonal skills required to do it. Law firm culture focuses almost exclusively on skills based in reason, logic, and intellect. Lawyers practice in an adversarial system where suspicion and rancor are rampant and too much trust can be hazardous. They tend to be strongly individualistic and highly competitive and like to fight every battle and argue every point. In personality assessments, lawyers rank very low on sociability and intimacy skills, which are important for establishing and maintaining relationships. Rather than invest time in getting to know people on a personal basis, they prefer to maintain role-to-role interactions, focusing on the task at hand and the individuals' responsibilities in getting the work accomplished.

Building trust in the low-trust environment of a law firm takes enormous effort. Good leaders forge personal relationships with as many people throughout the firm as possible, and to the extent feasible, all firm partners. The more trust and social capital you have with colleagues in the firm, the broader your span of influence and the greater your chances of being effective. This requires constant hard work and a great deal of time, but the people you lead must feel that you have invested the time and effort to know them personally and understand what is important to them. They want to believe that you care about them as individuals and are committed to helping them solve their problems, serve their clients, and advance their careers. As with any relationship, they must believe that your relationship with them is based on mutual respect. Because circumstances change quickly and new challenges and risks may arise, you need to prove again and again that the followers' trust in you is well placed. When you desire new changes or innovations, you may again have to convince them that your vision is a good one for them, so you need to continuously strengthen those relationships. That is why leaders

---

[2]Hurley, R.F. (Sept. 2006), The decision to trust, *Harvard Business Review*.

[3]Maister, D. (April 2006), Are law firms manageable?, *The American Lawyer*.

spend a great deal of time and energy walking the halls, schmoozing, listening, problem solving, and counseling people.

Establishing trust-based relationships requires more than getting to know the people you lead. They also need to know you. They need to feel that they know you as a person: what you stand for, what your values and priorities are. They want to know both your long-term vision for the firm and your immediate plans for handling today's hot issues. They need proof of your constancy so that they can predict what you will do and how it will impact their interests. They want to know how you make decisions and how they can influence you. They want evidence that you are sharing and not withholding information that might affect them. In order to meet these expectations you need to be forthcoming, highly visible, and accessible.

As a new leader, you can start to earn trust by extending your trust to your followers before expecting it from them. You can do this by inviting their ideas, criticism, and involvement. This is somewhat risky because you can't predict or control what they will say or do. However, it shows them that you are being open-minded and fair and that you believe in them and value their views. It is especially important for those partners who do not support you or are even hostile to your selection as leader. It may not be enough to win them over right away but it is a good foundation for moving ahead.

Trust between you and your followers is important but not enough. As a leader, you cannot get anything accomplished if the people you lead do not trust each other. Given the low-trust environment, leaders have a steep road to climb to spread trust throughout the firm. Partners need to work together openly to execute firm strategy. Leading by example is an important place to start. In particular, leaders build trust by demonstrating their personal integrity and professional excellence and by holding others to the same high standards and values which they set for themselves.

§ 6:3 Leadership requires integrity

People need to believe that their leaders have integrity. To put your future in the hands of someone else is taking a big chance. No sensible lawyer would willingly be led by someone with questionable moral values or conduct. Nevertheless, every time we trust someone to act in our interests, we run the risk that we are making a mistake, so we must believe that the person whom we have chosen to lead us has integrity and is worthy of our trust. We must believe that the leader will be honest, do what she says, and keep promises and secrets.

Integrity requires "saying what you mean and meaning what you say." Leaders with integrity are straight talkers. In order to believe in you, people need to know what you stand for and what you believe in. If you equivocate, cannot explain your thinking, or repeatedly change directions, people become suspicious of your ability and your intentions.

A leader with integrity has motives and intentions that are honorable. She focuses on the goals of others in the firm and the collective goals of the firm. She believes that the firm is more important than any single individual, including her. To be seen as a leader with integrity, the people you lead must feel confident that you decided to become a leader in order to serve the firm, not to increase your own power or rewards; that you will use the power you have in an ethical way; and that you do not have a hidden agenda to advance your own interests at the firm's expense.

Integrity also depends on setting and maintaining high values and standards. A leader with integrity holds strong personal values and high standards of professionalism and ethical conduct for herself and others. Most importantly, her conduct is consistent with those values and standards. In *Practice What You Preach*,[1] David Maister describes research he conducted that proved what a powerful influence this consistency can have on a law firm. Maister found that the distinguishing characteristics of leaders in the most financially successful firms were their honesty and integrity: they lived according to the values and standards which they advocated. When other people in the firm saw this, they realized that the leaders really meant what they said. Followers were more likely to take those values seriously, believe and accept them, and work together to further the firm's business objectives. Maister concluded that a leader's influence is directly and positively related to behavior that is consistent with the values which the leader espouses.

Integrity is especially critical in law firms because so many decisions require a consensus of the partnership. Even when leaders are authorized and prepared to make a decision on their own, they often try first to solicit concurrence from other partners, especially those whose support and cooperation they need. Being known as honest and ethical helps you earn partners' confidence and get their buy-in more readily. A leader with integrity can

---

[Section 6:3]

[1]Maister, D.H. (2001), *Practice what you preach: what managers must do to create a high achievement culture* (New York: The Free Press).

more easily make partners feel that she is protecting each one's personal interests at the same time that she is asking them to act for the good of the firm.

§ 6:4   Leadership requires professional excellence

Professional excellence, i.e., being an outstanding lawyer, is the sine qua non of law firm leadership. It is what gives you credibility in the eyes of your partners. You cannot be a leader in a law firm unless you are highly respected for your legal abilities and success. Being known as a brilliant and extraordinary lawyer can get you the leader's mantle even if you lack the skills and attributes of leadership. In contrast, if your partners do not respect you as a lawyer, they will not let you lead them.

One of the most significant ways that lawyers demonstrate their professional excellence is through their client relationships. Because a lawyer's primary professional obligation is to clients, respect from your peers requires that you first earn respect from your clients. Strong relationships with satisfied clients are the lifeblood of any law firm. Without them, firms cannot survive, much less achieve their long-term goals. A history of good client relations may, in fact, be a good indicator of leadership potential. Some lawyers have a superior ability to attract lucrative clients. Others have the ability to manage major client relationships, whether it is their client or someone else's. Still other lawyers gain admiration because of their work on behalf of pro bono clients. Any lawyer who maintains excellent client relationships may be able to apply similar talents in leading the firm.

However, many lawyers with a strong client following do not have the temperament, patience, or people skills needed for leadership. Good client relationships do not necessarily translate into good interpersonal relationships with peers and subordinates. Many rainmakers, for example, are not as considerate to the people they work with in the office as they are to their clients. Some rainmakers show clients only one side of their personalities while the people with whom they interact every day experience the whole partner, warts and all. While good client relationships may indicate excellence in some regards, they are not necessarily proof of the kind of skills or relationship-building required for leadership.

Women often misconstrue what professional excellence means. They assume that excellence refers to diligence, intellectual superiority, and high quality work, so they mistakenly concentrate exclusively on legal expertise and brilliant work product. They follow the rules, put in the expected hours, do everything that is asked of them, dot all the i's, and cross the t's. This kind of excellence is important for a woman's sense of accomplishment and to earn respect and referrals from colleagues, but it is not the excellence required to make you a leader.

Leadership excellence is about driving and achieving results. It requires practical street smarts, political savvy, and other abilities that are not taught in any law school class or CLE course. It means getting out from behind your desk and building the personal relationships that form social capital. Excellence means understanding that leading a law firm means leading a business and acting as if the future of that business depends on you—because it does.

To be recognized as excellent for purposes of leadership, people need to know that your excellence as a lawyer translates into excellence as a leader. They may know that you are smart and you work hard, but that is also true for most of the other lawyers in your firm. You have to establish a reputation and perception that causes people to think of you as someone who stands out above the others. They need to believe that when it comes to both law and leadership, you know what you are doing and do it very well. This means making sure that your excellent results, your client relationships, and your business acumen are out in the open where others can see them. Leaders have no use for excessive modesty. If you are excellent but no one realizes it, you will not be thought of as leadership material.

Excellence in a leader is also demonstrated by good judgment. Judgment is the ability to perceive and measure relative values and make good choices based on those values. It involves the ability to distinguish between reasonable alternatives and wise ones. It uses both what you know and what you intuit about a given situation, and it often requires retrieving and applying relevant knowledge derived from past situations.

Good judgment is the ability to perceive and evaluate the consequences of behavior (your own and others) and to make wise decisions based on that assessment. It involves knowing when to make short-term sacrifices for the sake of long-term gains and being creative in solving problems and turning adversity to your advantage. To accept you as a leader, partners must trust your judgment. They must see you as thoughtful yet decisive and apt to make well-reasoned decisions. Having good judgment is not the same as being smart, especially when it comes to leading lawyers. There are many lawyers with an encyclopedic knowledge of the law who should not be making strategic business decisions about your firm or managing its people.

Good judgment is developed through observation, analysis, and learning from your own and others' successes and failures. It is the product of accumulated knowledge and experience shaped by ever-increasing wisdom and is acquired over time through self-awareness, practical experience, and continual learning. As these processes deepen your understanding, the options available to you for addressing a problem or creating a strategy expand.

A leader with good judgment is mature and wise enough to deal with a wide array of difficult business and people issues. Many complex problems have multiple possible solutions, each of which has different consequences. A leader with good judgment can appreciate the ramifications of the various possibilities and choose those that will be best for the people involved and the firm. She knows when to move on a decision independently and when to consult her partners; how to frame an issue so that it produces acceptance (even if grudging) without inflaming a difficult situation; how to approach an adversary without generating anger or dissatisfaction. She is versatile and can use different styles, adapting to the particular issue, circumstances, and people involved. In addition, more often than not, her choices are sound. People can see the underlying wisdom of her decision or approach even when they disagree with it.

§ 6:5 Leadership and management

Most aspects of leadership in law firms have nothing to do with charisma or inspirational speeches. Law firm leadership is more about the details of managing a complex organization effectively. In most law firms' organizational structure, the lines between leadership and management are blurred. The two functions are intertwined and hard to separate. Harvard Business School Professor and leadership authority John Kotter has provided a construct that well describes the relationship between them.[1]

Kotter explains that leadership is about creating, channeling, and coping with change, while management is about coping with complexity. Both leaders and managers decide what must be done, create networks of people and relationships to accomplish their agenda, and try to ensure that those people actually do the job. The major differences are that leading change begins with a vision, setting a direction, and developing strategies to get there. Managing complexity is done through planning and budgeting. Both roles require working through others but in different ways.

[Section 6:5]

[1]Kotter, J.P. (Dec. 2001), What leaders really do, *Harvard Business Review.*

Leaders concentrate on articulating goals and aligning people with those goals by communicating a vision, building coalitions, and inspiring and empowering people to do what is necessary for their accomplishment. Managers focus on organizing people and processes in ways that can implement the firm's plans as precisely and efficiently as possible. Whereas leaders tolerate chaos and lack of structure, and may even thrive on them, managers try to accomplish firm goals by maintaining order and solving problems.

Seen in this way, true leadership is scarce in law firms—not because the talent is not there, but because few lawyers are permitted to exercise leadership this way. The structure and nature of law firms and the aversion of lawyers to change force would-be leaders with bold ideas to behave more like managers. Law firms expect their leaders to stay the course rather than come up with innovative new initiatives. Even in these turbulent days of recession and law firm contraction, most firms that consider trying new approaches are making small, hesitant moves. When one makes a change of any significance, such as taking associates off lockstep or using fixed-fee billing, it is considered a radical departure even though the ideas have been circulating and tried in some quarters for many years. In this environment, leaders need to be very strong and very determined to be agents of change.

Relatively few law firms are led by a chair, senior partner, or managing partner with far-reaching powers to institute change single-handedly. That occurs most often in firms where the founding partners maintain tight control until they decide to relinquish it, usually when they are ready to retire. Some firms also have strong leaders who have led the firm so successfully over the years that they have accumulated considerable power. Even in those firms, though, other partners balk at the idea of power being concentrated in too few hands. They resent the lack of leadership opportunities for themselves or others or distrust concentrated power as a matter of principle.

In most law firms, the management structure creates multiple leadership positions. Partners hold leadership roles at several management levels with no strict hierarchies or lines of authority. In multi-office firms, some leadership roles are firm wide (e.g., department chairs, practice group leaders) while others are local (e.g., office managing partners). Firms may be organized around specialized substantive law groups, which may have their own subspecialty groups and separate management structures. They may be organized by client or industry groups, or they may use a matrix structure with overlapping organizational units. All of these subdivisions are led by partners of the firm. At these various levels of management, leaders participate in decision making and oversee implementation of the decisions and policies they adopt. Individually or as leaders of committees, they focus on particular functions (e.g., setting compensation, hiring, marketing) or groups (e.g., offices, departments, practice areas) to ensure that the firm conducts its business so as to achieve its strategic goals. All of these management positions open up possibilities for leadership.

At the top, there are only a few executive leadership positions. The Chair, Senior Partner, or Firm-Wide Managing Partner holds the clearest and highest designated slot. Typically that leader reports to a Board of Directors or the firm's highest governing committee (usually called the Executive, Policy, or Management Committee) and ultimately to the partnership as a whole. Together with the highest executive committee, the top leader oversees the firm's financial health and sets policies and strategic objectives for the entire firm. In large and multi-office firms, the principal governance, strategy, and policy making committees may be comprised of managing partners and other leaders from the firm's different offices. Many partners rotate through these executive level committees and most partners participate to some degree in strategic decision making.

Women are rarely found at this top level of leadership. According to the 2009 National Association of Women Lawyers Survey, only six percent of managing partners are women, and hardly any women sit on executive-level governance committees. The median size of the highest governing committees at AmLaw 200 law firms is 10 members, with many committees reporting more than 25 members. Yet women currently constitute only 15% of those committee members and 14% of firms have no women at all on these committees.[2] In law firms considered "best" for women, the representation of women on top governing committees is no more than 20%.[3] With so many leadership possibilities, it is intolerable to have so few women in the highest leadership positions or on the highest management committees. There is no question that women are qualified for leadership and many are motivated to do it. Women are present and performing skillfully as leaders at every level of firm management—except the top. It is imperative that women achieve parity at the most elevated levels not just in the middle ranks.

---

[2]The National Association of Women Lawyers [NAWL] (Oct. 2009), *Report of the fourth annual national survey on retention and promotion of women in law firms.*

[3]Yale Law Women (2009), 2009 Top ten family friendly firms list, key statistics from the top ten survey, http://www.law.yale.edu/stuorgs/topten.htm.

§ 6:6 Leadership and power

"Power is what calls the shots, and power is a white male game."
— Ann Richards

Leadership is about power. Leaders use their power to get others to act in certain ways and they bear the responsibility to ensure that those actions benefit the group being led. In a law firm power is the ability to get something done, not control over the people who do it. It is the ability to influence—not coerce—outcomes. Power is a resource to be used to accomplish goals, to enable others, and to move people along toward desired ends. In a law firm, a leader's power flows not from manipulation or self-aggrandizement but from trust, integrity, and professional excellence.

In a law firm, your power as a leader is derived from the belief of others that you are trustworthy and capable to lead and their willingness to let you act on their behalf. As Common Cause founder John Gardner has pointed out, "leadership is conferred by followers." Even the most driven and successful lawyer cannot become a powerful leader—or a leader at all—if others are not willing to follow her.

Some lawyers find it hard to lead in a law firm because there is so much that they cannot control. Partners may grant a leader substantial authority but that does not mean that they will abide by her decisions or follow her directives. In your daily law practice, you can control a great deal. When you lead a client team, most team members will do what you tell them to do. Conversely, as a firm leader, you have little control over others. You cannot command your partners and often must defer to them. A managing partner who is also a trial lawyer explained the difference this way: *"When I go to trial, I am the star, director, and producer of my own play, but as a managing partner, I cannot decide everything. I cannot solve everything alone. I have to listen to everyone else. I have to move from decision maker to consensus builder to parent and other roles. At trial, I control the agenda in order to be out in front. As a leader, I do it so no one sees it happen."*

However, a lack of control does not mean that law firm leaders lack power. Effective leaders do wield power by using their good reputation and keen political skills to influence, persuade, and coax others to act in desired ways. They accumulate power by understanding where it comes from and strategically establishing their own power-generating sources and relationships. They recognize that they must do this in order to carry out their responsibilities as a leader.

Many women shy away from power but little good comes from being powerless. If women do not place much importance on having power, it may be because they do not have it and therefore do not realize what it can do for them. Women need a taste of power in order to appreciate how valuable and liberating it can be. As one leader said, *"Once I was in a position of power, it became more and more attractive to have that power."* Power gives you greater control over your life and the ability to set your priorities, do the things that are most important to you, and approach them on your own terms. It gives you a voice and the ability to have a greater impact on the firm and the world around you. Power brings more opportunities your way and enables you to take smarter risks. If you want to make a difference you must have power.

In a law firm, there are three principal sources of power: rainmaking, positions of authority, and personal attributes.

§6:7 Rainmaking power

Rainmakers rule. The greatest source of individual power in a law firm is revenue generation. It has been said that law firms follow the golden rule—those who have the gold make the rules. There is no question that those partners who generate the most revenue have enormous power. Their control of clients, which gives them control over work and business, makes them powerful whether or not they hold important management or leadership positions. One rainmaker who has held almost every major leadership position in her Texas firm said that she never thought about the power these positions gave her. As she put it, *"I have power because clients have given it to me."*

Rainmakers bring in clients which firms depend on for revenues. Clients may retain the firm but individual partners usually control the client relationship. If a rainmaker's demands go unanswered or she is dissatisfied with how the firm treats her she can take her clients and leave. This can be devastating to a law firm. When a corporation loses a leader, it may be disruptive but it usually does not threaten the company's existence. In contrast, when a major rainmaker leaves it can destroy a law firm or a major part if it. The rainmaker may take other valuable lawyers with her and the impact of the loss on colleagues, clients, work, and profits can have damaging repercussions throughout the firm. This gives rainmakers a great deal of power when negotiating with the firm for what they want. The more revenue their clients generate the more leverage they have to get their way.

Rainmakers who put responsibility for the greater good of the firm ahead of their own interests are often the firm's most respected leaders. But rainmaking power does not necessarily translate into leadership. Law firms are filled with powerful rainmakers who are not perceived or respected as leaders. They are the partners who elevate self-interest over the interests of the collective, using economic threats to pressure others to act or decide a certain way and get the outcomes that they want for themselves. It is up to strong and diplomatic firm leaders to manage these narcissistic partners and curb their demands. Giving in can doom a firm. Firms whose leaders allow bullying rainmakers to determine management decisions are destined to suffer constant instability, conflict, and inability to attract good leaders.

The primary source of a rainmaker's power is the ability to bring in new clients. However, rainmakers do not always service all of the business that they bring in. Sometimes other partners are given day-to-day responsibility for the client. Over time, these partners are often able to originate new work from the client. A strong ongoing relationship with such a client can be a significant source of power for the partner who manages the client relationship. In some firms, business expansion is recognized as a form of business development and rewarded in some way. However, many firms do not give relationship partners who grow the business any credit—unless they assert their client-derived power strategically.

There are many sources for this client-based power, including the firm's continual need for talent, the large number of women lawyers in most firms, the growing number of women decision makers and buyers of legal services, and corporate and government diversity initiatives. Women who have solid client relationships, robust business networks, or strong relationship-building skills can exploit them by expanding relationships with clients and referral sources. One leader described how another woman in her firm gained power by making effective use of relationships with existing clients and partners: *"We have one woman practice group leader who is extremely valued and powerful in the firm, though not as powerful as other rainmakers or practice group leaders. She's in labor and employment, which is usually not very powerful because they have to have lower rates, but she has built that department and drives the value of the department in a way that has given her tremendous respect and power."*

Very few women rank among the top rainmakers in their firms. According to the 2009 NAWL Survey, almost three-quarters of law firms (72%) have no women among their top five rainmakers and almost half (46%) have no women among their top 10. This is a problem, of course, but also an opportunity for women who want to step up and be counted as players. Whether seeking new clients or existing business from current clients, women need to be conscious of the power they hold and the potential to increase it.

§ 6:8 Positional power

The decentralized and flat structure of law firms creates many leadership positions, including office and department heads, practice leaders, and committee chairs. Partners in individual leadership positions and members of high-level committees hold positions that give them authority to act and decide for the firm. When you are elected or appointed to a management position, you assume the authority and responsibilities that go with it.

Positional power may be based on authority that is actual or simply perceived. A position of actual authority is one that gives you direct control over resources (such as bonuses, budgets, or staffing), control over clients, the authority to make appointments, or access to critical information or people. Being on the committee that sets partner compensation is a very powerful position because it gives you control over partners' income and the ability to reward or penalize their performance and behavior. Being on the committee that recommends associates for partnership is also powerful. Not only are you influencing the future of the firm, you are also making decisions among candidates being pushed by competing partners and practice groups. In interviews, three practice group leaders described different kinds of power which they enjoyed by virtue of the authority vested in their position:

- *Since I am the head of my practice group, plus my large client base, opportunities come to me. I can help someone else get those opportunities—or not.*
- *As a practice group leader, I can make decisions on a smaller scale for my teams and practice group members about how we practice. I also help decide strategic goals that will expand market share. I want to make changes that are better for women and for my group, and I am in a position to do that.*
- *When I said I would step down as co-chair of the litigation department after seven years, they asked me, "Who would be a good person to do this after you?" My response definitely influenced their choice.*

Not all management positions are inherently powerful. The power given to a leader is often more perceived than real. Some lawyers have titles that sound impressive, earn them some deference, and create the perception of power. However, while the position may confer certain status and autonomy that suggests power, it confers no meaningful authority to direct outcomes since most leaders cannot impose their will or enforce their decisions without their partners' active consent. Yet even in those positions, you still may be able to demonstrate leadership and exert power. One leader found that *"It's exhilarating to realize you have power —even if it's only a perception of power."* You can use the advantages that the position gives you to influence change, raise your visibility, and benefit the people whom you care about. Your ability to have a real and direct impact depends on how you use your perceived power to drive change or produce positive results.

A professional development director in a national firm explained how her position gave her access to powerful partners and how she used that access strategically in order to advance associates' careers. Here are three situations she described:

- *I knew I had seven minutes to walk with the firm chair from one conference location to another. I knew he had two extra seats at his table at an upcoming luncheon, and I wanted him to invite two certain minority associates to sit with him. He did.*
- *Then the managing partner came to me and said: I eat lunch every day. I can take 3 associates to lunch every week. Tell me who to take. I did.*
- *Then I briefed the associates on what to do and not to do: Use this time as a golden opportunity to make an impression, start a relationship, pique the managing partner's interest. This is your one shot!*

In these seemingly small but highly strategic episodes, she used her position to have a significant and favorable impact on the associates for whom she was responsible. At the same time, she enhanced her reputation and relationships with the leaders and associates because she was able to help them.

Perception can also work against a leader. For instance, the perception that a leader does not deserve a leadership position can undermine the authority which she actually has. Firms sometimes place partners in positions of leadership because they are rainmakers who insist on it, because they represent powerful interests in the firm (e.g., a vital practice group), or through their close relationships with other powerful people. Those who did not "earn" their positions are often disregarded by partners and their ability to lead is negated. In one example, the protégé of a powerful rainmaker was appointed managing partner of one of the firm's offices because her mentor insisted on it. While she was known to be a good lawyer, she worked only on the mentor's cases and had never accomplished anything on her own. She was considered a lackey who basically took direction from her mentor, and in spite of her title, she was neither respected nor influential in the position.

The specific authority that accompanies leadership positions in law firms is rarely spelled out, and most law firm partners in executive leadership positions lack specific guidance about the scope of their responsibilities and authority. In one survey of managing partners in midsize and large law firms, only 26% of respondents had formal job descriptions.[1] In another informal survey of practice group leaders from firms with more than 100 lawyers, the percentage was even smaller.[2] When firms do write job descriptions for leadership positions, they are vague at best. As a consequence, leaders often do not know how much authority they have to act independently. A managing partner or practice group leader may have generally acknowledged areas of responsibility but her authority is rarely commensurate with those responsibilities. Although she may be held accountable for outcomes, she has only limited control over the actions of others. I interviewed one leader who was head of the largest practice group in her international firm and who had the authority to ask underperforming partners in her group to leave. However, in most firms, a leader cannot unilaterally fire a current partner, hire a lateral partner, decide on pay increases or decreases, or open or close an office. Partnership agreements, compensation committees, or executive committees control those decisions. The inability of leaders to control these matters was illustrated by the 2009 story of a law firm whose management committee called a partnership meeting to oust an equity partner but could not generate the votes needed to do it under the partnership agree-

---

[Section 6:8]

[1]Remsen, J. (Oct./Nov. 2008), The evolving role of today's law firm leaders, *ABA Law Practice Magazine* 34(7), 28.

[2]McKenna, P.J. (Apr. 2009), What does a practice group leader actually do? *Law firm leadership rants, raves, rebuttals, reflections, revelations & ruminations*, post #388, http://www.patrickmckenna.com/ PatrickJMcKennaBrainmatterRantsRaves9.aspx.

ment (80% of the partnership), so the disfavored partner
remained at the firm.[3]

Because of this uncertainty, many new leaders act with caution
until they get a sense of their limits, but experienced leaders use
the ambiguity to their advantage. One leader who had held high
leadership posts in law firms, corporations, and government commented that *"Power isn't given to you—you just exercise it! Someone else will tell you if you've gone too far."*

§ 6:9   Power through personal attributes

Many partners have considerable power even though they lack
any specific authority. Their power is informally derived from
certain personal traits that command special respect and attention, such as professionalism, expertise, dedication, and (rarely in
law firms) charisma. Many law firm partners have no formal
titles or major clients but are considered leaders and enjoy
unshakable loyalty because others respect them, trust them to
protect and promote the firm's best interests, and are prepared to
follow their lead. By example and inspiration, these leaders are
able to persuade people to act in a desired way for the benefit of
the larger group.

These informal leaders include lawyers who are:

1. Action takers who successfully spearhead special projects,
2. Lawyers whose professional reputation, community ties, or
   political connections are critical to the firm's business success,
3. Specialists whose technical expertise is essential to the firm
   or members of the firm, and/or
4. Lawyers with unique leadership skills that the firm needs
   at a particular time.

These people can have substantial influence over the firm's
strategic direction, policies, and revenues. Even if they have little
or no formal authority to act, they can make things happen (or
prevent them), influence strategy and policy, and serve as
catalysts for change. Their power may derive from their reputation and following in the firm or from personal attributes that
give them the ability to direct or persuade others to act in certain
ways. The degree of their influence and power varies depending
upon the issue involved and the source of their authority. When
their skills, capacities, or attributes match what is needed for a

---

[3]Neil, M. (Oct. 2009), Firm calls meeting to remove partner, but doesn't
get enough votes, *ABA Journal*, http://www.abajournal.com/news/firm_calls_
meeting_to_remove_partner_but_doesnt_get_enough_votes.

particular situation, these people can be extremely powerful. The expert mediator who is called on to help resolve a serious dispute between two major practice groups can have a significant impact on the firm, albeit in a limited sphere or for a brief time. But doing high-quality work and earning the trust of those involved in the dispute can increase her reputation and influence as a leader.

There are many sources of informal power. If others have to rely on you for money, information, work, or access to key people, even if you do not have the direct power to make things happen, their dependence on you causes them to view and relate to you in ways that give you power. If you occupy a central position in a team or network and others must go through you for information or access to key players, your power may be disproportionately greater than your position would suggest. It is not simply having access or information that generates power; the perception of power comes from the way in which you control and communicate the information. One leader explained how she gained informal power by drafting the report that her practice group leader had to submit to the management committee. *"Initially, my power came from setting the agenda. In our firm, practice group leaders report to the Management Committee twice a year. My practice group leader had no patience to prepare a report, so he always asked me to help. What I wrote shaped his presentation and agenda, so I emphasized what I thought was important."* By drafting the report, she was able to influence the discussion in the management committee. At the same time, she learned what her practice group leader thought was important and the way a leader looks at the issues.

Informal power is often a matter of perception and associated with nonverbal symbols and behaviors. Sometimes even physical location may confer power. One leader noted how men in her firm understood this principle while she did not: *"I was managing partner for many years and never sat at the head of the table. Two men jointly assumed the job when I stepped down. They always sat at the head of the table."* That position told others that they were in charge. Similarly, proximity to powerful individuals can give you an aura of power. In one illustrative situation, a mentor believed that the male minority associate she was mentoring was on the wrong floor and too far out of the way; no one would see the associate there. The mentor (who happened to be the office managing partner) arranged to have the associate move to a more centrally located office on the same floor as hers. The associate found that his relationship with the mentor became stronger because they were able to spend more time together. As his connection to the managing partner became known, other partners began to give him better assignments than he had ever received before.

Chapter 7

Special Challenges in Leading Partners

§ 7:1   Lawyers' personality traits
§ 7:2   Attitudes toward leadership
§ 7:3   Leadership selection
§ 7:4   Need or desire to maintain a client practice

KeyCiteᴿ: Cases and other legal materials listed in KeyCite Scope can be researched through the KeyCite service on Westlawᴿ. Use KeyCite to check citations for form, parallel references, prior and later history, and comprehensive citator information, including citations to other decisions and secondary materials.

---

§ 7:1   Lawyers' personality traits

Lawyers' personalities and their attitudes toward management and leadership make it especially arduous to be a law firm leader. Partners make it difficult for anyone, male or female, to lead them. They do not see themselves as followers and do not want to be led. The leaders they select are their peers who are at most considered "first among equals." Partners are highly trained and successful lawyers who see themselves as elite—and, in fact, they are. As law professor Jeswald Salacuse notes, lawyers are "smart, talented, rich and powerful."[1] They possess a low tolerance for ceding authority to others even if they have elected those individuals to be their leaders.

Law firm partners are high achievers who expect a great deal of personal autonomy. They insist on maintaining their sense of independence, and they vigorously challenge efforts to direct them or rein them in. They see no reason to follow one of their peers whose qualifications for leadership are no greater than their own. Moreover, they feel little obligation to the people whom they place into leadership positions. To the contrary, since they elected or appointed the leader, they see the leader as beholden

---

[Section 7:1]

[1]Salacuse, J.W. (2006), *Leading leaders: how to manage smart, talented, rich, and powerful people* (New York: AMACOM).

to them. They see themselves to be leaders in their own right and expect to be treated as such by everyone around them—including those in designated leadership roles.

New law firm leaders are often surprised when they realize that partners' actions or positions are ruled by their egos, not the best interests of the firm. One leader who was appointed to the firm-wide management committee arrived with no agenda or sense of self-importance and was surprised to find that she was the only member who thought that way: *"The other committee members seemed to feel, 'I'm on the committee because I deserve to be, and I'm the most powerful person other than the chair.'"*

Lawyers are also skeptical and trained to be argumentative. This makes it difficult to get them to accept new ideas, reach agreement, or make decisions. If leadership is about change, law firm leaders must be very patient because change happens very slowly in law firms. Lawyers have a tendency to analyze everything in painstaking detail, focus on the flaws in every idea, and challenge every proposal. This leads to lengthy, tedious debates and helps them avoid making tough decisions. The plethora of committees in many firms compounds the delay as it slows down decision making. Moreover, it makes the leader's job more time consuming and difficult. One managing partner said that she has to prepare for monthly partner meetings *"as thoroughly as I would for a court hearing. I can't afford to be unprepared for partners' questions. I need to prove I'm on top of all office issues so they'll respect me, not rattle me."*

Lawyers' skepticism also has a negative impact on interactions that depend on trust and collaboration, such as personal, team, and partnership relations. Personality tests show that lawyers' skepticism is extreme. In the Caliper Personality Profile, a leading personality assessment tool, lawyers score in the 90th percentile for skepticism. Their skepticism is compounded by their pessimism. In tests conducted by psychologist Martin Seligman, lawyers distinguished themselves by scoring the highest among any professional group on pessimism.[2] While that trait may be a positive attribute in law practice, where lawyers need to consider worst-case scenarios, it has a negative impact on their resilience and ability to maintain personal and professional relationships. What's more, lawyers rank low on social skills and empathy, making it hard for them to get along well with others. Combine these traits with a very high-stress work environment

---

[2]Seligman, M.P. (2002), *Authentic happiness: using the new positive psychology to realize your potential for lasting fulfillment* (New York: Free Press).

and it is not surprising that leaders of lawyers have such a difficult time. Said one leader, *"Management is a thankless job. Lawyers focus on problems; they complain. No one knows what you do to prevent problems or to make things work because they don't see it, but when there's a problem, they complain and blame management. They are skeptics: it's 'management' versus 'us.'"*

Most lawyers are also risk averse. Being a leader requires taking risks and persuading those risk-averse lawyers that the risks you propose are worth taking. Any change or innovation requires risk. In business, innovative thinking and action are considered primary requirements for success. Companies seek strategic ideas, products, and services that competitors have not yet discovered; they encourage entrepreneurial thinking. But in law firms, no one wants to go first. When you suggest an idea to a law firm, the first question asked is, "Who else is doing it?" Firms take comfort in knowing that they and their competitors all do the same things basically the same way. As Richard Susskind observes, "law firms are more anxious to avoid competitive disadvantage than to secure a lead. Even the finest firms are happy to be part of an elite grouping rather than to lead the pack."[3] We had a recent example of this in the spring of 2009. As the recession deepened, firms knew that they should decrease associate salaries but did not want to be the first firm to do it for fear that it would hurt their stature or future recruiting efforts. However, as soon as the first firm announced a salary decrease many others quickly followed suit. David Maister suggests that this may be the reason that firms have been successful in spite of being badly managed: since they compete only against other law firms and there is so little variation among them, even egregious organizational behavior does not cause a competitive disadvantage.[4]

Lawyers are expert problem solvers and many think creatively about the law. However, because they avoid risk, most lawyers are not entrepreneurial, especially in established corporate firms. Lawyers do not often engage in "out of the box" thinking about how to best run their firms, and few law firms are early adopters, much less change leaders, when it comes to new approaches to firm management. In a time of rapid change, however, like the one we are in now, it may be riskier to maintain the status quo than to initiate creative changes.

---

[3]Susskind, R. (2008), *The end of lawyers? Rethinking the nature of legal services* (Oxford: Oxford University Press), 177.

[4]Maister, D. (Apr. 2006), Are law firms manageable?, *The American Lawyer*.

Innovation combines problem solving with creative thinking. It extends beyond the immediate problem to connecting dots, looking for patterns and bigger pictures, anticipating future needs, and finding or developing new approaches. Innovative thinkers are also entrepreneurial, always looking for better—and different—ways to do things, not simply to tweak the current system. The need for entrepreneurial and innovative thinking was well described in this quote from Henry Ford: "If I asked customers what they wanted, it would be a faster horse."

Firms need to be innovative in order to advance their competitive advantage, but it is rare to see a law firm do anything other than follow or implement variations of what their competitors do. Good law firm leaders appreciate the need for innovation and try to convince their followers to do the same. Leaders listen to clients, follow trends, stay current on new developments that other firms and businesses are employing, and seek outside help to generate and apply creative ideas in their own firm. They pay attention to what is said in the media, the local and professional communities, and the industries which the firm serves. They use this information to foresee the possible outcomes of decisions, strategies, and market trends and try to stay several steps ahead. In addition, they place a premium on originality and new perspectives. Individual leaders may or may not be innovative thinkers themselves, but they encourage and reward innovative thinking in others.

§ 7:2   Attitudes toward leadership

Considering the size, complexity, and revenues of law firms today, it is remarkable that lawyers place such a low value on leadership. Many lawyers view leadership work as drudgery not a desired prize. Partners want to be treated as leaders and rewarded with titles that reflect their importance and status in the firm, and they want to retain oversight and control over what happens in the firm. But most lawyers have no interest in taking on leadership responsibilities. First and foremost, partners like to practice law and serve clients. They succeeded as lawyers because they were good at solving clients' problems. That is what they love to do, what they are good at, and what they feel confident about. It is often near impossible to get partners to focus on leadership when they would rather be doing client work.

Many leaders complain that partner resistance is not as much a problem as partner passivity. They cannot get partners engaged in management activities. One managing partner noted that few of her partners are interested in leading the firm and laughed,

"They're relieved that I'm doing it." Another leader who serves on her firm's executive and compensation committees explained, *"I did not aspire to leadership, but the firm can only succeed if I and others help it succeed. This requires time and is my obligation as a partner."*

The lack of partners interested in leadership can have devastating effects on a firm. Not long ago, a law firm announced it was closing its doors because when the managing partner retired, no one else in the firm was willing to move into the role. Another firm attracted successful lawyers with promises that they would not be distracted by management responsibilities. Instead, the sole equity partner handled management unilaterally—until he was arrested for fraud. The firm's coffers had been depleted and the firm dissolved.

§ 7:3 Leadership selection

Some leaders are born women.

—Anonymous

The lack of respect for leadership in law firms is reflected in the flawed process by which law firms choose their leaders. Most law firms do little formal succession planning to identify and groom leaders. A 2006 survey by Robert Half Legal found that a majority of law firms do not engage in formal succession planning[1] and a 2008 study by Altman Weil found that only 20% of large law firms have leadership development programs.[2] Firms do not articulate what they need in a leader or the competencies of leaders who could fill those needs. Formal succession planning using objective selection criteria has been shown to reduce favoritism and promote equal advancement opportunities for women,[3] but in most firms the process of selecting leaders lacks objectivity, transparency, and scrutiny. This is one of the main reasons that so few women are law firm leaders.

The process for choosing leaders varies from firm to firm. In some firms, leaders for key positions and committees are appointed by the Managing Partner or a designated committee. In

---

[Section 7:3]

[1]Robert Half Legal (Dec. 2006), *Who will follow the leaders? Survey shows majority of law firms, legal departments lack succession plans.*

[2]Richardson, D.B., & Coopersmith, D.P. (July 2008), Learning to lead, *The American Lawyer.*

[3]Howard, A., & Wellins, R.S. (2009), *Holding women back: troubling discoveries and best practices for helping women leaders succeed*, Development Dimensions International, Inc.

other firms leaders are elected, but elections are seldom contested, and the voting is merely a formality. Partners active in management walk the halls, seek input from other partners, and operate behind the scenes before selecting candidates. After a consensus is reached about the best candidate, the slate is presented, and the partners vote. Some partners see this as a good thing because *"the intent is not to have representative government but to have the best people to maximize profits and manage the business."* However, without objective criteria and vetting for well-qualified leaders, this process may reflect biased notions of who makes a good leader. The partners who are selecting candidates may not know many qualified but more junior women, especially if they are senior partners or in a large firm or practice group. They are likely to pick people like themselves, perpetuating the dominance of white men in leadership positions.

This type of system further discourages new faces from appearing in leadership because in many firms it is considered "bad form" to actively campaign for a significant leadership position or even to announce that you are interested in it. Partners tend to be suspicious of a lawyer who openly wants to be a leader. Several leaders who were interviewed said they would never announce that they wanted an executive-level leadership position because they would be criticized for being "too ambitious." As one former Managing Partner stated, *"I would never have said I wanted it. They would never have elected me."* Instead, she discussed it with a close ally who started to talk about her to other partners as a good candidate for the position. It was the behind-the-scenes politicking that eventually led key firm leaders to approach her and urge her to run for a position that she had wanted all along.

When elections are contested some women who want the job choose not to run. They are loath to put themselves in a position where they might lose and be stigmatized for their failure. They fear that losing an election will reinforce the stereotype that women are not as well suited for leadership as men. On the other hand, women who are self-confident and determined to be players are fearless even if they are not always successful. One woman who is a rainmaker and a highly visible and prominent lawyer in the community has told her firm leaders that she wants to be on the executive committee. She is very direct and outspoken about the need for change, especially on issues of concern to the women in her firm. However, they refuse to select her because her insistence on certain changes intimidates many partners. They have told her that she pushes too many buttons. She keeps pushing, however, because she wants to promote changes that she believes are essential for the firm to keep its women.

Because the leadership selection process in most firms is subjective and political, leadership roles frequently go to people for reasons unrelated to whether they are qualified for the job: the biggest rainmaker demands the position; the firm wants to reward a partner's practice performance; it wants to give a partner with a weak or failing practice something to do; or the position goes to the lawyer who will offend the fewest partners. In the first case, even the most successful rainmaker may be totally unsuited for a leadership role. Moreover, if a rainmaker intends to keep her clients, the source of her power, she may not have the time to devote to her leadership job. In the second instance, leadership should not be a reward; it requires specific abilities and attributes in order to carry out the leader's responsibilities. In the third situation, the lawyer may be well liked but is given the position out of sympathy, not for leadership ability, and may command little respect. In the last case, diplomacy is an important part of leadership, but leaders have to be more than just tactful. In all four cases a lawyer with many fine professional and human qualities may be completely ineffective as a leader. These are not appropriate bases for leadership selection.

When firms select good leaders, they sometimes do it accidentally, reinforcing David Maister's conclusion that law firms succeed in spite of how badly managed they are. One woman was told that the firm wanted her to be managing partner because "you are the one we distrust the least." Another woman was asked by the chair of her firm to become managing partner of two offices. She declined, saying that she loved her client work and that her trial schedule would make it impossible for her to do it. He persisted however, exclaiming: "You have to do it! Everyone else I asked has said no."

Individuals who are selected in these haphazard ways often turn out to be excellent leaders, but can law firms count on luck when they are entrusting the future of their enterprise to these people? This is an issue for all law firms. Without identifying and preparing future leaders, firms of all sizes may find themselves without obvious candidates or with leaders who are ill-equipped to handle the job. One woman explained the problem in her firm this way: *"There are only 18 equity partners in the firm. It is hard to find someone willing, able, and competent. Many partners are too polarizing. Do they have the skills? The gravitas? The patience? Will they be able to mediate between two powerful partners?"*

Many lawyers believe that leadership is a product of innate traits and therefore cannot be learned. They also assume that any lawyer who has become a partner in a law firm is smart enough and, therefore, sufficiently capable of being a leader. Until recently, partners also assumed that because their leaders are lawyers, they will be able to do whatever is necessary to keep the firm stable and profitable. However, the ever more complex challenges facing law firms in today's legal marketplace have caused forward-looking law firms to re-examine these faulty assumptions.

Increasingly, firms are paying close attention to all aspects of leadership, including what makes a good leader and how leadership is learned and developed. Firms are beginning to appreciate the business imperatives that depend on good leadership: strategic thinking, understanding of law firm and market economics, creation of talent management systems, preservation of client relationships, and optimization of a diverse work force. They are starting to realize that they need sophisticated leaders not just at the top of the organization but scattered throughout it at all levels and in all offices in order to ensure that the firm's strategy is sound and that it is effectively carried out. As a result, some firms have begun to allocate time and training resources to leadership development and management education. While this is a very promising move, these firms remain the exceptions rather than the rule.

Meanwhile, skilled law firm leaders are in short supply. Often one or more partners emerge as leaders; they appear to have the ability, temperament, and willingness to do the job. Usually they have demonstrated leadership ability through their previous work on committees or projects. However, many who might be good leaders are not motivated, face serious disincentives, or are better suited and happier to be practicing law than leading a law firm. One former managing partner noted that it was far easier to practice law: *"I thought of myself as a people person, but I couldn't stand the kinds of problems, the constant annoyance of trivial complaints, etc. I couldn't wait to get back to full-time practice."*

These points underscore the importance of succession planning and leadership development programs. When the firm develops leadership competencies and criteria and uses them to guide the process, women are more likely to emerge among the best candidates. In one example where a law firm used an outside consultant to facilitate the selection of the next managing partner, the candidate who was ultimately chosen would never have been considered under the firm's usual selection process. She was chosen because the consultant helped the firm identify its specific leadership needs and then find candidates who were best suited to address them. This objective process led them to her.

§ 7:4 Need or desire to maintain a client practice

In small law firms, it makes sense for leaders to maintain their practice because the responsibilities of running the firm are not as time consuming and can be shared among several partners. But highly complex organizations like large modern law firms need full-time leadership. The AmLaw 200 law firms are enterprises generating hundreds of millions—and in some cases, more than one or two billion—dollars in revenues, with offices all over the globe. In some of these firms, especially the larger ones, leadership is indeed a full-time job. Their managing partners and partners in some executive positions have no billing or client service expectations. However, throughout the legal industry, this is the exception. In a proposed (but ultimately unconsummated) merger of two high-profile firms in 2007, it was notable that the managing partner of one of the firms had not practiced law since 1992, while the managing partner of the other had logged 3,300 billable hours in the previous year.[1] Although the number of hours the latter billed is excessive, the choice to continue his practice while leading his law firm is the norm.

Most law firm leaders continue to carry a full or reduced caseload even when they have the option of being in management full-time. A 2004 study of managing partners in more than 100 law firms in the 150–600 lawyer range found that in the 43% of firms that responded, most managing partners did not manage the firm full-time.[2] Moreover, they had no clear job descriptions, limited formal leadership or management training, no formal evaluation process, and no established criteria for choosing their successors. What other business entity as large as these law firms would use such a model?

In some cases, leaders keep practicing law because client work gives them pleasure and rewards that leadership does not. They enjoy doing legal work, and for some partners, being a leader may also impress clients and enhance their business relationships. However, the primary reason is often that partners are more likely to trust a leader who maintains her law practice. Continuing to do the "real work" of a lawyer gives her legitimacy in the eyes of the partners she leads.

Many leaders also remain in practice as self-protection. When

---

[Section 7:4]

[1]Koppel, N. (Jan. 2007), Big law firms try new idea: the true CEO, *Wall Street Journal*.

[2]McKenna, P.J. (Sept.-Oct. 2004), What they do (and how they do it), *Legal Management*.

compensation is calculated, many firms place relatively little value on leadership contributions, so if partners reduce or give up their client work, they face multiple risks. They may take a hit in their compensation, and they may lose their clients to partners who take over the everyday responsibility for serving them. Thus, they need to protect themselves while in a leadership role but more importantly, for the time when their term in leadership ends and they have to return to practice. Very few law firm managing partners have well-defined exit strategies.[3] Even if they have negotiated a "practice re-entry" provision that guarantees a certain income while they rebuild their practice, having to rebuild a practice after a hiatus of several years is a daunting and difficult prospect. One leader who stepped down from a leadership role to focus on building her client base explained that she intends to move back into leadership later at a higher level. First, however, she wants to bring in enough business to create a secure financial cushion. Her plan is to maintain control over the client relationships when she goes into executive leadership but to delegate the day-to-day work to several junior partners.

The prevailing model in law firms of all sizes relies on high-performing practicing lawyers to fill demanding and time-consuming management roles. There is no separation between their management roles and their responsibilities as a partner to the firm. Partners are the rainmakers who bring in business and manage client relationships, producers who serve clients, managers who run the firm, talent developers who ensure that the firm has the talent and future leaders it needs, and owners who are responsible for the financial and cultural well-being of the firm. Contrast this to a corporation, where sales, production, training, and management are all separate functions. Because partners are ultimately responsible for the firm, they delegate few activities to professional managers. Even when they employ professional managers, partners resist giving up control over what is, after all, their firm. In areas where their expertise is limited, such as Information Technology, the firm may rely on specialists to guide and inform them, but partners still chair the IT committee. They may not have the skills, knowledge, or inclination to handle the IT function, but as owners, producers, and managers, all of these responsibilities fall on their shoulders.

Leadership is often made more difficult and less attractive because of the extra demands placed on leaders without concomi-

---

[3]Remsen, J. (Oct./Nov. 2008), The evolving role of today's law firm leaders, *ABA Law Practice Magazine* 24(7), 28.

tant rewards. In most law firms, there is no premium or financial reward for participating in law firm management. While the responsibilities of leaders have grown, the vast majority of large law firms pay their top leaders—who have both leadership and client service responsibilities—on a par with the amount that most senior partners make.[4] Most partners who take on significant leadership roles do not receive any additional compensation for their extra work. Some firms may discount billable hour expectations for partners in high-level leadership positions, but the discount is usually insufficient compared to the amount of time those partners devote to leadership. A 2007 Altman Weil survey found that partners with significant management responsibilities billed only 10% fewer hours than non-manager peers.

Many potential leaders cannot cope with the extra time demands of leadership on top of a busy practice and personal life. A managing partner of a global firm called management a "time-sink": *"Working in management is just as demanding, or more so, than a litigation or environmental practice area. The work never ends. Work fills all the available hours. It's also more demanding because you're dealing with personnel issues, which can be emotionally draining."* One of the reasons it is so demanding is that most of it has to be addressed during the workday and on-site. This is frustrating for some lawyers who are used to taking work home, working at night, or on weekends. They can do their client work that way, but they have to be in the office to handle staff disputes, operational issues, and other matters that require immediate and in-person attention.

This model of partner-managers makes it extremely difficult for mothers, especially those with young children, to become leaders. Lawyers who become partners in their 30s often start families soon after. At the same time, they are trying to build their own client base, which requires a substantial time commitment for business development. Women who are new partners are also frequently asked to accept appointments to committees or to take responsibility for projects that further stretch them— and they feel pressured to say yes.

These conflicting demands put women in a terrible bind. To assert their status as both a rainmaker and a leader deprives them of the ability to devote sufficient attention to either—or to their family or the many other demands on their lives. Some of the interviewed leaders were especially sensitive to these pressures on young partners. When these leaders are in positions to make

---

[4]Jones, L. (Nov. 2007), Should firm leaders get CEO pay?, *National Law Journal*.

leadership appointments, they often tell young women (and men) partners that if their priorities at the time are family or practice building, they should not feel pressured to participate in firm management now; they will be given other opportunities at a later time.

Maintaining a practice may occasionally put leaders in positions of direct conflict with the firm. The partner who is faced with too many responsibilities in both management and client service often feels that she is short-changing one or the other. If the firm values income generation over leadership, the leader may favor spending time attending to her clients even though she has management responsibilities to the firm. Some leaders try to manage this conflict by retaining only the clients they want to serve personally and transitioning other clients to lawyers in the firm but so long as leaders have incentives to maintain a substantial client base, especially if it makes a difference in their compensation and future career plans, these conflicts will remain. Most partners are willing to make some sacrifices for the good of the firm, but even dedicated leaders have a limit if it results in significant economic penalties.

Here is how five of the leaders I interviewed described some of the challenges they deal with:

- *The time demands on the managing partner of a small firm are enormous. I am running a business, which sucks up time, and I am working harder than ever. I take it very seriously, but the best part of being a lawyer is engagement with clients, and my practice is interfering with my management responsibilities.*
- *I am the first managing partner of my [global] firm to maintain a practice and maintain her client relationships. I practice one-third time; I bill about 1,000 hours and spend about 2,000 hours on nonbillable management time. I believe it is very important to continue my practice. It keeps the burdens that face practicing lawyers in my mind and reminds me of what I'm asking others to do.*
- *Since I moved into full-time leadership, the hard part is my self-image. My aspirations always focused on client service. It's hard to change, especially in the legal world where management is not highly valued. My actual power and responsibilities are greater in the firm in my management role, but among partners, management is viewed as a lesser role.*

- *Management is extremely hard. There are constant challenges and pressures. People want you to leave them alone and don't want to be told what to do. Being a lawyer is easier—it's fluid for me after 20 years and much less stressful.*
- *I'm really good at administrative stuff; it's a strength of mine. But I LOVE practicing law. I don't mind billing 2,600 hours. I wouldn't be happy just doing admin. I love clients, take pleasure in my relations with them, and long-term that's better for me. Leadership posts won't make me immensely successful.*

Chapter 8

How Law Firm Structure Affects Leadership

§ 8:1   Comparing leadership in law firms and corporations
§ 8:2   Impact on leadership as law firms become more corporate
§ 8:3   Impact of law firm culture on women

> **KeyCite®:** Cases and other legal materials listed in KeyCite Scope can be researched through the KeyCite service on Westlaw®. Use KeyCite to check citations for form, parallel references, prior and later history, and comprehensive citator information, including citations to other decisions and secondary materials.

§ 8:1   Comparing leadership in law firms and corporations

Most business books about leadership are written for leaders who operate within a corporate setting. However, leadership in a professional service firm, and especially in a law firm, presents unique challenges. While many leadership principles apply in any setting, it is important to consider the distinctive context of law firm partnerships. Corporate and law firm structures create very different work environments and it is helpful for law firm leaders to understand how they differ. See Table 8.1. Contrasting the differences highlights the distinctive nature of law firm leadership and puts it in a clearer perspective.

In both corporations and law firms, leaders are responsible for the profitability and continued success of the organization. In a corporation, leaders deal with the big picture. There are many layers of managers who carry out company initiatives and strategies through the employees whom they oversee. In a law firm, however, almost all leadership and management functions are carried out by the partners themselves.

In a corporation, the CEO is selected by the Board of Directors, acting on behalf of the shareholders, who are the owners of the company. The CEO may attend occasional employee or shareholder meetings but usually remains distant and insulated from them. In a law firm, leaders are selected by their partners, who also happen to be owners of the firm. Unlike corporate CEOs, law firm leaders are always in the midst of their partners and fellow owners. Even if they are in different offices, partners consider their leaders obliged to give them immediate access and attention. Whether elected or appointed to their positions, law firm leaders are chosen by, and accountable to, the very partners whom they lead. One global firm leader explained, *"I work for my partners, and they own this place. They are not distant shareholders. I might take guidance from HR and other departments, but my partners are my bosses."* Lorsch and Tierney describe this situation as "leading from within."[1]

This is especially challenging because, in leading their own partners, law firm leaders have responsibilities but little control or power to implement decisions or compel people to act. By virtue of her position, the CEO of a corporation has power to set the strategic direction for the company. She might consult subordinates and discuss the decision in advance but managers will typically defer to her judgment and employees will carry out the strategy. In stark contrast, law firm partner-owners are not inclined to be deferential. Instead, they feel entitled to debate every point, pursue their own agendas, and openly oppose or even ignore the leader's decisions. Moreover, because power is distributed throughout the partnership and partners want to study and debate most issues, issue analysis can continue endlessly, opposing sides can become hardened, decision making can become paralyzed, and firm cohesion can be undermined. Law firm leaders must be forceful enough to overcome resistance, generate consensus, and facilitate decisions. But they cannot be too forceful, because partners will reject efforts to impose on their autonomy. This requires a delicate balancing act.

Whereas corporate leaders enjoy power that comes with their position, law firm leaders must use persuasion, lobbying, cajoling, and peer pressure to implement strategic decisions and initiatives, and to align the interests of individuals with those of the firm. Law firm leaders are held accountable for producing expected results, but even at the highest executive levels, have little power or leverage to carry out their responsibilities. Instead of the positional power that a CEO enjoys, a law firm leader must use highly developed political skills in order to get partners to carry out strategic decisions and stay focused on building the collective success of the firm.

[Section 8:1]

[1]Lorsch, J.W., & Tierney, T.J. (2002), *Aligning the stars: how to succeed when professionals drive results* (Boston: Harvard Business School Press).

Table 8.1. Corporate vs. Law Firm Leadership		
Category	**Corporation**	**Law Firm**
Organization of leadership	Leadership and management are separate from production and from ownership	Managers and leaders are also producers and owners
Leadership selection	By a board of directors, on behalf of shareholder-owners	By partner-owners
Leadership responsibility	To act in shareholders' interests	To reconcile partners' self-interest and firm interests
Positional power	Clear lines of authority; sets strategic direction	No clear lines of authority; Sets strategic direction but partners have right to question, debate, oppose
Contact with constituents	Insulated from shareholders, rare interaction	Leads from within, works in midst of partner-owners
Implementing a decision or initiative	Leader decides; subordinates defer to leader, carry it out	Partners must concur, be willing to fund and carry out the effort
Leverage over constituents	Compensation, promises of promotion, threats of negative consequences	Persuasion, influence, peer pressure
Tenure	No set years or terms; Board may fire for poor performance	Leader serves at pleasure of partner-owners; some firms set length of term, require re-election, or limit terms

Corporations generally do not define a specific number of years or terms for CEOs. The Board may fire a CEO, but usually does so only for consistently bad decisions or poor performance. In contrast, law firm partners rotate in and out of leadership positions. Many law firms select leaders for specified terms and some limit the number of terms one partner can remain in a particular leadership position. Leaders may be turned out when they stand for re-election at the end of a term, or midterm if there is sufficient discontent, especially among powerful partners.

In addition to these differences, law firms are beset by ongoing tensions, particularly those between the self-interest of individual partners and the interests of the firm as a whole. Partners control the key resources of a law firm—legal knowledge, technical skills, professional reputation, and client relationships. They are the people who generate the firm's revenues. They also happen to be owners of the firm who are financially responsible and accountable for its actions. This combination of control over critical intangible resources, income-generating power and proprietary interest in the firm makes them feel entitled to participate directly in any decisions that affect them.

When a law firm adopts common values and all live by them, less time is wasted in internal negotiations and posturing. Strategies are implemented, not endlessly debated, and people are more likely to work as a team. However, partners expect to receive preferences and special treatment, so they constantly negotiate to receive the benefits, resources, and privileges that they deserve and that may serve their personal interests even at the expense of the firm's. Partners also tend to focus attention on their short-term self-interest. This short-term way of thinking is reinforced by the partnership structure, which disburses all profits at the end of each year rather than retaining funds for long-term projects.

It is up to firm leaders to maintain a well-functioning culture that achieves a healthy balance between that short-term thinking and the long-term collective good of the firm. One of a leader's responsibilities is to try to shape the behavior of individual partners so that on average they put the interests of the firm ahead of their own needs.[2] The firm's ability to achieve its objectives over time, and to endure as a successful entity depends on a large proportion of partners being willing to do this.

This often requires a great deal of diplomacy. One interviewed leader described a challenging situation that her firm had to resolve when a prominent and powerful founding partner of the firm brought in a new client that promised to be a huge money-maker, but the client's business was an anathema to many of the firm's lawyers and the representation would have gone against the values and political culture of the firm. The New Business Committee and the Executive Committee ultimately turned down the new engagement. In telling the founding partner that they

---

[2]Lorsch & Tierney (2002), *Aligning the stars.*

were rejecting the work, they emphasized his longstanding role in the firm and community, persuaded him that he did not want to be a cause for tearing the firm apart, and appealed to his concern for the long-term well-being of the firm. Other partners were willing to forego the profit, and in the end, so was he.

§ 8:2 Impact on leadership as law firms become more corporate

Almost all law firms operate as partnerships of professionals. Even law firms that are legally organized as corporations perceive themselves as partnerships whether they refer to lawyer-owners as partners or shareholders. However, many law firms are becoming more corporate in their management structure. Firms that have numerous offices throughout the country and around the world, with multiple practice groups and industry teams, have complicated organizational structures and operational systems. They have become so large and complex that they can no longer be run effectively by practicing partners who are "enthusiastic amateurs."

Many firms acknowledge that their partners do not have sufficient training or preparation to deal with many aspects of leadership. Those firms hire professionals with expertise in fields such as finance, operations, business management, marketing, technology, professional development, and project management to run various organizational functions. Although firms remain organized by specialized practice areas and client teams rather than functional areas found in corporations (e.g., sales, marketing, financial services, production), law firms' addition of full-time professional managers is creating more of a corporate structure than ever before.

In Australia and the U.K., law firms are actually becoming public corporations. Two Australian law firms have gone public since outside ownership of law firms was allowed in 2007. In the U.K., the Legal Services Act, which takes full effect in 2011, will no longer restrict law firm ownership to lawyers and will permit both public investment in law firms and new types of legal service firms known as "alternative business structures." Several private equity firms in the U.K. have raised millions of dollars to buy ownership stakes in law firms as soon as it is permitted. The legislation currently permits law firms to become alternative business structures. One British firm that has already made this change has admitted to the partnership their IT director and facilities director, neither of whom are lawyers. While the regulatory scheme in the United States makes it highly unlikely that

American law firms will become publicly held corporations or make other professionals partners any time soon, these changes abroad will have a significant impact on the management of American law firms.

At present, however, with few exceptions, even the largest law firms manage themselves as partnerships. They laud the collegiality that is the hallmark of partnerships, although their cultures are becoming less and less collegial all the time. However, even in firms whose "eat what you kill" cultures tend toward the cutthroat or where they de-equitize or expel partners without hesitation, lawyers typically describe their firms as "collegial." They place great importance on partners being friendly, mutually respectful, and supportive, whether or not they actually are. This "partnership ethos," as Professor Laura Empson calls it, is "a powerful unifying force" in a law firm that "serves to counteract the potentially self-serving impulses that drive each partner individually."[1] That unifying force takes on great importance for leaders because of the underlying tensions that challenge law firm unity. Those tensions are disruptive whether they are in a one-office firm where all the partners fit into one conference room or in large firms with hundreds of partners spread across many offices and throughout the world. One of the critical challenges for law firm leaders today is how to make leadership more capable and respected and management more professional without destroying the collegiality and consensus that firms find so important.

Unfortunately, the collegiality upon which firms pride themselves is under increasing strain and in many firms it is more myth than reality. Lawyers are competitive. They are into scoring points and comparing what they make to what their peers make, and some firms have adopted compensation systems that encourage internal competition. The idea is to drive partners to maximize their contributions; the more work and money you bring in, the more you and the firm will earn. However, when partners compete against each other for business and personal rewards they undermine the trust and teamwork needed for the partnership to move ahead as a whole. In the worst of these firms, leaders face a constant struggle to maintain a common vision and cooperative action while the intrafirm rivalries threaten to tear the firm apart. Even in the best firms, it is hard to keep everyone focused on the collective good.

[Section 8:2]

[1]Empson, L. (Ed.) (2007), *Managing the modern law firm: new challenges, new perspectives* (Oxford: Oxford University Press), 21.

Paradoxically, this may create new leadership opportunities for women. The high value that lawyers place on collegiality plays to women's strengths. To the extent that women use leadership styles that are collaborative and supportive and have greater facility and interest in building relationships, they are well equipped to foster the kind of work environment and culture that lawyers want. The increasing number of professional management positions may also attract some women who have specialized expertise and are interested in moving into full-time management.

§ 8:3 Impact of law firm culture on women

Leaders have a great deal of influence on a law firm's culture. The way leaders deal with firm issues and policies makes a difference in the experience and opportunities available to women. Having a large number of women in leadership roles can shape the culture of a firm. Many firms have great maternity leave, on-ramping programs, and part-time policies, but a supervising partner who believes that new mothers lose focus, commitment, and brain cells can sabotage a woman's career by giving her tedious work assignments, forcing her to work more than her agreed-upon schedule, and making her feel marginalized. Leaders who make it a priority to prevent such bias from derailing women's careers will institute management systems that prevent such abuse and hold partners accountable for their actions.

Law firm cultures vary significantly. Some firms are genuinely good places for women to work. Women succeed in many ways because the firm is open to diverse leadership styles and behaviors. Men encourage, mentor, and support women without hesitation and with positive results. Women hold numerous important leadership roles in the firm, and there are no token "women's seats" on important committees. Women are valued for their contributions, not just their hours or origination credits, and flexibility is woven into the fabric of firm life. These firms are not common but they do exist.

At the other end of the spectrum are firms where women still face sexist comments, offensive behavior, and overt discrimination. Fortunately, women today do not work in firms where firm meetings are held in male-only clubs or the firm's managing partner wears suspenders with naked women on them. These flagrantly degrading types of behavior are no longer tolerated but more subtle and insidious activities continue. Many firms have a rigidly masculine mental model of leadership and only those who fit that model are accepted. In those firms, it is rare for women to become leaders, and if they do, they tend to adapt in ways that many other women find unappealing. In order to be perceived as a strong leader, many of these women become "more manly than the men."

Most firm cultures fit somewhere between these two extremes. Each year, Working Mother Magazine and FlexTime Lawyers jointly publish a list of "Best Law Firms for Women," as does Yale Law Women. The lists are derived from surveys that focus on policies and work conditions that are deemed to be women friendly or family friendly. That firms want to appear on the lists reflects the competitive marketplace for women lawyers and the imperative to respond to women's needs. Firms that appear in one survey do not always appear on the other, but the fact that firms feel it is important to be listed at all is highly significant and underscores the value of publishing these lists. Law firms want to have reputations as being good places for women to practice. The surveys put pressure on them to adopt progressive policies and to make those policies work. They reveal patterns and trends. Most importantly, the surveys provide account-ability—what is measured is what gets done—and enable the profession to track progress over time.

However, it is tricky to categorize a firm culture as being good or bad for women. One leader explained it this way: "*Some obstacles are real; some are perceived. You need to know which it is in your firm. Say you don't see enough women in leadership roles or in equity partnership. In some firms, gender is not the is-sue at all—the firm is supportive of women, helps them with clients, etc. Women can succeed in those firms but get grabbed away or choose alternative paths. In other firms, it's a problem because women don't get any support. Men see no women leaders and say 'So what? What's the problem?'*"

We can—and should—look at law firm policies, practices, and demographics. Using that data, we can make generalizations, and firms with reputations as being good for women will undoubt-edly attract more of them. However, even in firms that are considered the best for women, not every woman will find the place culturally suited to her aspirations and personality. Some firms with outstanding policies on paper do not implement them fairly or at all. In contrast, others may lack certain policies and programs, or the number of women in leadership may be small, but the women in those firms have what they value and want and feel that they are in a great place for them.

When a firm is considered a good place for women generally, the basis for that assessment gives you important information about the kind of culture it has, but your career satisfaction and success depend on whether it is a good place for you personally. What matters to you may not be what polls and surveys measure, which is why it is important to understand yourself, your ambitions, and your values. If flexibility is a priority for you, a firm where flexible work arrangements are well established and part-time lawyers are successful may be the right place for you. If you are more interested in advancing quickly and becoming the firm's top-earning lawyer, you may prefer a culture that rewards high individual achievement, long hours, and tireless effort.

If you have risen through the ranks of your firm to partnership, you are undoubtedly familiar with its culture and whether it will support your move into leadership. If you are considering a move to another firm, it is important to know whether the culture of that firm will make it easy or hard for you to be a leader. If you are an associate deciding whether you want to stay and try for partnership or move to another firm where the chances might be better, you also need to compare different law firm cultures. When you are deciding whether a firm is a good place for you, it is vital to look beyond the firm's policies, reputation, and published statistics. Talk with women leaders in the firm about their experience and ask specific questions that relate to your ambitions. Table 8.2 provides some questions to consider.

In addition, observe the way that people treat each other. You can tell a lot about whether a firm's culture will be conducive to your career ambitions from small, everyday things. Casual interactions and observations provide clues about the cultural environment of the firm. For example, a lesbian who joined a firm as Counsel was impressed by the fact that staff stayed at the firm a very long time, which signaled to her an environment of mutual respect and good work relationships. She also knew that the firm held another lesbian partner in high esteem and had appointed her to an important leadership position. That signaled to her that this was a safe place where she could be herself. Her feelings were further reinforced by an experience at her first partner meeting. She felt totally lost at the meeting. The managing partner saw her and invited her to sit next to him. *"It made me feel so welcome. You always remember those small things."*

Table 8.2. Questions About Firm Culture

- Is the culture of this firm conducive to my career, my life, and my personal aspirations?
- Is this a firm that values leaders, both women and men?
- What kind of lawyers does the firm select to be leaders?
- Do many lawyers seek leadership roles, or do they have to be prodded into leadership?
- How diverse are firm leaders?
- How many leaders are women? Are women encouraged to seek leadership?
- Does the firm value women as leaders, or is it putting women into leadership positions to make its diversity numbers look better?
- Is leadership rewarded?
- Are leaders respected?
- Do I think I can have a real impact as a leader in this firm? How hard would it be? Is it worth the effort?

The leaders I interviewed related many ways that they were affected by the culture of the firms in which they practiced. A leader who has been managing partner in two firms attributed the starkly dissimilar experiences she had to differences in the firms' cultures. In her first firm, *"there were lots of bullies, all of them men; they pushed back on everything. If they weren't bullies, they were paternalistic. They would tell me to keep quiet. I had to fight fire with fire and had to be very tough."* She changed firms. At her current firm, *"People are nicer. They assume we're all on an equal footing. They push back, but I can deal with them."*

Being in a culture where women are respected is terrific, but being where women are actively championed is sublime. It leads to an inclusive environment where women are truly judged on their skills and talents, not their gender. One leader's experience illustrates how the support of one male partner made a huge impression on her and created a culture where women leaders could flourish. As a new associate in a large firm, this woman was assigned to a client team led by this male partner, who was also the practice group leader. His client was the biggest client in the firm. This powerful male partner made a woman partner his second in command on this team and placed women in leadership on many other teams. The leader I interviewed said of him, *"He was a wonderful leader and had many women on his teams in prominent roles, so the whole practice group was used to working with women at every level, and I had many role models. In his practice group, everyone—young and old, women and men—was comfortable working with women and being supervised and led by women."*

Chapter 9

Mastering Law Firm Politics

§ 9:1 Politics is not a dirty word
§ 9:2 Reciprocity
§ 9:3 Picking your battles
§ 9:4 The power of networks
§ 9:5 Building alliances and coalitions

KeyCite®: Cases and other legal materials listed in KeyCite Scope can be researched through the KeyCite service on Westlaw®. Use KeyCite to check citations for form, parallel references, prior and later history, and comprehensive citator information, including citations to other decisions and secondary materials.

---

§ 9:1 Politics is not a dirty word

You can't ignore politics, no matter how much you'd like to.
—Molly Ivins

Leaders must get partners to act together, but they do not have the power to force them to comply. The power of law firm leaders is only "the potential ability to influence behavior, to change the course of events, to overcome resistance, and to get people to do things that they would not otherwise do."[1] Politics is the way leaders use that potential power to achieve results. As Stanford Business School Professor Jeffrey Pfeffer explains, "politics and influence are the processes, the actions, the behaviors through which this potential power is utilized and realized."[2]

Within law firms there is a continuous interplay between interests, conflict, and power. Lawyers practice in a law firm to serve their clients, make a living, and develop their careers. They join together because they prefer to have common structures, systems, and resources, which makes it easier for them than to practice on their own. They share interests in the firm, but

---

[Section 9:1]

[1]Pfeffer, J. (1994), *Managing with power: politics and influence in organizations* (Boston: Harvard Business School Press).

[2]Pfeffer (1994), *Managing with power.*

sometimes their interests diverge. If the divergent interests are compatible and can be reconciled easily, most of their decisions will be rational and for the common good of the enterprise. However, when their interests clash, all bets are off. Partners exert whatever personal power they have and the power they can marshal from others in order to protect themselves and get their way.

The attempt to resolve the tensions among competing partners and interests is a political process. When individual or group interests diverge, politics is a means to reconcile differences through consultation and negotiation. To many ears, politics sounds pejorative and "dirty," but it is necessary and common in any organization, especially in law firms where few people have the power to act alone. It is a natural part of every firm and is not an optional activity for law firm leaders. It has been said of firm politics that "Declaring yourself out of the game doesn't get you out of the game. You can't 'not play'—you can only play competently or incompetently."[3]

Since reconciling competing interests is part of a leader's job, leaders must be politically savvy. Being respected for your competence is essential for a leader, but if we look at two equally competent leaders, "the one who has political savvy, agility in the use of power, and the ability to influence others will go further."[4] To be politically adept, a leader needs to understand what competing interests exist and be able to square individuals' personal interests with the collective interests of the firm in order to protect and advance the latter. Political astuteness involves recognizing the political nature of the firm and knowing how to build a critical mass of support for something you care about, whether it is your personal goal or part of your leadership agenda. It acknowledges that people tend to do what they believe is in their best interests and that conflict can be a positive force for change and growth, but that it must be managed.

Many law firm leaders are slow to recognize the importance of firm politics. Several leaders who were interviewed noted that they could have been more effective sooner if they had understood more about the political nature of their firms. They started in leadership with idealism and political naïveté. One leader believed that the firm was a meritocracy; that partners were compensated on the basis of stated, objective criteria; and that

---

[3]Albrecht, K. (2006), *Social intelligence: the new science of success* (San Francisco: Jossey-Bass).

[4]Reardon, K.K. (2001), *The secret handshake: mastering the politics of the business inner circle* (New York: Currency Books), 2.

partners always acted in the firm's best interests. Another leader who was in charge of the committee to select new partners learned that final decisions were made by the biggest rainmakers in each practice group after discussions from which she was excluded. Yet another leader thought that if firm leadership committed to doing something, then it would get done and was surprised by the disconnect between words and action. Once these women gained leadership experience, they learned how the system really worked. Had they been less naive, they might have become more effective more quickly. Here are comments from two leaders about hare they increased their political awareness:

- *I learned what really matters by becoming a leader. I sat in on compensation reviews for partners and associates and learned that there was a big difference between what partners say and what they really value. They listed 12 criteria/ metrics, but only a few really counted: billings, hours, the kind of clients you have, and the margin of profit, so some work might be more profitable even if you work less because you staff more efficiently or have more leverage. You can be better compensated even if the total dollars brought in are less than another practice group.*

- *When I came up through the ranks, I chaired various committees, including the committee to select new partners. At each step, I did not have access to the people with "real power" who were making decisions, pulling strings behind the scenes. When I became managing partner, I realized how many discussions had been held without me about which associates to elevate to partnership. They're the most powerful people in the firm because they control most of the business. I didn't know how involved they were before. I had to push my way into their discussions—now I'm in a position to do it. They're including me in decisions for the first time.*

In a law firm, where every partner is a leader, "[e]ffective leadership lies in recognizing other leaders' interests, understanding them in all their complexity, influencing them, and then finding modes of action that will satisfy those interests while achieving desired organizational goals."[5] In order to be politically savvy, you need to know who the power brokers are and know them well enough to size them up. What are their agendas? What is important to them? What do they want and need? Who are your potential supporters or opponents?

On any issue, you must be able to anticipate what you will be

---

[5]Salacuse, J.W. (2006), *Leading leaders: how to manage smart, talented, rich, and powerful people* (New York: AMACOM).

up against and who can help you or stop you from succeeding. You may want to build alliances with partners who support your goals. If you know who your opponents are, you can develop strategies and tactics to overcome or neutralize their objections. Perhaps you want a position that is elected or appointed. Who should you have in your corner? If you want to get a new initiative passed, start a new practice area, or change the firm's bonus policy, whose support will you need and what will you have to do to procure that support? You need all this information in order to increase your ability to take effective action. How will you gather the "intelligence" you need to answer these questions accurately?

Answering these questions can be extremely challenging because of the complexity of individual interests and the many competing interests that arise between and among partners and the firm as a whole. These conflicts may just be about the partner's personal needs or desires, but they may also include those of the partner's clients, practice group, or team. Only when you fully understand what all the interests are can you develop approaches to influence and satisfy those interests while achieving desired firm goals. This is inherently a political process. It involves employing persuasion, building coalitions, enlisting ambassadors and champions, and engaging in lengthy, often tedious, discussions and negotiations.

All of these steps are essential to getting things done in your firm. Suppose you have studied every aspect of an issue and feel certain you know the best way to solve a problem that has been plaguing the firm, but you cannot implement that solution without the support of the group, many of whom are undoubtedly of different views. Even those who share your conclusion may challenge you about how you plan to implement the solution you suggest. You are unlikely to persuade opponents about a controversial new move with just a well-reasoned argument. You will need to take actions that are plainly political. The Washington, D.C. office managing partner of a large regional firm explained it this way:

> Every organization has its own dynamic. To become politically savvy, you need to figure out the dynamic at your firm. What is the agenda of the people in your constituency, what drives them, what are their needs? How do you get people to work together? How do you get your objectives through? Even in my leadership role, I need to make sure that my objectives are aligned with those in higher leadership roles, those controlling firm-wide issues. The firm-wide managing partner and I coach each other regularly. We differ politically but respect our common goal for the firm.

One leader showed political savvy when she wanted to start a new practice group. Over a period of years, she had done the groundwork to develop a "clean energy" practice in her firm. At some point, she felt that the firm had enough related business and interested partners to create a separate practice group. She felt that she should chair the group but a powerful male partner also wanted to be the chair. She knew that if he used his clout, he would get the position, so she found another way to maintain a leadership presence. She spoke to each of the other partners who would be in the new practice group and suggested that the group be led by a steering committee, not by one person. They all agreed and selected a 12-person steering committee, of which she is a member. Their collaborative governance has been so successful that other practice groups in the firm are thinking about switching to the same approach.

All firms have rules about how things are supposed to happen, like how lawyers are promoted or selected for leadership, the criteria for compensation awards, and who makes hiring and firing decisions, but sometimes the written or established rules have less relevance than who you know or who owes you a favor. This is where politics comes into play. Politics helps you get things done outside the rules. It means having the ear of people with power and influence to help you get what you want. It means being better able to gauge the impact that decisions and changes will have on other powerful partners, what their reactions might be, and how it will affect your chances of success. It ensures you are on "the inside track" and helps you come to sound conclusions because you have open and useful communication channels.

Even if you know the firm's "official" rules, one big question is whether everyone plays by the rules. Many new leaders may be surprised by this question, yet you need to know whether rules in your firm are enforced uniformly, and if not, who follows them and who is permitted to deviate or ignore them. Because lawyers are constantly negotiating for what they see as the privileges that come with their status as partners or rainmakers, some lawyers play by a separate set of rules or feel entitled to be treated differently. This is often the case with partners who demand the largest office, insist on using certain associates when it is not in the firm's or the associate's best interests, or expect the firm to pay for their monthly parking. However, rules may also be applied inconsistently because some partners are simply more politically attuned to possibilities than others. They ask for credits, positions, or favors that others simply fail to request. Be sure that you understand which rules matter, which are merely suggestions, and which are not even expressed, and learn how to make all of those rules work for you.

To be an effective leader, you need to know how to go through established channels to achieve desired ends, but you also have to understand the firm's unwritten rules and use them to get things done. So how do you learn the unwritten rules? One way is by being in leadership. When you are in charge of a project or committee, you see things that you otherwise would not see; you learn how to deal with them and how the game is played. People interact with leaders differently than with other peers because they want things from leaders for themselves, their clients, or other people whom they favor. You learn that while some partners ask for nothing and are taken for granted, others demand—and often receive—outrageous preferences. At first this may be shocking, but you soon learn how firm leaders deal with these demands and how they determine whether a partner is creating sufficient value for the firm to warrant special treatment. You learn that what you believe to be a meritocracy values and rewards some achievements as more meritorious than others.

If you obey all the rules, you miss all the fun.

— Katherine Hepburn

§ 9:2   Reciprocity

The politics of leadership often involves reciprocity: the principle that if you do something for someone, they will return the favor. We hear it in many common sayings, such as "One good turn deserves another." We see it when we walk down the street and smile at an approaching stranger; most likely she will smile back. This principle has a social basis and is found in virtually all societies.[1] Reciprocity facilitates transactions among individuals and across time because it means that individuals are obligated to repay what they have received. It is commonly called a "favor bank" because it involves an exchange of support or resources that can be banked, owed, or redeemed. But reciprocity is not a direct quid pro quo exchange. An immediate exchange of favors is not necessarily sought or desired, the extent of the future obligation is not specified at the time when the favor is granted, and the gift creates no specific expectation but rather a diffuse, generalized obligation.

Reciprocity—both in what you have to give and what you want to get—is a key factor in all relationships. It is manifested by doing a good turn, showing kindness, or providing help. When an-

---

[Section 9:2]

[1]Cialdini, R.B. (Oct. 2001), Harnessing the science of persuasion, *Harvard Business Review*.

other person does something for you, you usually show your appreciation and automatically consider how you can help them. Similarly, when you show generosity and consideration to others, they think of you positively and are more willing to extend favors to you. You never know when you will need to ask another person for help, so it is a good idea to be generous with information, introductions, contacts, or anything else that will benefit the other person before you need their help. Unexpected favors can be especially powerful, as can hard-to-obtain benefits, whether it is an opportunity to take the lead on a high profile client matter or tickets to a sold-out concert.

Reciprocity can take many forms. Sometimes it involves making concessions to people who make concessions to us: if I concede a small point now, the other person will be more willing to concede to me later. Sometimes it is putting people in a better position: if I give another person a chance to look good, they will likely return the favor one day. Sometimes it is making an important introduction: if I refer a client to another lawyer, that lawyer may send business to me. One leader I interviewed described how she used reciprocity: "*When I needed help for an important client in a legal area that I didn't know, I went to a partner on the management committee who practices in that area. I did it to raise my visibility with him. We are in different practice areas . . .. Now he knows me, and maybe he'll reciprocate when he has work for one of his clients that I can handle.*"

In a political context, reciprocity is used to support desired ends. Just as in government politics, law firm leaders have particular proposals, decisions, or policies that they want to enact or prevent. Supporting Partner A on one measure may persuade her to support your position on the next. If Partner B opposes your position, you may be able to offer her something that will get her to back off and take no position.

As a leader, you are in a prime position to be helpful to others. Learn what key people need to get their projects implemented, and let them know what you can do for them. At the same time that you are helping them, you are also laying the groundwork for help with your own future needs. In a sense it is a bargaining process: what can you give them if they support you on this? Understanding what is most important to people in the firm allows you to decide what to offer as well as when and whom to press on certain points.

As with any leadership technique, reciprocity should not be overplayed. It is not about keeping score or being obvious in granting or asking for favors. When it works well, it is a subtle, barely noticeable process. Also, if you do too many favors, too often, they may become off-putting or lose significance. One managing partner who did a great deal to help one of her partners described what happened when he began to take her support for granted. It also shows the way a leader can exert power to help or hinder another's career: *"This guy is someone I championed. I traded many favors to get him into the partnership. I hired him, got him elevated to partner, then to equity partner. I made sure his compensation was high."* The managing partner expected that he would appreciate her help and behave in a way that would make her proud of him. Instead he became arrogant and demanding, and angered other partners. She felt that he was not holding up his end of the bargain: *"I'm the one with credibility and power; I can choose to keep or expel him; I have a tremendous impact on his career. He needs my support, and I know it. When he started acting like a jerk, I simply stopped advocating for him. That gave others the signal that it was OK to tell him to go."*

Many women fail to use reciprocity as a political tool. They are hesitant about asking for favors from colleagues in the firm, and they are willing to do favors for others without expecting any sort of payback. For example, women agree to take on time-consuming responsibilities or assignments even though it takes time away from their own work. Someone who wants your time should be willing to give you something in return, but most women do not use such requests as a bargaining chip; they do not treat their time as a valuable resource that can be traded for something else.

Two other points to remember about reciprocity. First, you must collect in a timely fashion. Otherwise, the reciprocity principle fades, and it will be less persuasive when you ask for a favor later. Second, while most people will naturally reciprocate according to the norm, some do not. They merely exploit those who are generous. If you do a good turn for someone who fails to assist you in return, you should resist when they ask you again or remind them that they owe you.

§ 9:3   Picking your battles

You only have a certain amount of political capital and do not want to squander it on unimportant issues. You need to decide when to speak up and when to stay silent, which projects to sponsor and which battles to fight. Regardless of how much or how little power you wield, you can have considerable influence over the policies and practices that are most important to you. You want to be a person whose opinions others care about, seek, and listen to when they are making decisions. Sometimes timing is critical; choosing the right moment to raise an issue may make success more likely. On the other hand, taking a stand now may win you support on a particular issue but destroy your ability to achieve more important long-term goals.

This is why it is important to be clear about what matters the most to you, and to think politically and strategically. When dealing with controversial issues, consider:

- What do you care about and how important is it to you?
- What do the power players in the firm care about and how important is it to them?
- What do your constituents care about and how important is it to them?
- Can these various interests be reconciled? If so, how?
- If the interests cannot be reconciled, what are the risks, benefits, and likely results of supporting each position?
- Are there events, conditions, concerns, or other factors within the firm, in the marketplace, or pertaining to certain clients that have a bearing on the controversy?

In addition to the political calculations that all leaders must make, women leaders often come under pressure to give top priority to issues of special interest to women. As noted previously, most women leaders want to support other women but not necessarily on every issue. They may have to take positions that displease women constituents, or they may have important priorities on their agenda besides those of special interest to women. Sometimes two interests which may both be important to women compete for limited resources, and leaders have to choose between them. As one leader, a woman of color, pointed out, *It's good to be empathetic, but too much empathy can be dangerous. You get swept up in other people's issues. You cannot fight every battle. You only have so many chits to play. For example, part-time is important to some people but not to me. I don't want to focus on it. Diversity is what I care about. I can't be all things to all people.*

§ 9:4 The power of networks

In organizations, real power and energy is generated through relationships. The patterns of relationships and the capacities to form them are more important than tasks, functions, roles, and positions.

— Margaret Wheatley

The importance of networks cannot be overstated. Research

shows that belonging to successful networks is crucial for women to achieve leadership and that exclusion from influential networks holds women back.[1] The inability to access such networks serves as a barrier for women trying to achieve leadership roles and it persists for women even after they become leaders. Women lawyers experience exclusion and isolation far more than their male counterparts. An ABA study found that 60% of white women and 62% of women of color—but only four percent of white men—feel excluded from formal and informal networking opportunities.[2] In a 2009 study by the Minority Corporate Counsel Association more than 25% of women partners said that they experienced exclusion from informal networking opportunities. This was the highest exclusion rate of any demographic group surveyed.[3]

Networks are critical to your ability to become a leader and to be effective as a leader. They give you access to resources and information, and to people who can make things happen for you—whether getting you the right work assignment, introducing you to a potential client, or influencing the amount of your compensation. They also put you close to powerful partners, and that proximity confers power to you by putting you in the center of communications, social relations, and decision making. Having a broad network of influential people means that you are well connected and those connections give you the ability to get what you need to produce the results that you want. The power derived from your network relationships can help you advance your leadership aspirations, your agenda, and the firm's business goals.

Networks are based on relationships formed for different reasons, personal as well as professional. Within the firm, the quality of your relationships—your social capital—determines how quickly and how high you move into leadership. If powerful partners support you, you will be able to call on them for information, expertise, ideas, assistance, and support, and your entry

---

[Section 9:4]

[1]Schipani, C.A., Dworkin, T.M., & Kwolek-Folland, A. (Jan. 2009), Pathways for women to obtain positions of organizational leadership: the significance of mentoring and networking, *Duke Journal of Gender Law and Policy* 16(1).

[2]ABA Commission on Women in the Profession (2006), *Visible invisibility: women of color in law firms* (American Bar Association).

[3]Minority Corporate Counsel Association (2009), *Sustaining pathways to diversity: the next steps in understanding & increasing diversity and inclusion in large law firms*.

into leadership circles will be faster and smoother. Without that kind of support, you may go nowhere.

Networks are powerful because they give you both the means to get ahead and rewards for getting there. Politically savvy leaders cultivate personal relationships with partners, especially those who are power brokers, within their practice and office and throughout the firm. When they get appointed to leadership roles as a result of those connections, it gives them higher status and also reflects the fact that they have powerful friends—which reinforces their image as a powerful partner. Then they use their power to have their followers appointed to important positions, which further expands their influence in the firm. As their influence grows they are rewarded with new opportunities for leadership that enable them to advance even further.

The problem is that the most powerful partner networks in law firms are populated and controlled by men. They go out for lunch together, play golf or poker together, and belong to the same clubs. While some men deliberately exclude women, most of the time they are simply more comfortable in these settings with other men. In addition to the strong bonds that form within a powerful group of men, many men are uncomfortable having to watch what they say and do when women are nearby. New male leaders fit in naturally; they are "one of the guys." Moreover, their gender does not call their qualifications into question as it does for women. Because men are presumed more likely than women to succeed as leaders, the men who are in these networks and who control the law firm tend to channel career development opportunities and support to other men—thereby facilitating male success and creating self-fulfilling prophecies that validate their thinking and perpetuate male dominance.

Men have used networks this way to build and hold onto power for generations. Women do not have the same power base—yet. Women must find ways to get into leadership networks and then use their positions to expand opportunities for other women. It has been said that women's networks have deeper but fewer relationships, while men's networks are shallower but more expansive. Women need both kinds of networks. It is good to have a small circle of several close friends and clients, but you also need broad networks with many contacts. You have to have a wide spectrum of network contacts who can help you in many different ways, from finding a dog walker to introducing you to a new CEO.

One of the reasons women's networks are more limited than men's is that women think of relationships in terms of friendships and they do not like to impose on their friends. However, in a business context, networking relationships are based on reciprocal benefits, not friendship (even when the people involved are friends). Networking relationships are more transactional than personal. They are a manifestation of the reciprocity principle because both parties recognize that they can potentially benefit from the relationship. They are not exploitative because each member of the relationship respects and helps the other. Good networkers always look for ways to do something helpful for the other person, but they also realize that in business, once a relationship forms, people regularly extend favors and seek favors in return. The connections between them do not have to be very profound or personal; they may be purely professional or social. However, once you have demonstrated your helpfulness or willingness to help, it is not an imposition to ask the person for an introduction, a committee appointment, or a vote. Therefore, from a political standpoint, you want people in your network—and you want to be in the networks of others —who are in positions to provide, or provide access to, the kinds of support, information, opportunities, people, and influence that you need now or in the future.

Belonging or having direct access to powerful networks is necessary in order to carry out your leadership responsibilities. Your power as a leader is to a large extent a function of your links to the powerful individuals in these networks. They are the partners who make decisions about firm issues through informal conversations and activities behind the scenes long before other partners meet to decide. If you are excluded from these networks, it will be hard to wield your authority or even to maintain a perception that you have any significant authority. On the other hand, if you are well connected and can exert your influence in and through these networks, you can increase your credibility as a leader and your span of influence within the firm. You can lobby thought leaders and power brokers directly and solicit their help to get your policies adopted, your decisions implemented, and your goals achieved. Networks can leverage your knowledge and effort by serving as vehicles for directing communications, coordinating efforts, and sending signals to your partners about what they need to do, how to behave, and which initiatives and goals have the highest priority.

Networks are also important sources of influential mentors and champions for women leaders. Both female and male mentors can provide inside information, contacts, and political support that make women leaders more readily accepted, admired, and effectual. However, so long as men control the power structure in law firms, having senior male mentors is especially important for women leaders. One of the greatest benefits of having a male mentor is gaining access to his network.

There are many formally organized networks that you can join, like internal affinity groups, college and law firm alumni associations, bar associations, and professional organizations. Some require certain professional qualifications but many are open to anyone who is interested. Networks outside the firm can be sources of business, advice, leadership opportunities, and recognition for your leadership skills. These networks are useful because of the people you meet and the interactions that can lead to personal and professional opportunities.

Informal networks, especially those in your firm, are harder to access. Informal networks are simply webs of relationships with no formal structure. Members share common interests, experience, or concerns, know who else is a part of the group, and may socialize together, but they do not necessarily hold meetings or have a list of members. They operate through personal relationships, outside the structures of committees, practice groups, or other organizational units. Members share familiarity and a common understanding. These networks may be politically neutral (e.g., all lawyers who started at the firm together), but the ones that matter for leadership are those that control decisions, policies, and strategy in your firm.

Those networks represent the inner circles of power, and women have more difficulty than men gaining entry to them. In many cases, the door to those inner circles opens up to women only after they achieve a high level of authority in the firm. When doors do open, they are only slightly ajar, and even women who manage to enter may still not be fully accepted. One managing partner I interviewed who attended a two-day, firm-wide management committee meeting learned on the morning of the second day that the other committee members—all men—had gone out together the night before but had not invited her. Although she was a part of the group at one level she was excluded from full membership.

Gaining access to powerful networks is one area where you cannot afford to wait for an invitation. You have to be highly conscious of the importance of networks and connections and willing to push open the door and take your seat at the table. This requires thinking about networking strategically. An expert on strategic networking notes that, "It's less about working the room and more about being in the right room."[4] One bold technique is simply to invite yourself into that room—repeatedly if necessary. When the men meet alone, call them on it. When you have the clout to insist on being included, use it.

Another approach is more political. Networks operate in many ways as barter systems where knowledge, resources, favors, or other valuables are exchanged. To gain acceptance, you need to have something that members of the network deem worth trading. Most often, this involves power, and most power is based on client relationships and revenue generation. But there are other factors that may make you attractive to a network, such as having the loyalty of an important constituency, having highly specialized and desirable legal expertise, or having control over vital resources (e.g., information, contacts) or groups (e.g., a key practice group or committee). Your own external networks may be valuable consideration if they enable you to offer your partners access to important people in the community or the profession. Whatever leverage you have should be used to make and strengthen connections to members of the networks that matter to you. Use those connections to break through the barriers and into those networks.

§ 9:5   Building alliances and coalitions

As a leader, you need allies you can trust and rely on for guidance, advice, and support. Allies are helpful in any situation, but when you are dealing with issues that are especially sensitive or controversial, having allies behind you is essential. Successful leaders have allies, both women and men, who will support them in their ordinary work and to whom they can turn in a crisis. Allies are trusted advisors who will tell you the truth even when it hurts. They are individuals who bolster your strength when you have to push back against clients or partners whose actions have the potential to impede your objectives or erode your self-confidence. Allies are your champions and defenders. They can serve as diplomats, messengers, catalysts, conciliators, or almost any role that supports your agenda.

Leaders cultivate their closest allies through shared interests and long-term relationships. They identify and do favors for partners whose help they might need in the future. As a leader, you may have the authority to hire or appoint people to key posi-

---

[4]Rhys, G. (June 2009), Being in the right room: networking professionally for professional women, *The Glass Hammer*, http://www.theglasshammer.com/n ews/2009/06/23/being-in-the-right-room-networking-professionally-for-profession al-women/.

tions where they can be of help to you; push through a promotion for someone who will support your agenda; or bestow resources upon someone, for which they will remain grateful. The people you help should be reliable supporters for you down the road.

Some controversial issues are best handled by forming coalitions with influential partners and groups in the firm. Coalitions arise when groups of individuals unite and cooperate on specific issues, events, or decisions or to advance particular values and principles. They consist of people in formal or informal groups who unite for a single purpose because they have a shared interest or stake in a specific outcome even though their goals and interests may vary greatly on other matters. Coalitions are based on mutual dependency and exchange. They are often short term or temporary, forming around a particular issue or set of issues and then disengaging. Therefore, to be effective, the force that unites them must be unambiguously articulated and the goal must be agreed upon.

Coalition building is an important strategy for advancing interests, power, and influence in the firm. If your position is weak, having a coalition behind you gives you broader support. If you are in a position of strength, it helps you to consolidate your power. An example of a successful coalition was described by a lesbian leader who wanted her firm to change its partnership agreement, which required that in order to inherit a partner's interest in the firm, a survivor had to be legally married to the partner. One group of supporters who helped her push through this change was composed of unmarried heterosexual couples who had the same interest in extending benefits to their life partners.

Part III

BECOMING THE LEADER YOU ASPIRE TO BE

Chapter 10

Introduction

§ 10:1   ASPIRE

KeyCite®: Cases and other legal materials listed in KeyCite Scope can be researched through the KeyCite service on Westlaw®. Use KeyCite to check citations for form, parallel references, prior and later history, and comprehensive citator information, including citations to other decisions and secondary materials.

---

§ 10:1   ASPIRE

Life isn't about finding yourself. Life is about creating yourself.
— George Bernard Shaw

Once you understand the challenges and context of law firm leadership, you can move ahead with greater forethought and discernment to shape your career as a leader. If you are heading toward leadership, how will you get there? When you become a leader, how can you be most effective and successful at it? Part 3 of this book will help you answer those questions. We explore six areas that are critical to your progress toward leadership and your performance as a leader. These are the building blocks that will help you become the leader you **ASPIRE** to be: **A**mbition, **S**trategy, **P**ersonal power, **I**nterpersonal dynamics, **R**esilience, and **E**mpowerment.

Chapter 11

Ambition

> **KeyCite[R]:** Cases and other legal materials listed in KeyCite Scope can be researched through the KeyCite service on Westlaw[R]. Use KeyCite to check citations for form, parallel references, prior and later history, and comprehensive citator information, including citations to other decisions and secondary materials.

---

§ 11:1 Acknowledge your ambitions

The greater danger for most of us lies not in setting our aim too high and falling short, but in setting our aim too low and achieving our mark.

—Michelangelo

You need to be ambitious to be a law firm leader. If this disturbs you because ambition sounds like a character flaw, you may misunderstand what ambition is. Ambition is nothing more than a strong desire to succeed and be recognized as successful. If you are interested in becoming a leader, you must come to terms with your personal ambitions. The way you begin this process is by becoming more self-aware. Awareness involves recognizing and understanding what your values, strengths, and limitations are so that you can find a way to achieve your ambitions and feel good about yourself and what you are doing at the same time. Having a clear vision of who you are, what you want, and where you want to go is the beginning of your journey to leadership.

Psychiatrist Anna Fels explains that ambition simply combines a desire for mastery (i.e., being skilled) with a desire for approval from others—in this case, your law firm. Acquiring mastery gives you control over your destiny; recognition affirms your accomplishments and shows that others value and appreciate you.

Without mastery, you cannot be effective or enjoy the respect of your peers; without approval, you feel isolated and, ultimately, demoralized. When in balance—when your need for recognition does not outweigh your need for mastery—you can be incredibly productive and realizing your ambitions can be extremely fulfilling.[1]

Ambitious lawyers work hard and are driven to achieve. They have a clear sense of purpose and are persistent, well-prepared, and optimistic. With single-minded devotion, they embrace challenges and overcome obstacles. They are determined to excel and be considered the best in their field. For many lawyers, these personal ambitions are sufficient. However, other lawyers seek more. They couple their personal ambitions with a desire to make a difference in something they care about. It is their focus on something larger than themselves that motivates many to step forward and become leaders. For women leaders in particular, contributing to something larger than oneself is an important source of motivation, meaning, and satisfaction. It sustains women as they strive toward leadership and keeps them engaged and passionate about their work once they achieve it.[2]

In a law firm, leaders who feel this way care deeply about the firm and the people in it. They view themselves as stewards of the firm's resources, including its people, its physical assets such as finances and property, and its intangible assets such as good will and reputation. They understand that each individual is part of the larger organization and that their actions have consequences for others and for the firm as a whole. These leaders have a strong commitment to the firm's future and make every effort to ensure that the firm is a better place and in better shape when they leave than when they start. The higher a leader's role in the firm, the farther her perspective extends beyond today to encompass future generations of lawyers and clients.

Women lawyers begin their careers with ambitions similar to men's.[3] Their psychological needs for power and autonomy are no

---

[Section 11:1]

[1]Fels, A. (2005), *Necessary dreams: ambition in women's changing lives* (Harpswell, ME: Anchor).

[2]Barsh, J., & Cranston, S. (Oct. 2008), Centered leadership: how talented women thrive, *McKinsey Quarterly*.

[3]Hildebrandt International (2007), *Understanding associates: new perspectives on associate satisfaction and morale*.

different than men's.[4] They are high achievers and top performers, and they expect that their performance and value will be
recognized and appreciated by the firm. They have a strong desire
to control their own destiny, which requires acting assertively on
their own behalf. However, when they promote themselves, challenge practices that do not support their goals, or openly pursue
firm leadership, they are criticized as "overly ambitious." Law
firm partners are suspicious of anyone they view as ambitious,
both women and men, because it suggests egotism, self-
aggrandizement, or manipulative use of others for selfish ends.
However, women carry a heavier burden. Ambition in men is
seen as necessary and desirable for career success and treated as
"a hallmark and virtue of manhood."[5] In women, ambition is
considered unfeminine and unnatural. While men are expected to
be ambitious and merely have to manage their ambitions, women
have to mask theirs.[6] So women downplay their ambition because
the implications make them uncomfortable and open them up to
criticism.

The suppression of women's aspirations is one of the reasons
for the dearth of women leaders in law firms. As their careers
progress many women become discouraged. Unable to give full
expression to their ambitions, or disparaged when they do, women
feel unfairly constrained and isolated. They may attain a very
high degree of mastery as lawyers but still find that the career
possibilities for them are limited. They see few women at the top
in their firms, they do not feel valued by the firm, and they do
not see a meaningful career end point considering the work they
are putting into their practice. They lose confidence in their ability to attain their goals or believe that to do so would require
them to betray or unduly compromise their core values. Women
who feel discouraged and start to lose their ambition often leave
the firm for more conducive work environments. Those women
who overcome or escape these feelings and maintain the drive to
forge ahead can become productive and successful leaders.

When women downplay their ambition, rather than envision
great things for themselves, they accept roles and rewards that
are merely "good enough." As an aspiring leader, you should want
to be, and be recognized as, great, the best, the top. I was in a
hospital recently where a sign directed at patients and visitors

---

[4]Austin, L.S. (2000), *What's holding you back? Eight critical choices for
women's success* (New York: Basic Books).

[5]Wilson, M.C. (2007), *Closing the leadership gap: why women can and
must help run the world* (New York: Penguin Books).

[6]Wilson (2007), *Closing the leadership gap*, p. 53.

said, "It is our mission to give you very good service." Somehow that message was uninspiring. Leaders do not settle for "very good"; they strive to make their firms "excellent," "superior," "outstanding." Likewise, that's what you should expect in your career.

A large majority of the leaders I interviewed knew early in their careers that they wanted to be leaders. One of them said, *"I knew that being a leader would give me more control—as well as accountability—for my own success. If I'm going to bet on anyone, it's better to bet on myself."* Another said, *"I wanted to be managing partner of this firm because I want to make a difference for the people here, help them become the best they can be in their jobs, help them realize their dreams and their goals."* Whether or not they set their sights on particular leadership positions or goals, these women knew they would be excellent leaders, valued being leaders, and expected to become leaders in their firms. Even those who were surprised when they were offered leadership positions had proven their leadership abilities through their contributions to the firm and welcomed the new responsibilities—as well as the firm's recognition.

Virtually all of the women I interviewed felt that as leaders, they could and did make a difference in many different ways, e.g., setting strategic direction for their firm, making the firm a better workplace for everyone, and advancing the interests of women and/or minority lawyers. Most of the interviewed leaders also took personal satisfaction in leadership. They loved what they did, felt they were good at it, and took pride in their accomplishments. As one women said, *"I've achieved it! My kids admire me for it."*

If you become a partner in a law firm, you have demonstrated your intellectual abilities and been acknowledged for your professional accomplishments. This distinguishes you from most other lawyers, both women and men. More importantly, you have already shown that you are ambitious because it took a powerful desire, perseverance, and hard work to pursue and achieve partnership. Moving into leadership is a logical next step, although not for everyone. Leadership means continued hard work, new challenges, and perhaps steeper obstacles than you faced before. However, if you aspire to greatness, not just goodness, then muster the courage to move ahead, fulfill your ambitions, and fully express your talents. You have come so far; don't stop now!

> • *Early on, I saw there's an A Team and a B Team, and I was determined to be on the A Team.*
> • *I saw other lawyers happy to be sitting in the second chair, in a service role, and I thought: Maybe that's good enough for them, but I want to be the #1 person, the lead trial lawyer.*
> • *As a litigator, I knew I was good—better than the more experienced guys I saw in court. I always wanted to be first chair, always thought I could do well. I wanted to stand out.*
> • *I saw women partners dependent on male partners and I said, Not me! If I'm going to be a great lawyer, I want to depend on me, not him. I won't be intimidated. Otherwise, why bother?*
> • *There's nothing like being the [practice group leader] who decides what marketing initiatives to pursue, sets group objectives for the year, decides what support the group will get, and focuses the group members' energies on what they really do best. You get to shape the direction of your group and influence the growth of your own practice.*
> • *I want to diversify firm leadership worldwide. If I'm in a leadership role with a lot of influence, I'll be better positioned to do it.*

§11:2 Increase your self-awareness

If your success is not on your own terms, if it looks good to the world but does not feel good in your heart, it is not success at all.

—Anna Quindlen

You have to do what's good for you. No one else can do it. Ultimately, your life is your own, and you have to decide what you want that life to be. You will have to make choices repeatedly and to make smart choices requires understanding what is really important to you—not what others think you should want, or what you feel you *should* want, but what genuinely gives you pleasure, gets you intellectually and emotionally excited, makes you happy, gives your life meaning, and brings you serenity. To know this requires introspection that makes you acutely conscious of your core values. As you build your life and career, these values become the foundation for your decisions.

The more aware you are of your values the more effective you can be in making career and leadership decisions and in being a successful leader. In general, lawyers do not place great significance on self-awareness when starting a developmental journey.[1] However, self-awareness is essential for authentic and successful leadership. It makes you better able to manage your own behavior, your expectations of other people, their expectations of you, and the way you relate to others. Being self-aware enables you to exert more control over your future and optimize your abilities. You become more agile in reacting to new situations, smarter about when and whom to ask for help, and able to find ways to complement and reduce your shortcomings. Without self-awareness, you miss opportunities that could give you great satisfaction. If you accept an unexamined life as your "default" mode, you will rely on what comes along and never know if you could be doing something better.

This holds true for any career woman but it is especially important if you hope to become a leader. Passive leadership is an inherent contradiction. As Will Rogers said, "Even if you're on the right track, you'll get run over if you just sit there." If you wait to see what comes along, you might be lucky and land a dream job or a fabulous leadership position. However, you are at the mercy of others which limits your possibilities. Unless that appeals to you, you need to take control of your career. This means deciding what kind of career you want and then deliberately taking steps to achieve your desired future. When you know what you want and are ready to go after it, you will be able to find, create, and maximize advantageous opportunities. The sooner you start, the more time you will have to develop and execute a strategy, to make and correct mistakes, and to change your mind and shift direction if you are unhappy with your initial choices.

The journey to leadership requires careful analysis of your ambitions and values, developing a vision of your future as a leader, and finding the courage to achieve it. The first question to ask yourself is, "Is it important to me to be a leader?" Leadership can be stimulating, exciting, and highly rewarding, but to be effective as a leader, you must be highly motivated to lead. It is too hard and risky to do half-heartedly, so you should only do it if you genuinely want to and if you are committed to doing it well. If you do not have the drive to do it, do not enjoy it, or agree to do it out of a feeling of obligation rather than desire, it will take a great deal out of you with no corresponding reward. One leader

---

[Section 11:2]

[1]Smith, R.B., & Marrow, P.B. (Sept. 2008), The changing nature of leadership in law firms, *NYSBA Journal*.

stated: *"I really love what I do. Otherwise it would be too much and I would quit."*

If you are unsure whether you want to be a leader, consider what will happen to you if you stay where you are. You may be satisfied with your work and your status right now as a partner, counsel, associate, or in some other position. If the prospect of holding steady appeals to you, leadership may not seem like an important goal—at least for the time being. However, becoming a leader takes a while, and if you think you might want it some time in the future, it is best to start planning now. So think long-term: where do you want to be in three, five, or 10 years? The answer does not need to be very specific; you just need to know how much control you want over your career and how much influence you want in the firm. Some of the questions you might ask yourself to help you decide are in Table 11.1.

Table 11.1. Questions if you are undecided about leadership

- What will life be like for me in the future if I do not become a leader?
- Have I missed out on any opportunities because I am not a leader?
- What opportunities will be available to me if I become a leader?
- What benefits and advantages will I enjoy as a leader?
- What will be the costs—to my family and myself—if I move into leadership—or if I don't?

Assuming you decide that you want to be a leader, the next question is, "Why is it important to me?" Being aware of and able to articulate your values, ambitions, and goals will help you envision what personal and career fulfillment will look like for you. You will be able to decide how being a leader will help you achieve your vision and what will be necessary to make it meaningful for you.

Once you understand why, you will be prepared to answer the next question: "How will I become the leader I want to be?" Your self-awareness will help you envision yourself as the leader you would like to be, assess your strengths and resources, and determine what path will help you achieve your objectives. Understanding your strengths will help you capitalize on them and compensate for any limitations. Understanding the resources you will need (e.g., time, assistants, sponsors, technology) will help you utilize those you have and figure out how to acquire those you lack. As you travel along your path to leadership, not only will you make smarter choices with less anxiety, you will be more purposeful and successful in getting what you want in your personal life and your career.

A related and critical question is, "What is holding me back?" You will face impediments to your ambitions even after you reach leadership. They may be externally imposed or the result of conscious or unconscious internal processes. Some external constraints might relate to your personal situation such as family needs or health problems. Many other external barriers and constraints include an unpleasant work environment, gender bias, or work demands that you cannot meet. Gender bias is particularly insidious, because not only is it manifested in the way you are treated at work, you may also unconsciously internalize the limitations that it insinuates.

Many women hold fears, uncertainties, and doubts that prevent their actions from furthering their ambitions. Often unconscious, these feelings are manifested as both patterns of behavior and negative "self-talk", i.e., messages that a woman tells herself that make her uncomfortable with ambition and reluctant to promote herself. These self-restraints form internal barriers to women's successors. They include fear of failure or loss, ambivalence about her practice, or doubt about her abilities. She worries that she is not good enough, ready enough, or worthy enough to move into leadership; or she suffers from "imposter syndrome," fearing that others will discover that she is not as smart or qualified as they seem to think. When she receives feedback that includes some criticism, she hears the message as negative and dwells on the minor critique even when the overall message is positive. When something goes wrong, her inner voice replays it repeatedly, intensifying her self-doubt.

These negative thoughts undermine a woman's ability to be a leader. They "lead you to cooperate rather than initiate; produce but not invent; participate but not lead; reflect but not create."[2] They keep you searching for external validation rather than relying on your own strengths and powers. Because these patterns cause you to compromise your ambitions and limit your contributions, they stop you from achieving your highest potential.

Most of the time, these self-limiting behaviors and thoughts can be overcome through self-awareness, planning, determination to move forward, and confidence-building support from friends or coaches. Sometimes just making yourself conscious of

---

[2]Austin (2000), *What's holding you back?* at xxiii.

them deflates their power. From there, you can begin to recognize and take pride in your own talents, power, and wisdom; become your own champion; and harness the courage you need to move ahead.

If you do not face up to these self-restraints, they will prevent you from getting where you want to go. You may avoid choices and miss opportunities to assert your power and authority. You may hide behind excuses and accept lesser roles rather than soar to the great heights of which you are capable. However, if you acknowledge and deal with them, find confidence and security in yourself, and have a positive attitude, your strength and clarity of purpose can increase your resilience and bring you success.

§ 11:3 Articulate your values

Who you are, what your values are, what you stand for . . . they are your anchor, your north star. You won't find them in a book. You'll find them in your soul.
—Anne M. Mulcahy

Self-awareness requires an understanding of your most deeply held values. When you are passionate about what you do, your work is more enjoyable and fulfilling. In contrast, when your work is not aligned with your values, it increases your stress and depletes your energy. However, being clear about what matters most to you makes it easier for you to find and undertake leadership responsibilities that add meaning and purpose to your work and avoid or turn down those that do not. By choosing to do things that are aligned with your values you can reduce your stress and be more energetic and vigorous. You are happier and more effective because you move closer to achieving your highest aspirations. Katherine Graham, the first woman CEO of a Fortune 500 company, the Washington Post, said it well: "To love what you do and feel that it matters—how could anything be more fun?"

Many people who try to understand themselves begin by assessing their strengths and weaknesses, which is an important analysis and should be done. However, understanding your personal values is equally important and sometimes gets overlooked when people focus on their competencies. Finding our strengths is often easier than identifying our values. We need to know what we are good at to get our daily work done, so we tend to be more conscious of what our strengths are and fret over our deficiencies. Values do not always get the same degree of attention.

Values go deeper and are harder to articulate than strengths.

At times, we operate from values that are externally imposed—by family, the legal profession, or the community in which we live. The pressure to conform to external expectations drives many people to make choices that leave them unhappy or unsatisfied, even though they adapt and can perform their duties very well. When you are good at something, even if you feel ambivalent about doing it, you may characterize that strength as a value in order to justify your choices. For example, let's say you specialize in a field of law that bores you but is highly lucrative. You can still do a fine job as a lawyer, and your superior knowledge and performance may lead to further work in that area. You may feel pressured to stay in the field because the money is so good even though you do not enjoy it. However, how much happier would you be if you recognized and pursued the work you really love rather than remain shackled by golden handcuffs?

People are motivated by a myriad of values: wealth, fame, social responsibility, equality, justice, career success, family, autonomy, loyalty, having fun, just to name a few. Studies that seek to understand what values motivate women professionals and lawyers in particular come up with mixed results.[1] Some research finds that women place the highest value on flexibility while in other studies, that factor ranks lower than values like high quality work, making a difference, being challenged, and authenticity.

There are many books and instruments available to help you identify and prioritize your values. Table 11.2 presents one such tool, a list of personal values.[2] You may add to the list any other values that you hold. Review the listed values and consider how important each one is to you; then choose the four or five values that you hold most dear. The values you choose as "very important," and especially those you rate as the top values within that group, will reflect what is important to you at this moment in your life and can provide useful insight as you craft your leadership strategy.

[Section 11:3]

[1]Wittenberg-Cox, A., & Maitland, A. (2008) *Why women mean business: understanding the emergence of our next economic revolution* (John Wiley and Sons); Hewlett, S.A. (2007), *Off-ramps and on-ramps: keeping talented women on the road to success* (Boston: Harvard Business School Press); Harrington, M., & Hsi, H. (2007), *Women lawyers and obstacles to leadership: a report of MIT workplace center surveys on comparative career decisions and attrition rates of women and men in Massachusetts law firms*, MIT Workplace Center.

[2]Based on figure 4.1 from Lee, R.J., & King, S.N. (2001), *Discovering the leader in you: a guide to realizing your personal leadership potential* (San Francisco: Jossey-Bass/a Wiley Imprint). Adapted and republished by permission.

Table 11.2. Personal Values

Categorize the values below into three groups: *Less Important, Important,* and *Very Important.* Then reduce those in your *Very Important* list to your top four or five values. Add to the list any other values that you prize.

Achievement—a sense of accomplishment, mastery, goal attainment

Activity—fast-paced, highly active work

Advancement—growth, seniority, and promotion resulting from work well done

Adventure—new and challenging opportunities, excitement, risk

Aesthetics —appreciation of the beauty in things, ideas, surroundings, personal space

Affiliation—interaction with other people; recognition as a member of a particular group; involvement, belonging

Affluence—high income, financial success, prosperity

Authority—position and power to control events and other people's activities

Autonomy—ability to act independently with few constraints; self-sufficiency; self-reliance; ability to make most decisions and choices

Balance—lifestyle that allows balancing of time for self, family, work, and community

Challenge—continually facing complex and demanding tasks and problems

Change and Variation—absence of routine; work responsibilities, daily activities, or settings that change frequently; unpredictability

Collaboration—close, cooperative working relations with people

Community—serving and supporting a purpose that supersedes personal desires, making a difference

Competence—demonstrating high proficiency and knowledge; showing above-average effectiveness and efficiency at tasks

Competition—rivalry, with winning as the goal

Courage—willingness to stand up for one's beliefs

Creativity—discovering, developing, or designing new ideas, formats, programs, or things; demonstrating innovation and imagination

Duty—respect for authority, rules, and regulations

Economic Security—steady and secure employment, adequate financial reward, low risk

Enjoyment—fun, joy, and laughter

Fame—prominence, being well known

Family—spending time with partner, children, parents, or extended family

Friendship—close personal relationships with others

Health—physical and mental well-being, vitality

Helping Others—helping people attain their goals; providing care and support

Humor—the ability to laugh at oneself and life

Influence—having an impact or effect on the attitudes or opinions of other people; persuasiveness

Inner Harmony—happiness, contentment, being at peace with oneself

Integrity—acting in accordance with moral and ethical standards; honesty, sincerity, truth; trustworthiness

Justice—fairness, equality, doing the right thing

Knowledge—the pursuit of understanding; skill and expertise; continuous learning

Location—choice of a place to live that is conducive to one's lifestyle

Love—involvement in close, affectionate relationships; intimacy

Loyalty—faithfulness; dedication to individuals, traditions, or organizations

Order—stability, routine, predictability; clear lines of authority; standardized procedures

Personal Development—dedication to maximizing one's potential

Physical Fitness—staying in shape through exercise and physical activity

Recognition—positive feedback and public credit for work well done; respect and admiration

Responsibility—dependability, reliability, accountability for results

Self-respect—pride, self-esteem, sense of personal identity

Spirituality—strong spiritual or religious beliefs; moral fulfillment

Status—being respected for one's job or one's association with a prestigious group or organization

> **Wisdom**—sound judgment based on knowledge, experience, and understanding
>
>
> **Additional values:**
>
> _____
> _____
> _____

Most of the leaders who were interviewed for this book held values that were directed at improving the firm through their ability to influence goals and drive results. One value they shared was the desire for a more diverse workplace. Many of the interviewed leaders also held values that were related to personal achievement, such as a desire for validation and increased self-esteem through leadership recognition, or the exhilaration that comes with power. A few women said that making a lot of money was vital; others considered money less important, not an end in itself, but a symbol of respect and value. These leaders' firm-oriented and personal achievement goals sometimes appeared incompatible, but the women were able to reconcile them, often through trade-offs. For example, some stepped down from management roles for periods of time to build up their books of business, after which they returned to positions of leadership.

The values you hold will be reflected in what you do as a leader, so being clear about your values helps you maneuver through the conflicts and complexities of your job. As lawyers, we are led to believe that rational thought and analytical processes are the best way to approach any question or dilemma. Scientific research, however, shows that emotional and rational processes are closely intertwined and that both aspects of the brain are involved in decision-making.[3] It shows the power of intuitive approaches based on experience and deeply held values. Many situations you face as a leader will test your values, and your decisions will be affected as much or more by those values than by reasoned analysis. Your values influence your priorities and what gets your attention, the people and positions you support and oppose, and your leadership choices and actions. If your values are not aligned with what you are doing as a leader, the tension will make it harder for you to act. If, for example, you place great value on autonomy, and your firm is moving to a practice model

---

[3]Lehrer, J. (2009), *How we decide* (Boston: Houghton Mifflin Harcourt); Pink, D.H. (2006), *A whole new mind* (New York: Riverhead Books).

that emphasizes teamwork, you may have trouble persuading your colleagues to be more collaborative.

Core values generally remain constant, although some may change over time as your personal views and circumstances change. Accumulating wealth may be most important to you at 30, but at 60, shaping your legacy may take precedence. If you have accumulated enough wealth by then, or if a life event leads you to believe that there are more important things than being rich, you may choose to pursue activities that are more generative, such as mentoring and teaching young lawyers.

Sometimes, your values hold steady, but come into conflict, and you have to make choices that reorder their priority. When you are young and unattached, you may have a driving passion to succeed, enjoy what you do, and place the highest value on becoming a successful lawyer no matter how hard or how late you have to work. Should you decide to have children or need to care for a sick relative, you may devote less time to work, and your career may take a back seat for a while. You might also change where and how you manifest the same value at different times in your career. If serving the community is important to you, you might do a lot of pro bono work during the early part of your career, and at another point take a more active role on community boards or in politics. One of the leaders I interviewed took great solace in work when she became a widow. Her law practice had always been important to her but her husband's death made it more central.

§ 11:4 Appreciate your strengths

If we did all the things we are capable of, we would literally astound ourselves.

— Thomas A. Edison

You can only achieve true excellence by applying your strengths, so you need to be clear about what they are. Self-awareness includes being conscious of the particular characteristics that make you a good leader or hinder your effectiveness. Appreciating your leadership strengths and limitations allows you to choose the smartest approaches for moving into leadership and increases your effectiveness once in the role. You can select assignments, work environments, and activities that bring out the best in you and use your strengths to produce optimal results. One leader knew she had trouble in a particular area: *"It's hard for me to read people. I'm really bad at it. So I quit being on the hiring committee. I wasn't very good at making selections and found it boring."* She opted for other leadership positions where she could use the management strengths she did have. Exploring your strengths means taking a personal inventory of your gifts and learning to trust your wisdom.

One of your early decisions will be which path to leadership suits you best. Are you charismatic? Does your outgoing personality draw clients and others to you? Do you enjoy schmoozing, going to meetings, and having conversations with people; or would you rather deal with numbers than people, and with analyzing issues in a brief, rather than in a committee meeting? If you have strong preferences or dislikes, it may influence your choice of leadership through rainmaking, management, or some other path. Several women leaders realized at some point in their career that they were not doing what they were best at. One prominent leader started out as a litigator. When she found herself crying at work every night, she decided litigation was not for her and switched to the business department, where she soon became a top lawyer and highly successful rainmaker. Another woman left practice altogether: *"After so many years of practice, I thought, is this really me? And I stepped away from practice and into a full time management role in my firm."*

Knowing yourself is important for law firm leaders because of the tensions inherent in the job. Without a self-aware and solid grounding in your personal values and abilities, the constant pushes and pulls of leadership can be grueling. Leadership in a law firm requires a set of complex, seemingly contradictory skills. To be a leader, you need a high IQ and high EQ (emotional intelligence); you need to be devoted to your own success and to helping others succeed; you have to be hands-on and a good delegator, decisive and consultative, detail-oriented and a big-picture thinker, analytical and empathetic, a 24/7 worker, and someone who is balanced. Lawyers with all these qualities are extremely rare, so how can you live up to your followers' expectations? You can only manage their expectations if you know your best self.

Awareness of your preferred leadership roles and your favored leadership styles helps you recognize when they work well and when they are counterproductive. With this knowledge, you can utilize them when they are most effective but also learn other styles that will expand your repertoire and give you greater versatility. Knowing and being comfortable with your abilities enables you to know what interests you and what you find tedious; what you do with little effort and what is strenuous or frustrating; what you need to learn and how you can best learn it; and what draws people to you and what drives them away. This self-knowledge strengthens your ability to lead and helps you withstand the pressures of the job. When work presents obstacles or gets you down, being confident of your abilities enables you to meet the challenges and go on without letting self-doubt derail you.

Recognizing what you are good at in a leadership position can also help you focus your attention on what you need to learn and improve and when to seek appropriate help. Knowing you have low energy levels or have a hard time speaking in front of a group may put some leadership positions out of reach—unless you find ways to build up your stamina or improve your public speaking skills. Knowing that you are a big-picture, strategic thinker who hates details or is bad with numbers may lead you to recruit people to your leadership team who complement these shortcomings.

To help you discover your strengths, look for patterns at work, in the activities and projects where you have succeeded and at those that have not worked out. Analyze them and see if you can spot recurring factors that seem to work for and against you. It is helpful to get feedback from others about what you are good at, which may not be exactly what you think. Ask someone you trust to give you their assessment and compare it with your own. You might also find it useful to hire a coach to conduct a 360 review or ask trusted colleagues and clients about their perception of your leadership talents. Most people are pleased when you ask for feedback and glad to help you improve your leadership capabilities and performance.

Keep in mind that what you consider your strength as a lawyer may not be helpful to you as a leader. Leading a client team and leading an office, practice group, or law firm are very different exercises. For instance, as a lawyer, being a detail-oriented perfectionist is valued because clients and colleagues can rely on you to do a careful and thorough job. However, as a leader, perfectionism can undercut your effectiveness. In a leadership role, you are running a business, dealing with people and emotions, sometimes having to make quick decisions, and engaging in sensitive communications when crises arise. You do not have the luxury of studying every issue in painstaking detail or worrying about the perfect language or ideal solution. Even if you have considerable experience leading client teams or complex client matters, when you transition into firm leadership, you have to shift your thinking and utilize a different set of skills.

Table 11.3[1] shows some of the differences between leading a team on a client matter and leading partners in a law firm. In handling a client matter, the client's needs and objectives control the way you manage the matter. That matter has a beginning and an end as the deal is concluded or the case results in a verdict or settlement. Within the team, there is a clear hierarchy of authority, with the partner in charge making key decisions, and particular tasks being delegated down along the line. Information and decisions can be communicated efficiently to all members of the team through e-mail, memos, occasional meetings, and conferences. Likewise, the partner in charge is clearly accountable to the client for the work and its outcome.

TABLE 11.3. Comparing Client Team Leadership with Law Firm Leadership	
Client Team Leadership	Law Firm Leadership
Client sets objectives	Group creates objectives
Beginning and end	No clear beginning or end
Accepted hierarchy	Partners question authority
Efficient communication	Inefficient communication
Clear accountability	Unclear accountability

Leading a law firm or group within the firm is far more ambiguous and complicated. The dynamics of leadership, including the difficulty of leading leaders, is discussed in Chapter 7. While some leadership positions may be for designated terms, others are open-ended. Problems and projects may have no specific time frame; indeed, for reasons discussed earlier, generating change in a law firm may take many months or years without clear resolution. The leader's authority is constantly being questioned, and leaders are frequently powerless to pressure partners to act. Because the process of leading is political, is based on individual relationships, and requires walking the halls to persuade partners and build consensus, the communication process takes a great deal of time and effort and is extremely inefficient. Likewise, while leaders may ultimately be accountable to their partners, the nature and implications of that accountability are often unclear.

[Section 11:4]

[1]Adapted and published with permission from Tim Leishman, Firm Leader Inc.

Being a woman may on occasion turn out to be one of your strengths. Many women use their gender to their advantage when others underestimate or patronize them because they are women. You may not like it but don't be afraid to use it. Being the only woman in the room may make you uncomfortable, but it also makes you memorable and distinctive and enables you to call attention to yourself or your client's position.

§ 11:5   Create your vision

A vision is not just a picture of what could be; it is an appeal to our better selves, a call to become something more.

— Rosabeth Moss Kanter

To bring your ambitions to life, you have to be able to articulate a vision of what you hope your life will be. That vision, based on your values, ambitions, and strengths, will enable you to determine where you can make your greatest contribution as a leader. It will allow you to focus your energy on what is most important to you. Throughout your career, you will have opportunities that arouse various degrees of interest, excitement, and discomfort; some will be a result of careful planning while others may be completely unexpected, a matter of luck, or being in the right place at the right time. When you have a clear vision of what is important to you and where you are heading, you can better evaluate and select among the leadership options that you encounter along the way. You can calculate the trade-offs; decide what to accept, decline, avoid, or pursue; and negotiate from strength and conviction. Instead of wasting your energy on trivial concerns and insignificant pursuits, you can maintain your vitality and drive toward the goals you have set.

When your values, ambitions, and strengths are clear to you, it becomes easier to envision your ideal future and figure out how to get there. Anna Fels wrote that "The first step in creating a future is to imagine it."[1] There are so many possibilities! Little is mapped out for you. When you are mired in the daily responsibilities of work and life, it is hard to think about a larger vision. When you step back and contemplate all the possibilities, you may feel overwhelmed. However, actively envisioning what you want the future to be and how you will achieve it gives you a sense of agency and control over your life. The things that are genuinely and profoundly important to you become the founda-

---

[Section 11:5]

[1]Fels (2005), *Necessary dreams*, p. xvi.

tion upon which you hone your skills, strengthen your leadership abilities, build your confidence, and make wise leadership choices. As you work on developing your personal vision, ask yourself:

- What is important to me?
- What do I want to become in my personal and professional life?
- Do I enjoy being a leader? Am I good at it? Does it feel natural? Does it energize me?
- What kind of leader do I want to be?
- How will being a leader help me become the person I want to be?

Defining your vision requires giving yourself time, distance, and emotional space, as well as purposeful effort. You work awfully hard at your profession. You undoubtedly do excellent work and already enjoy some success whether or not you think about what you are passionate about, what drives you, and what makes all that hard work worthwhile. Once you know what those things are, then instead of working just for an income, doing what clients and partners expect of you, or plugging along for some other undefined reason, you can put your vision to work for you. You can create a plan based on that vision that will help you define and achieve success on your own terms.

Defining your success will also open your eyes to the trade-offs that may be necessary and help you decide which compromises you are and are not willing to make. For instance, current law firm career tracks assume that lawyers will work full-time, consistently, and without interruption. If you work less or drop out for a while, then the odds are you will advance more slowly than your peers. If your vision is to have a family and become a leader in your firm, you will have to make choices. Some of those choices will be constrained by your firm's culture and policies and your home situation; some will be negotiable, and others will not. The clearer you are about what matters most to you, the clearer your choices will be. That doesn't mean it will be easy, but you will appreciate the likely costs and be able to decide which you will accept and which are too great and must be rejected. You will be the person calling the shots to shape your future.

Regardless of what you decide, remember that there are no perfect values or paths. Anthropologist Ruth Benedict said that "The trouble with life is not that there is no answer, it's that there are so many answers." Every woman's values, vision of leadership, and the way she chooses to achieve it are very personal. What is important for you is to be able to use your ambitions, values, and strengths as assets to help you form a vision of leadership and achieve your leadership goals.

CASE STUDY: Envisioning Success

Mary Cranston of Pillsbury Winthrop, the first woman to chair a global law firm, often describes her journey and the steps she took to create and achieve her leadership vision. She sets out four principles for aspiring leaders:

1. *Get clear on career and personal goals that resonate with you.*
2. *Find the courage to believe that nothing will stop you.*
3. *Do not stop until you get there.*
4. *Once you accomplish your initial goals, set new goals that add greater meaning to your life.*

Getting to the point where she could have a clear vision of the leader she wanted to be required considerable self-study. Mary describes the process as "watching her thoughts," bringing her biases, fears, and ambitions to consciousness so that she could understand and address them. An initial step was to distinguish between what she really wanted to do and what she thought she *should* do. Recognizing that she had been socialized to become a "good girl" and live according to the prevailing expectations for women, she had to reprogram her thinking to eliminate thoughts that might limit or sabotage her leadership prospects. She accepted the fact that she enjoyed competition, winning, and building new things, and that pursuing those strengths was not selfish, but served the greater good of the firm. Once she did that, she was able to envision herself as a top litigator and formidable rainmaker with a $10 million book of business.

Then she had to muster the courage to achieve that vision. She had to overcome the "million unconscious reasons why these goals were impossible." She had to face up to her fears that she didn't have the skills to do it, and that success would take up all her time and hurt her family. To overcome these negative thoughts, she adopted a more positive frame of mind, looking for possibilities, not obstacles. She convinced herself that she really could do it. She learned to say no to assignments that did not support her goals. When things did not work out well, she found meaning in failure. There were stumbles along the way, but she took small steps every day that moved her in the direction she had set; and she kept at it relentlessly until she achieved her vision.

Having attained the professional success she had defined, Mary discovered that achieving career goals was not a source of fulfillment in her life. There are always new goals and the journey is never ending. Her career was always very important to her, but her top priorities were and remain family first, friends second, and career third. Maintaining her health and serving her community round out her priorities. Mary resets her goals around these five priorities every year and carves out time for all of them.

Chapter 12

Strategy

> **KeyCite**ʳ: Cases and other legal materials listed in KeyCite Scope can be researched through the KeyCite service on Westlawʳ. Use KeyCite to check citations for form, parallel references, prior and later history, and comprehensive citator information, including citations to other decisions and secondary materials.

§ 12:1 Develop a strategy for leadership success

Vision is not enough, it must be combined with venture. It is not enough to stare up the steps, we must step up the stairs.

—Vaclav Havel

To become a leader, you must approach your career strategically. This means setting your sights on long-term leadership goals and determining which actions and choices will help you reach those goals. The planning process is straightforward, but it requires disciplined thinking. There is no single formula that addresses all women's ambitions and circumstances, and each woman's ultimate plan is unique to her. Because the strategy may take years to execute, staying on track is challenging, and many women lose heart. Having a clear vision and a defined plan will remind you that you are working toward something important. This chapter will look at the process and components of developing a strategy for your leadership success. Table 12.1 presents questions for you to consider as you develop that strategy.

After discussing how to create a strategy, this chapter looks at the two most common paths to leadership: rainmaking and law firm management. Along either path, a great deal of leadership activity and opportunity takes place in law firm committees. So this chapter gives special attention to how to think strategically when you choose or are tapped for a committee assignment.

In addition, planning your strategy requires you to examine the current state of affairs in the firm, the obstacles you may face, and the resources you will need in order to make your strategy work. Gathering "intelligence" about current business conditions in the firm, its future direction, and the agendas of the firm's leaders and powerful partners informs you about the current playing field and what to anticipate in the future. When you know the lay of the land, you can avoid hazards and exploit or create conditions that make your efforts more likely to succeed. As one leader said, *"If you see obstacles, create alternatives."* The resources you need include mentors, champions, and role models, as well as supporters who will help you be recognized and accepted as a leader.

The latter part of this chapter addresses several areas where strategic thought and planning will facilitate your work as a leader. In order to carry out all of your leadership obligations, you need to acquire the skills and knowledge that you do not already possess. To manage effectively at work and at home, you must be extremely focused, efficient, and well organized. Delegating work to others and using assistants to do some work for you or help you to do it more expeditiously are important habits to learn. For women who have families, this chapter also looks at ways to manage your work and family life.

TABLE 12.1. Developing Your Strategy to Leadership
- What is my leadership vision? What will it look like when it is realized?
- Is my vision compatible with the firm's future direction?
- What is the best path to take to realize my vision?
- What goals will help me achieve it?
- What obstacles will I face?
- What fears, uncertainties, and doubts are holding me back?
- What resources will I need?
- What sacrifices will I have to make in other aspects of my life in order to be a leader in my firm? Which am I willing to make?
- Will I have to compromise any of my values? Which compromises am I willing to make? Which values are non-negotiable?
- What are my strengths as a leader? What are my shortcomings?
- What knowledge, abilities, and skills do I have that will make me effective as a leader?
- What knowledge, abilities, and skills will I need to acquire? How will I acquire them?
- Can I tolerate the risks I will face to become a leader and when I am a leader? How will I be able to deal with those risks? How can I minimize the chances of failure?

---

§ 12:2   Plan for leadership

If you don't know where you are going, you might wind up someplace else.

— Yogi Berra

When you are clear about what you want, you can start to translate your ambitions into action by developing a strategic leadership plan. The plan can be very simple, stating the general direction you want your career to take, or quite detailed, with specific, measurable goals, action steps, and a timeline. It will always be a work in progress, reflecting current priorities that will change as your life proceeds. The plan should be revisited regularly, and you can make midcourse corrections or add new goals as current goals are attained. The important thing is to shape an agenda for your future that reflects your values and ambitions, emphasizes your competitive strengths, and gets you where you want to go.

To plan strategically is to think critically about how you will bridge the gap between where you are now and where you want to be. Your strategy outlines how you will get from the present to the future. The steps are logical:

- assess your values, strengths, and motivation
- define your vision and goals
- choose a path
- consider possible obstacles (internal and external)
- identify the resources and support you will need
- outline your action steps

The plan you create will be uniquely yours, and to a large degree you will make it up as you go along. There are no maps to guide you to successful leadership nor even clear road signs. The good news is that this allows for "multiple paths to effectiveness."[1] You can create your own strategies and styles or study what works for others and combine those that appeal to you. You can try and adapt various approaches as situations and dynamics change. The downside, however, is that the multitude of possibilities can be frustrating, scary, and a barrier to your ability to bring all your talents to the forefront. It will help if you treat constructing your career as a grand and exciting adventure.

Leaders must be able to think strategically, and planning your career in leadership is a good place to practice your strategic skills. Understanding the context is critical, as discussed in Part II. After looking inward to see how your ambitions, values, and strengths fit into leadership possibilities in your law firm, you are ready to create your leadership strategy. To be successful, that strategy must be compatible with the culture and business objectives of the firm. Looking carefully at the demands of leadership within your firm helps you understand the rewards and costs, determine what is worth pursuing and at what sacrifice, and prepare the foundation necessary to support your aspirations and your strategy.

One key piece of information is your firm's strategic plan. Knowing the firm's strategic business goals allows you to test your own goals against the firm's to ensure that they are compatible. A related and important item is where your department or practice specialty stands with regard to the firm's future direction. You probably selected your practice out of personal preference for the area and enjoy it. However, if you intend to po-

---

[Section 12:2]

[1]Ruderman, M.N., & Ohlott, P.J. (July/Aug. 2005), Leading roles: what coaches of women need to know, *Leadership in Action*, Center for Creative Leadership.

sition yourself for a leadership role, the current and long-term status of your practice group will be a factor. It will make a huge difference to your planning if your practice area is seen as critical to the firm's future growth, or if it is going to be phased out. Related indicators that are important to consider as you sketch out your plan include: client information (e.g., which firm clients are the largest revenue generators and which of those you serve), internal firm trends (e.g., where most of the firm's revenue has been coming from, how much of the firm's revenues are generated by your practice group), and marketplace trends (e.g., changes in client expectations, increase or slowdown in particular practice areas).

Many of the leaders I interviewed placed great importance on setting specific goals, saying the sooner you have a clear strategy and objectives, the better your chances of reaching your goals. However, goal setting is not the only way to proceed. When approaching the future, leadership researcher Annie McKee found that people use three different leadership planning styles: goal-oriented, direction-oriented, and action-oriented.[2]

- The *goal-oriented* approach is the one most lawyers are familiar with. You identify specific short-term and/or long-term goals and set concrete action steps to move toward them. This is the style most commonly used in other planning aspects of legal work and is supported by most law firm performance review systems.
- The *direction-oriented* approach to planning is planning toward a goal without the linear details. People who use this approach are big-picture thinkers and know the general direction they want to go in, but they stop short of getting too specific about goals. Guided by "an overarching set of principles, values, or a vision,"[3] they watch out instead for opportunities they can leverage in pursuit of their objectives.
- The *action-oriented* planning approach is used by people who live in the moment without paying great heed to the future or to long-term planning. They see planning as a series of tasks and activities without worrying about where the steps will lead. Instead of planning for the future, they focus on the present, concentrating on who they are as leaders now rather than on who they might be, or what they might do in the future. A subset of this group "choose[s] each action according to the logic of the moment and base[s]

---

[2]McKee, A., Boyatzis, R., & Johnston, F. (2008), *Becoming a resonant leader* (Boston: Harvard Business School Press).

[3]McKee, Boyatzis, & Johnston (2008), *Becoming a resonant leader.*

the next decision on outcomes of recent past actions." In other words, if they like what they are doing, they continue to do more of it or take it to the next level. If they do not, they move on to something else.

McKee emphasizes that each planning style has benefits and employs skills that are useful in planning for the future. She encourages leaders to be aware of their natural preference but to learn and include elements from all three styles. For example, if you tend to be highly goal-oriented, it would be useful to make room for some unplanned leadership-oriented activities. Adhering too strictly to your plan might cause you to overlook interesting opportunities that come your way. If you are direction- or action-oriented, you might include a few measurable goals that support your progress. Without any framework at all, you may find yourself wasting time on activities that get you nowhere.

The leaders I interviewed used all three planning styles. While some were very systematic, set goals, and worked assiduously toward them, others had no clear plans but a general direction; and a few had not considered leadership at all until they did it. Sometimes leadership opportunities fell into their laps and they rose to the occasion and made the most of it. One managing partner was surprised when she was approached about the position. She was not a major rainmaker, held no important management posts, and as a lateral, had only been practicing at the firm a few years. However, the firm was going through a difficult time, and partners were unhappy with their current leaders: prominent rainmakers whose main focus was on clients, not firm management. Partners realized they needed a different type of leader, a strategic thinker with outstanding communication, management, and people skills. In considering all the partners in the firm, they saw her as the most promising candidate. Despite initial wariness, she agreed to do it, liked it, and found she was good at it.

The women I interviewed who knew they wanted to be leaders took more proactive approaches:

- Women who were determined to play important leadership roles set and achieved specific business goals that enabled them to attain the positions they desired.
- Some women methodically found practice niches where they could use their attributes to their best advantage. One African-American leader successfully transferred out of employment law, where there were many women of color, and moved into IP law, where there were few, and she would stand out. Another woman switched from a large practice

group to a smaller one where there were fewer senior associates blocking her advancement to partnership.

- Several women became prominent leaders outside the firm, primarily in local, state, and national bar associations, which raised their profiles as leaders inside the firm.
- A few women used their previous experience in government or corporate legal departments to become leaders when they joined their firms as laterals. Some came to firms with established reputations as leaders, while others negotiated leadership roles as part of their agreement to join the firm.
- Several women got leadership experience by leaving their firms and moving to business, government, or nonprofits. They then returned to private practice in a higher leadership position, either in their former firms or more often, in other firms.

Whichever planning approach you use, having a vision of where you want to go makes it easier and more likely for you to spot serendipitous opportunities. It makes you alert to openings that other people miss. You can grab those opportunities directly, or if that isn't possible, you can develop a strategy to make it possible. For example, if there is a vacancy on the finance committee, and you are not an obvious candidate, you can put your name in the hat to be considered. Alternatively, you can ask an influential partner to nominate and lobby for you. To be in a position to do that, you need to lay the groundwork in advance: think ahead about what you want, know who the players are in that area, and start or solidify relationships with people who might be able to help you. Unless you build those relationships first, you cannot assume that they will know your capabilities or leadership desires, or that they will help you just because you ask them to; nor can you expect that opportunities will be available when you are ready or want them.

Keep your eyes and ears alert for existing openings and for developments, trends, and upcoming events that may signal a future leadership need in the firm. To ensure that you are in the best possible position for these opportunities, take stock of leadership experiences that have prepared you to take on new levels of responsibility. Ask yourself the following questions:

- What leadership positions do you hold now?
- What leadership roles have you held in the past?
- Which leadership roles do you find interesting and challenging?
- At which leadership roles do you feel especially effective?
- What are the aspects of leadership that you find exciting?

- Which aspects of leadership give you the most satisfaction?
- What parts of being a leader present the hardest challenges for you?
- Which leadership abilities do you want to improve?

Take advantage of leadership opportunities whenever you can, because demonstrating your leadership ability will open paths toward higher leadership responsibilities. When you see an opportunity, let decision-makers know your aspirations and readiness and ask them for the chance to prove yourself. If you are eager but inexperienced, ask a current leader how the leadership advancement process works in the firm, and what you can do to develop your leadership abilities and raise your visibility so that you will be well positioned when something appears in the future.

Also consider whether any of your current activities are natural preludes to other leadership roles. Some positions are stepping-stones to others. When the opportunity to move up presents itself, you can step right in. For example, many lawyers who head up the summer associate program go on to become hiring partners. Is that something that would appeal to you? If so, throw your hat into the ring; volunteer to chair the summer program.

The most focused and disciplined form of planning is the goal-oriented approach: You set the end points and decide how you will get there. Once you have a strategy, you can convert it into specific steps that carry you toward your goals. Consistent action toward your desired result generates momentum, keeps you motivated, and helps you get through any rough spots as you move forward toward completion. A general plan of action may suffice, but the more precise and concrete you make the steps, the better able you will be to execute the plan and measure your progress. No matter how broad or detailed you make it, keep your plan flexible because there are many things you cannot anticipate or plan for. Your strategy may be beautifully crafted, but it is subject to the forces of time and circumstance. So let your goals guide you but not restrict you. Pay attention to shifts and trends in the firm, the market, and the profession that may require you to rethink your goals or your strategy. Stay nimble, observant, and receptive to possible changes.

Being strategic means always being alert to unexpected opportunities that may not be part of your plan but will move you toward your goals—or to new goals—in a different way. When you are open to possibilities, surprising opportunities come your way. If you are offered a chance to do something that is not in line with your plan, your goals can help you evaluate whether this surprise offer or situation is worth pursuing. You may want to become a practice group leader but are asked to join a political administration. You can decide whether this diversion will set your plans back too far for comfort and you should stay put, or if it is simply too exciting to turn down. If you accept the political post, your plan can be revisited and revised when the time comes for you to return to practice. At that time, you may decide to pick up where you left off in your original plan to become a firm leader, or scrap the plan entirely and stay in politics. One of the leaders I interviewed realized that the normal path to leadership in her law firm would take too long for her ambitions. So she left the firm for the public sector where she built a strong reputation and made important political contacts in a niche practice. When she returned to private practice, her experience, reputation, and client base catapulted her into a powerful leadership role.

Appendix A is a simple template for a leadership plan that you can use to state your leadership goals and the steps you will take to achieve them. It starts with a statement of your vision, which encompasses your ultimate goals. It then asks you to list two or three long-term objectives. For each objective, list interim goals and milestones. Interim goals may take a year or more while milestones are shorter-term, six months to a year from now. Reaching a milestone indicates that you have successfully taken the short-term steps that move you toward achieving your ultimate vision. The template also calls for you to identify people who may be able to help you and resources or experiences you may need. It contemplates that you may already know that these people can help you, or you may have to ask for their help, so you need to indicate when and how you will do that. The same is true for resources and experiences: indicate which you can put to use right away and which you will need to acquire.

Executing your leadership plan is a continual process that requires discipline and dedication. Not every plan goes smoothly. If you don't reach a milestone, or one of your goals does not work out, it does not mean you have failed. Try to figure out what happened. Was the goal too ambitious or unrealistic? Was it a lack of preparation? Did you allocate insufficient time to make it happen? Was there an external factor that you could not control, like a drop in demand for your practice specialty? Learn what you can from the experience and revise your plan according to the lessons learned. Then adjust your expectations, set new goals and milestones, and move on.

Planning and carrying out your leadership ambitions is serious business. However, it is good to maintain a healthy perspective and sense of humor about it. Said one leader: *"I am deeply seri-*

ous about what I want, which is to succeed at top levels. But I also see it as a big game and can be light about it too."

It might be helpful to hear what women leaders said about some of the strategies they used and the advice they offer about choosing the right work, helpful people, and purposeful activities:

> *Distinguish yourself. Look for hot growth areas. Look for growth potential. What needs attention?*

> *Go into a field where there aren't lots of other junior partners ahead of you who will block your way up, or work with someone who is retiring soon and will need to pass along his practice.*

> *You need to think how you will jockey for succession to other partners' clients. You need to let the partner and client know you are interested in transitioning into the leadership role. Build on the client relationship. Turn it into an opportunity for you and the client.*

> *Read business journals, not just law. Business trends lead to legal work. What do corporations and corporate counsel care about?*

> *I'm strategic about choosing activities. I volunteered for the MCLE committee. It was easy to do without a lot of extra time. If I heard of a good program, I suggested to a partner that he should send someone. It showed the partner I was looking out for the firm's interests.*

> *Don't limit yourself to what you know and are good at. Take a chance. Look for fields you don't see—there are so many possibilities; explore them.*

> *Read the firm's new client and new matter openings. What's going on? What clients will need service? What do I know about the client or the law that others might not know about? Who's bringing in interesting work? Reach out to those partners directly, even if it crosses practice group lines.*

Align yourself with premium, high-profile growth practices that the firm values. The firm will value you, too. It's hard to be distinctive doing commodity work and hard to distinguish you from your peers. Also, the compensation is not as high because of pressure on rates.

If you want to be a leader, tell people. Find mentors; take strategic assignments. The results will be better. Be in charge of your own agenda, and be sure you know how you're going to do it so that you do it well. Do not do everything the firm wants you to do but what you want to do. If the senior partner asks for your help get something in return.

I offered to help plan the firm retreat. I arrived early and had lunch with the planning group which included the founding partner of the firm, who is the most powerful person in the firm. Many people suck up to him. I knew that if he thought I was worth keeping, he would help me. At the retreat, I was associated with people he respects, and he saw that I was working for the good of the firm.

§12:3 Choose a leadership path: rainmaking vs. management

The two most common paths to law firm leadership are through rainmaking and management. Women who are preeminent rainmakers in law firms are still rare, and most women who bring in substantial business are concentrated in the middle ranks of the rainmaking elite. Most women leaders take the second route, serving in a series of management roles, especially on committees. There are pros and cons for either leadership path; you need to consider them and then choose the one that suits you best.

Both rainmaking and management require a large and steady investment of time and energy. Depending on your priorities—and those priorities may change over time—one or the other may be more appealing to you. If what is important to you is status, autonomy, and compensation, rainmaking is for you. However, if you like to work collaboratively, lead change efforts, or find solutions to firm problems, management is the way to go.

These two leadership paths are not mutually exclusive and, in fact, you may need to be a rainmaker at even a modest level in

order to be considered for leadership in some firms. Most successful women leaders do both rainmaking and management. A 2004
study[1] found that women who held leadership positions in
management were also more effective rainmakers, and that being
in leadership was a "pivotal success factor" for rainmaking.
Women at every level who held leadership positions reported
significantly higher business origination than their peers who did
not. Many leadership activities provided them networking opportunities that they used to build relationships with more
partners and thereby expand their internal referral sources. High
visibility leadership positions helped them become known
throughout the office or firm, again increasing possible referrals.
Some committees and positions enabled them to become more
visible to clients and business prospects and allowed them to
meet new contacts. In all these ways, being leaders through
management gave them greater prominence and confidence,
which also made them more successful at business development.

Timing is a key factor in choosing the rainmaking or management route to leadership. Depending on your priorities and the
status of your career, you may choose different directions at different times in your life. As a junior partner, concentrating on
business development is essential in order to give you the power
to decide what you want to do later. When your client base is
stable, and your rainmaking abilities established, you may decide
you want to do something else—such as take on more management responsibility; or, if you have done a lot of management
work, you might want to switch in the other direction. Many
women leaders who have been in significant management roles
for several years step down for a while to focus on business
development. They feel that with a more substantial book of business, they will be able to move into higher and more powerful
levels of leadership. The experience of one woman I interviewed
bears this out. This leader stepped down as office managing
partner in order to focus on bringing in business. When she successfully established a robust and lucrative client base, she
returned to management and was able to operate from a position
of greater strength and credibility. Her practice benefited
everyone: she kept other partners busy doing work for her clients,
which made her partners and clients happy and freed her up to
do the firm leadership work that she enjoyed.

[Section 12:3]

[1]MacDonagh, C.A., & Borgal Shunk, M.L. (Dec. 2007), Women rainmakers:
keys to business development success, *National Magazine*, Canadian Bar Association, http://www.cba.org/CBA/PracticeLink/leadership__marketing/wome
n__rainmakers.aspx.

§ 12:4 Rainmaking

Rainmaking is the principal source of power in a law firm. As noted in Chapter 6, the more business you control, and the more work you provide for others, the more power you have. This comes as no surprise. Law is, after all, a professional service business, and without clients to serve, there would be no business. Those who produce business for the firm, and a livelihood for others, are valued most highly.

For women who aspire to leadership, rainmaking power opens many doors. You may want to wield that power in a formal leadership role, such as a seat on the Executive Committee. You may prefer to be an informal leader, lobbying for projects and policies you care most about and knowing that people will listen to you; or you may choose to operate indirectly by having your protégé placed in a leadership position. Being a rainmaker does not ensure that you will get what you want but it definitely gives you negotiating power.

Rainmaking sounds riskier than management, but it actually provides greater security. In fact, a solid client base is the only source of security for lawyers today. Management may seem safer because it carries less pressure for self-promotion and generating new business, but the feeling of safety is deceptive. Having a portable book of business allows you to move elsewhere if you need or want to leave your firm. Knowing that your client relationships will produce business and income may be the most important reason to make rainmaking your top priority.

However, many women with tremendous talent and potential for rainmaking deliberately avoid the rainmaking path. One unfortunate reason is that they approach rainmaking with a negative mind-set. Some women feel this way because they downplay their ambitions, as discussed in Chapter 2, or are afraid they will fail. Sometimes women face real stumbling blocks, but often they make up excuses to avoid it: "I don't like doing it," "I don't have time," "I'm not good at it," "I don't know any potential clients." In most cases, these inhibitions can be overcome with coaching, encouragement, and adoption of a more positive outlook.

The leaders I interviewed recognized early in their careers that having substantial books of business gave them access to leadership as well as control, independence, and respect. They emphasized that their firms are businesses and contributing to a healthy bottom line is imperative. They also understood that despite what firms say they value, what matters the most is money. One African-American partner was recruited to her firm in large part because of her national reputation for work on diversity, but she soon learned that her diversity work meant much less than the firm let on. *"I put the firm on the map for its work toward diversity. But they don't care. The only thing they care about is how big is your book?"*

Leaders who want to be change agents are especially sensitive to the connection between money and power. Unless they have a strong revenue base, they do not have the power to drive the changes they seek. One leader stated the relationship precisely: *"Power and influence in the firm are all about revenue. Male or female, leadership depends on bringing in revenue. Hours, clients, new business, it does not matter so long as it produces money. If you are not connected to money, you have no power in the firm, both perception and reality. And if you have no power, it's hard to bring along others you care about."* Another leader echoed those thoughts: *"You can be a change agent without money, but it is not easy. It's better to have the money first; then you can be involved in leading change."* Still another leader, an Asian-American woman who had been the president of several bar associations, said that respect as a leader within the firm eluded her until she became a "player" by virtue of the book of business she developed.

Being a rainmaker provides more than access to leadership opportunities. It gives you the freedom to take charge of your career and your schedule. Although client service demands may be greater when you are the responsible partner, being in charge of the client relationship gives you the ability to manage those demands. One leader with three young children observed that being in control of her own clients made her life easier because she could make her own decisions and daily plans; she did not have to clear them with other partners.

Rainmaking can also be a great source of personal and professional satisfaction. One leader explained that she found many benefits in having her own clients: *"I came from humble roots and couldn't rely on anyone to help me. I worked through college, always searched for the best jobs, the most money. I knew I wanted to get ahead, be in charge. I was ambitious. The firm I joined gave associates a percentage of the revenues they brought in and I saw that I could make more money if I had my own clients. It became like an addiction. I had more satisfaction at work and more control over my life and career with my own clients."*

One thing to keep in mind is that while being a rainmaker gives you power and may get you a top management position, it does not necessarily make you a leader. It may be easier for you to attain executive positions when you are recognized for your client relationships and business development success, but whether you will be accepted as a leader depends on your comportment in the role, and whether you gain the trust and respect of your colleagues.

In fact, being a rainmaker and being a leader may put you in a position of conflict with the firm. This may happen if your clients' interests conflict with those of the firm, or when you want to bring in a new client who creates a conflict of interest for other partners. As one leader said, *"When you are torn between your clients and your management responsibilities, you protect your client relationships."* This is one of the challenges of leading a law firm while remaining in practice.

§12:5 Management

It is conventional wisdom that partners require a substantial client base in order to become leaders but that is not always the case. While it is essential to be well respected by clients and have strong client relationships, many partners attain leadership without a large book of business. In most instances, these partners have particular leadership skills or talents that the firm needs, and they have proven their leadership abilities through dedicated service to the firm over the years. Many of them move into full-time management roles.

Many women leaders find that being involved in management enables them to exercise talents and skills they cannot express in practice or as rainmakers. They find satisfaction working with people, making the firm stronger, and making a difference in firm policies and in people's lives. They also find that although management takes up a great deal of time, it is easier to control their calendars, travel schedules, and time commitments. If the key to leadership is the ability to influence change, these women find that their management roles give them a different, more concentrated and focused kind of power that is highly meaningful to them, such as the ability to increase diversity in the firm.

The nature of leadership through management is substantially different than leading through rainmaking. Rainmaking is focused externally, on client engagements; management is internal and deals with the firm and its people. Rainmaking appeals to women who love the tension, intensity, and drama of legal work, and who find fun and excitement in the challenge to bring in new clients. The controversies and deals that they work on are business matters with a beginning, middle, and end. Once they are resolved, the rainmaker can close the file, send it to storage, and move on to the next matter. Management is different. It has plenty of tension, drama, and challenges, but they are decidedly dissimilar. Leaders in management are wrapped up in personal and emotional issues of partners and employees. The problems often defy easy resolution and have no clear end point; some have lingering effects that the leader and others in the firm have to live with for a long time.

Another distinction is that as a rainmaker, you can accomplish a lot on your own. In managing client work, you can make decisions about strategy and tactics and direct others on the team to carry them out. Leaders in management have less autonomy in carrying out their work. Committee chairs and practice group leaders cannot direct partners to act; they have to get their buy-in and agreement. To do that, they have to coach and listen more, and take time to build consensus. Manager-leaders have to have patience for the slower process of law firm management, which involves collaborative decision-making and often tedious analysis in a constant dance of planning, implementing, assessing, revising, and planning again.

Many large and mid-size firms are moving to a more corporate model that places greater importance on professional management and leadership. These firms hire professionals, with or without legal backgrounds, from consulting, corporate, or other fields to manage areas such as finance, marketing, technology, or professional development. They are beginning to recognize that people in specialized management areas have critically valuable expertise that their firms need. Increasingly, some of those talented managers are lawyers who leave practice to do it. Many practicing lawyers are moving into full-time management and developing the expertise needed for the positions they assume. It was rare in the past for lawyers to give up law practice to do this but it is becoming less unusual. It is no longer uncommon for managing partners and firm executives to be lawyers who have made this move. Few of these leaders have formal training in management; most learn about management on the job.

If you move into full-time management, your status in the firm and your relationship with other partners may change. Transitioning from "fee-earner" to "overhead" may have a negative effect on both your identity and your relationships with other partners. Some partners may also view your move into full-time management as a drop in status to "non-practicing" attorney and treat you differently. How low you drop is variable, depending on your firm's culture and the esteem in which you are held. However, the leaders I interviewed did not have that experience. Some remained partners while others gave up their partnership. In either case, they continued to have a warm relationship with their partners, and most continued to be invited to partnership meetings and retreats. In fact, many of these women found greater career satisfaction in firm management than they did in practicing law.

One leader I interviewed gave up her equity partnership to become her firm's Chief Diversity Officer. She had practiced at the firm for 25 years and had held numerous leadership positions in the firm including several years each on the Management and Executive Committees and as co-leader of her practice group. During that time, she was also actively engaged in efforts to increase diversity in the firm. When top firm leaders came to her and asked if she would consider becoming the Chief Diversity Officer, she thought long and hard. She decided to do it because she realized that the diversity-related work she had been doing gave her great personal satisfaction, and this new role would allow her to devote more time to something she cared about deeply and to do something new and different in her career. Her partners supported the move. They continue to include her in partnership activities and make her feel valued, respected, and appreciated. *"No one cares or notices that I'm not a partner anymore."*

§ 12:6 Choose committees strategically

Whether you prefer rainmaking or management, committee participation is the most common way to enter law firm leadership. Many women become recognized as leaders through the work they do as members or chairs of committees. Because they work so hard and make sure that everything that should be done does get done—and gets done right—their results impress other lawyers and enhance their reputation for effectiveness. A substantial majority of the women I interviewed had chaired important committees as they rose to prominence in their firms.

In some firms, especially those that have few committees, special projects or task forces may serve as vehicles for moving into leadership. They are usually one-time events of some importance to the firm. After all, the firm is investing time and resources to undertake a project or scrutinize an issue. Being appointed to a special group studying a significant issue may increase your visibility and enhance your status.

There is disagreement about the value of committee work for women. Many marketing experts and senior women partners advise women to avoid committee work and concentrate their efforts on building a book of business instead. After all, rainmaking gives you power in the firm as well as self-sufficiency, so that if you have to leave the firm, you can. Committee work takes a lot of nonbillable time, and for women whose lives are already too busy, it is an extra burden to be avoided.

On the other hand, committee work can launch women into leadership and make their work more meaningful. Committees provide ample opportunities for women to gain visibility and reputation as leaders. Some law firms consider being head of particular committees as a training ground for significant leadership positions. Many women also enjoy committee work, find it a good use of their talents and strengths, and are able to influence and drive changes and policies that are important to them and benefit the firm.

Here are three leaders' stories of how they benefited from their committee experience:

- *I am on the New Business Committee. We deal with new client matters, accounts receivable, collections, and fee discounts for 20 to 25 partners . . . This committee gives me a better appreciation and exposure to what others in the firm are doing. It increases my understanding of how the firm operates and increases my client development opportunities. I can tell my clients about the firm's capabilities and can also get work from other partners who know what I do.*
- *I was asked to head up the Billing and Collections Committee, which was awful in that I had to push partners to collect. But I got to know many partners and they saw that I was tactful and did it well. It was the best year for collections that the firm had ever had, and I got a lot of credit.*
- *I was on the firm's committee on charitable activities and got involved in fundraising. We tried to marry the firm's charitable interests with those of our clients, so we had lots of firm support and I had the chance to interact with client representatives and community leaders. In the process, I was able to increase the prominence of the firm and my practice.*

Some women also enjoy the power that comes with certain committee positions. They are energized by being in the room when big decisions are made. Because they are involved in addressing the firm's top priorities or most pressing problems, people perceive them as powerful, which increases their stature and influence. They like having whatever power the committee role offers them and are glad to participate even if it takes time away from other priorities. One leader in a global law firm described her power this way: *"My source of power? Access and credibility. People seek out my help to get things done because I am on the Management Committee. I can affect how much money they get for business development. I can get exceptions approved. And I have direct access to the firm's Managing Partner."*

There are other pros and cons about committee participation.

These are some of the advantages from the standpoint of leadership development:

- Increased status. Being selected for a key committee raises your standing in the firm. The appointment is perceived as both a reward for high achievement and an opportunity to showcase your leadership abilities.
- Inside information. You acquire valuable inside information about the firm, its people, finances, and strategies that help you make more informed decisions for your clients, your teams, and your career. You learn how the firm operates, how to get things done, and what the firm really values. You are privy to the interpersonal dynamics within and across practice groups.
- Connections. You learn who the players are, what's important to them, and what tensions exist between them. You get to know and work with them, which can help you find allies, mentors, and champions; break into the inner circle; and build your own networks. When you leave the committee, especially at the executive level, you will continue to have access to important partners through the relationships formed and the status gained as a co-member.
- Safe learning place. You can practice important leadership skills (e.g., collaborative decision-making, presentations, political give and take) on a small scale and in a relatively safe environment.
- Higher leadership. Some committees are incubators for developing leadership talent. The skills you learn, relationships you form with committee members, and visibility and respect you earn may lead to higher positions.
- Influence change. You have the ability to influence the future direction of the firm and can act as a catalyst for change. In certain key committees, you can reward those who do their best for the firm, discourage undesirable behavior, and get rid of bad apples.
- Access to resources. You gain access to resources and may have control of resources that can benefit your clients, your teams, and you.
- Validation. Some women find ego gratification in being acknowledged as a leader by chairing or serving on an important committee.
- Something new. If you feel the need for a break from the steady flow of client work, it gives you a chance to do something else of value.
- Compensation. Many firms look upon committee work as

firm-building. They expect lawyers to do it, and when setting compensation, treat significant contributions on committees as a positive factor.

Serving on committees can carry disadvantages as well. The drawbacks to committee work include the following:

- <u>More committee work</u>. If you are dependable and effective on one committee, you are invariably asked to be on others. This puts extra time pressure on you and forces you to reevaluate your priorities and repeatedly make hard choices. While it gives you many opportunities to show how good you are as a leader, it also distracts you from revenue-generating work that is the foundation for compensation and advancement.

- <u>Lack of reward</u>. Committees take a lot of nonbillable time, and you may not be rewarded for your effort, financially or otherwise. Contributions are hard to measure and usually undervalued and, in fact, you may be financially penalized for this distraction from client work. Besides, your partners will never be satisfied with anything your committee does.

- <u>Too much burden</u>. If you are not careful, you may get stuck doing the heavy lifting for the committee. Women frequently take on more responsibility than they need to out of habit, the desire to do things right, or an inability to delegate, say no, or let go.

- <u>Futility</u>. Your efforts may not be appreciated, your recommendations may be rejected, and your projects may be ignored. Despite your best efforts, you may not have the clout to enact the changes that are important to you.

Partners generally care little for taking on management responsibilities, and (except for executive committees) they dislike committee work most of all. Firms commonly find it hard to persuade partners to accept committee assignments and even harder to find someone willing to chair a committee. So if you volunteer, the chances are good that you will get an appointment. For various reasons, you might not be selected at the time you ask, e.g., you are too junior, there is already someone from your department or group on the committee, or the seat has already been promised to someone else. However, if it is known that you want to be on a committee, you are highly likely to be asked at some point. This is what one leader said about committee work:

> *The first year I was an income partner, I was appointed to the strategic planning committee, even though all the other members were capital partners. This helped me get a reputation as a leader. It's easy to do—few people in management actually follow through and*

get things done. So there were many opportunities to get things done, do them well, and become visible. Also, like many other women, I just want to get things off my desk, scratch off items on my to-do lists. And since most lawyers do not want management work, anyone who really wants it and likes it can usually get it.

If you are coming to a firm as a lateral partner, being on a committee is a good way to become integrated into the firm quickly, present your ideas, and establish yourself as a leader. You might make this part of the negotiation before you arrive. Consider the committees or other leadership positions that will bring you the most benefit. For instance, if the practice group you are joining is starting a strategic planning process, and you led that process in the firm you are leaving, ask to chair your practice group's effort.

Some firms include associates on committees. Associates who have leadership ambitions should not be shy about asking for committee assignments. It is never too soon to show your leadership potential and to get recognized and thought of as someone who works effectively with others and produces top results.

Sometimes you will be invited or appointed to serve on a committee; sometimes you will decide to volunteer. Before accepting or volunteering, think about it strategically: how will this committee advance your leadership goals? Here are several questions and suggestions to consider when assessing committee possibilities:

1. <u>What committees exist in the firm</u>? It is important to know what your options are. Many firms have numerous committees that address a wide variety of issues. If the firm has only a few committees, your choices will be limited.

2. <u>Which committees are important</u>? Committees have varying degrees of importance. Being a member of the Compensation or Executive Committee is powerful; being the chair of the Library Committee usually is not. Which committees are integral to the firm's core business strategy? Which committees control strategy, promotions, money, or critical resources? Those are the committees that are most important to the firm.

3. <u>Which committees are treated as high priority by powerful people in the firm?</u> Many committees have no real authority, no defined objectives, poor leadership, and are a waste of time. In contrast, if the committee is charged with doing something specific and important, and the chair is someone who takes it seriously and will ensure that you will have the resources to achieve its objectives, participating may be worthwhile. Being involved in a committee that gets the care and attention of people

in powerful positions is a good way to foster relationships with them and have them think favorably about you. One of the leaders I interviewed picked a project that she knew her managing partner was passionate about. Another woman selected the committee that made charitable contributions on behalf of her firm. She decided to join that committee because she and the chair of the firm both supported the same community group, and being on the committee together gave her a basis for more frequent interactions with him.

4. <u>Which of these committees interest you?</u> Considering that you will have to put in extra time, be sure that the committee's work interests you. If you really like working with associates, join the professional development committee. If you want to learn more about the business of the firm, be on a committee that will help educate you. As with anything else in life, do not join a committee dealing with something you dislike or find boring or unimportant. If you are interested and motivated, you will do well; if you are not, it will be an ordeal. Try to find committees that will challenge you and help you learn something new. It may feel comfortable to take on the same kind of committee assignments repeatedly, but rather than advancing your development, it will stymie you.

5. <u>Which committees will help advance your career?</u> Certain committees will advance your career goals while others will not. Whether a particular committee will help you depends on what your goals are and the responsibilities and opportunities you will be given. Any two women may view the same committee differently. For instance, some aspiring leaders want to be on the hiring committee while others avoid it. A few of the women I interviewed actively sought to become chair of their firms' hiring committee and used it as a springboard into higher leadership roles. They felt it gave them visibility because it is a committee that affects and interacts with lawyers at all levels across the firm. They characterized their work in leading the hiring process as taking responsibility for the future of the firm, and they gained insight into the firm's vision for the future by scrutinizing the factors that drove hiring decisions. Other women I spoke with resolutely avoided the hiring committee. They believed that committees related to personnel issues are too soft and stereotypically female. Instead, they sought positions on committees that deal with business, economics, and strategy. In their view, those business-oriented committees are more valued in the firm and more likely to demonstrate members' fitness and experience for leadership. One woman leader turned down being chair of the hiring committee, saying it *"did not fit with the image I want."* She lobbied to become a practice group leader instead.

6. <u>Who are the other committee members</u>? If the other members are influential, considered rising stars, or people you like or want to get to know, that's good. It may be of special importance for you to serve on committees with partners you want to get to know because you want their support, introductions to their clients, or other reasons that further your career plans. This is an important consideration if you need to develop relationships with these people but do not see them often because they are in another office or practice area. However, if they talk a good game but do little real work, or if they are uninspiring or contentious, you may become frustrated, bored, or overworked because you will end up doing their work as well as yours.

7. <u>Is this the right time</u>? If you are at the point in your career where your reputation as an expert in your practice area is taking off, or your practice is gaining momentum, this might not be the best time to shift your attention to committees and other significant management responsibilities. If you accept the appointment now, and your practice development efforts are diverted, it might have a negative long-term impact on your practice. However, if you say no too many times, the firm may decide you are not sufficiently interested and will stop asking. Before declining, consider the likely consequences. If you do not take the position now, what are the chances this position—or something better—will be offered again in the future?

8. <u>Who is asking you to take the position?</u> The person who asks might make a difference in your response. If a valued mentor or key player in the firm wants to sponsor you or offers to appoint you to an important position, it is hard to say no. However, you still may be able to negotiate some limits on your obligations or other aspects of the work that will be required.

9. <u>How will your compensation be affected</u>? Some committees take a great deal of time away from your client work. How will your participation affect your compensation and your client relationships? How will you protect yourself against losing control of your clients? Will your income be reduced? Can you negotiate for more?

§ 12:7 Make yourself known as leadership material

Part of your strategy for becoming a leader requires creating the perception that you are leadership material. You need to develop a reputation as someone who is reliable and effective, is respected by clients and peers, understands the business of law, and is committed to the firm's success. Your abilities and contributions must be recognized and appreciated. Only when that happens can you achieve the results that are important to you.

If you want to be a leader, you cannot be overly shy or modest. You must be known as a potential leader and it is up to you to make others think of you that way. Self-promotion makes many women uncomfortable, but it is a necessary part of a leadership development strategy.

Making yourself known as an emerging leader does not require you to broadcast your accomplishments although you should find a way to tell others about them. Some women find it easier to praise someone else than to talk about themselves. If that is more comfortable for you, team up with one or more colleagues to do internal PR for each other, or use the firm's women's initiative, network, or affinity group to highlight your achievements. If mentors and clients want to help you, ask them to give you public credit. When a client lauds you in writing, forward the note to the head of your group. One interviewed leader was surprised and thrilled when the firm's senior partner sent a memo around the firm praising her for an important victory she won in court. Whatever you do, do not shy away from the limelight; a leader's place is out front.

There are many ways to increase your visibility as a rising leader:

- Show up. It is essential to be present at firm meetings, events, and social gatherings. People must see you as an active participant in the firm. Many women do not attend partner meetings or major firm events. Partner meetings may be tedious and frustrating; firm social events may be boring to you; and you would probably prefer to be out with your friends or home with your family. You are undoubtedly overworked, overcommitted, and pressed for time. It is important to set limits, but if you ever want to be considered for a leadership role, it is equally important to be known, active, and engaged in managing the firm and participating in its activities.

- Take the initiative. Do not wait to be tapped on the shoulder or given permission to initiate a project that you think is worthwhile. If you see that something needs to be done, do it—or get someone else to do it. This will show that you are a self-starter who makes things happen. One interviewed leader acted as a change agent with every minor management role she took. When she was asked to administer summer associate assignments, she revamped the entire work assignment system; she did the same thing when she was given responsibility for associate assignments. Partners saw her as someone who did not just carry out the administrative aspects of the job; they saw her as someone who thought about them, saw better solutions, and produced beneficial change.

- <u>Be alert to opportunities and exploit them</u>. Look for critical moments when you can make yourself memorable or prove yourself. Ask smart questions, and show that you are knowledgeable, a quick learner, and a deep thinker. Let others see that you are capable, dependable, and willing to be helpful. Here is the experience of one leader in a global firm: *"All the managing partners and practice group leaders were going to Harvard for a leadership program. Someone dropped out and I was invited to take their place. I was the youngest person in the room. This gave me an opportunity to meet people, get known, and make an impression. I soaked up knowledge and learned what leaders of the firm said and thought. Part of the program involved small groups. One of the senior managing partners in my group was impressed with me and recommended me to be the U.S. relationship partner for a global company they were pitching. When the business came in, I became the global client relations manager."*
- <u>Develop a reputation as a leader who achieves great results</u>. Choose to lead activities that are important to decision-makers in the firm and produce the results they want. Many lawyers in management positions fail to follow through, so if you take your responsibilities seriously and get the job done, you will stand out. Get your name associated with positive projects and results, and make sure people realize you are looking out for the firm's best interests, not just your own. To do your best work with the least exertion, choose activities that you enjoy and are good at—and be shrewd about your choices. As one leader cautioned, *"Do not do something if the managing partner thinks it's stupid."*

- *A fifth-year associate and I were working together on a project. My co-worker sent status memos to partners that told them what was happening on it. She highlighted herself, but in a subtle way. She made sure the partners knew her and associated her with what was getting done. That way she got attention and credit. I was shocked. I realized that I should do this too . . . so I would be noticed.*
- *A management team member asked me who I thought might be good in the role of leader for the firm's largest practice group. I was open with the fact that I thought I would be good. I also thought a few others would be as well and mentioned them. At the end of the day, they asked me to step up.*
- *As a new lateral partner, I got on the managing partner's radar screen by telling him that my practice group needed to be reorganized. I suggested a retreat for the sub-groups in the department where we could discuss it—and invited him to join us. He came to the retreat and saw how well I handled it. Soon the partners in powerful positions knew who I was.*

§ 12:8 Get connected through internal networks

Leaders must be well-connected and gain entry to powerful networks. (See Chapter 9.) Maintaining a visible presence in the firm and building a reputation as a rising leader will help you access those networks. Partners will see you in action and respect your work. Over time, they will be more interested in knowing you and more willing to talk with you, but you have to actively seek and use opportunities to connect with the partners who can open doors for you and bring you into their networks. At the same time, you should start building your own network within the firm. That network includes your mentors and champions as well as other leaders in the firm, partners who will introduce you to clients and business contacts, and others who can help you as your career progresses.

Committee participation in the firm can afford access to influential networks through relationships that you form with other members. As noted earlier, one of the reasons to join firm committees is the chance to work with other present and future firm leaders, but turning a committee membership into network access requires a strategic approach. When you are on a committee, form relationships with other members and find a role that enables you to demonstrate your leadership ability or to stand out memorably in a favorable way. Forming relationships with any members of a committee may be helpful, but to gain access to important networks target partners who are influential and powerful.

Here are some additional ways to build network connections in the firm:

- <u>Start immediately.</u> Don't wait. An old proverb says that the best time to plant a tree is 20 years ago; the second best time is today. You should have started making strategic connections as an associate. If you are starting now, lay the groundwork by forming personal relationships and proving your value to others. If you have begun to build a strong network, continue and increase your efforts. In either case, be purposeful and shrewd, targeting the partners who hold the keys to the networks you need to enter and the business contacts you want to meet.

- <u>Know what you have to trade</u>. As discussed in Chapter 9, the price of admission to many influential networks is something of value that draws others to you. Be aware of what you have that others may view as valuable, such as specialized legal expertise, client contacts, or political connections.

- <u>Reach out to partners with power and influence</u>. Choose your network members purposefully. Keep a list of colleagues you know and others you want to know. Seek out partners who are already leaders or rising stars, and make it a point to meet them at firm activities, or give them a call. When you plan to visit another office of your firm, let them know in advance that you will drop in to say hello. When they are visiting your office, make it a point to see them. Develop relationships with them just as you would with clients. Ask about their practices, clients, and family. Give them small courtesies and favors, such as offering them speaking engagements, or sending them a book they might like. Use these interactions as the groundwork for building personal and professional relationships.

- <u>Make smart introductions to others</u>. One of the most appreciated gifts you can give people is introductions to others who can benefit them in some way. When you connect partners with business contacts, clients, or even members of your firm in other offices, they expand their own networks. They also see you as influential and well-connected—which makes you more intriguing to them.

- <u>Become an information agent</u>. Decide what information is important to the partners to whom you want access or by whom you want to be noticed. Put yourself in a place to

control who receives new information and related business,
opportunities, or clients. Position yourself so that your
personal information network affords you access to this information and allows you to distribute it. You might become
a subject matter expert, engage in political activity, or
become head of a firm task force. It should be a position or
activity that gives you unique, little-known, and relevant
information. Then become a conduit for informing others.
Create a reputation for being the go-to person for the best
information.

- Offer your time. The greatest gift you can give many
  partners is your time. Offer to assist a colleague on a project, take over a task, or get involved in a cause they care
  about. Giving some of your valuable time to help them is
  always appreciated and remembered.

- Introduce yourself to new lawyers. Mergers offer an excellent opportunity to start or enlarge personal networks. So ´
  does the arrival of any new partner. Make a special effort to
  meet all new partners who join the firm or at least those
  who join your office. Some of these partners will become
  rainmakers, stars, and leaders; and all are potential supporters and allies. People remember individuals who
  welcome them and are gracious when they have newly
  arrived.

- Socialize. Many network relationships develop casually,
  when people have lunch together, go out for a beer after
  work, attend firm social functions, or hang out to chat in
  someone's office at the end of the day. For strategic networking, devoting time to these casual social interactions is
  essential. One leader noted that men do more of this than
  women do (a fact that is borne out by research[1]): *"Male
  lawyers like to be in the "aura" of the rainmakers. They waste
  time hanging out with them and chatting. They do this more
  than women do. Women do what needs to be done and don't
  waste time by hanging out . . . But men will sit in the cafete-
  ria and hang out. That's how they get information and
  partners get to know them. Women associates hang out with
  their friends in the office, with peers rather than with
  partners who could be influential for them. I'd rather go*

[Section 12:8]

[1]See, e.g., Wilder, G.Z. (2007), *Women in the profession: findings from the
first wave of the after the JD study*, The NALP Foundation for Law Career
Research and Education and the National Association for Law Placement, Inc.
[NALP].

home, and since most women partners have kids, they would too." These relaxed encounters are important investments in relationship building and expanding your social capital. You may think they are a waste of time because they are social rather than productive. However, if you spend all your time doing your work and do not take part in casual social interactions, your network will suffer, and you will miss out on important advancement opportunities. Plus, aside from their strategic value, these activities can be fun and offer relief from the pressures of work.

- <u>Stay in touch.</u> Use communication channels to keep people informed about what you are doing and what you have achieved, especially if it relates to something they prize or take a special interest in.

§ 12:9   Build and use outside networks

Networks outside the office can also be useful to highlight your leadership abilities and increase your standing and reputation in the firm. For many women, holding leadership positions in outside organizations for lawyers and professional women has been a popular path to influence and leadership within their firms. Many women join local, state, or national bar associations, women's bar associations, specialty bar groups, political associations, women's organizations, and nonprofit boards. In addition to finding professional satisfaction in these activities, women gain networking and leadership opportunities that are either closed to them or too fraught with risk inside their firms.

Participation in outside organizations gives you a chance to polish your leadership skills in safe environments where members are grateful for your service and supportive of your efforts. You learn how to run a business, deal with budget shortfalls, and handle personnel problems. You also develop personal relationships with others who share your interests as you work and socialize together. The bonds that form can be a powerful source of professional and personal support that is invaluable to you as a leader now and in the future.

As you rise through the leadership ranks of an outside organization, partners in the law firm will take note. If your work in an association or nonprofit leads to heightened visibility and favorable publicity for the firm or better yet, new business, you are taken more seriously, and new opportunities inside the firm should appear for you. When you are identified as a leader in the community, your good reputation reflects well on the firm, which benefits from its connection to you. Your affiliation with political and bar leaders can make you attractive to partners who want access to those contacts because of clients' needs or personal aspirations; and most importantly, when you achieve prominence as a leader, your connections to important people in the community can become a rich source of business contacts, referrals, and potential clients. All of these connections can be a significant source of power for you in the firm, as others who desire access to your outside network see you as a player who must be reckoned with.

Leadership outside the firm can help you accomplish change inside the firm as well. One leader I interviewed specifically ran for president of her city's women's bar association so that it would force her firm to do more for its own women partners and associates. When she told the firm's managing partner that she intended to run for that office, *"He said great and helped me build support inside the firm. By endorsing my leadership of the Women's Bar he committed the firm to the goals we set for women during my time in office."* She won the election and held him to his promise of support to the benefit of the women in her firm.

Another way to participate in powerful networks is to create new ones. You can sidestep existing networks and start your own, either for women only or for men and women. Depending on what you want to achieve and what is feasible in your firm or community, this may be an option for you to consider. One leader recounted her experience as a new lawyer working in government relations in Washington, D.C., 30 years ago. Women were excluded from the networks that might have helped them learn how to maneuver through the many agencies and bureaucracies they had to deal with and avoid the traps that made it hard to do their jobs. So they started an organization of women who worked in the regulatory field on Capitol Hill. Today, that group, Women in Housing and Finance, has become a powerful network with 750 members.

Leadership success in external networks will give you excellent leadership experience, raise your visibility, and enhance your reputation within the firm; but do not neglect internal networks. In order to translate your external success to internal leadership, you will still need important partners to champion you inside the firm and welcome you into the inner circles of power.

§ 12:10   Find mentors and champions

Our chief want is someone who will inspire us to be what we know we could be.
—Ralph Waldo Emerson

Few lawyers become law firm leaders on their own. Most enjoy the sponsorship of influential mentors who advocate for them, ensure that they receive the exposure and leadership experience they need, and persuade others to add their support. If you have become a partner, it is likely that you have had at least one or more mentors.

The positive impact of mentoring on career advancement is well established.[1] Mentoring has been associated with favorable career outcomes, including higher rates of promotion and compensation, and with greater clarity of professional identity. This is especially true for women lawyers who have prominent senior mentors. These women have been shown to have higher compensation and career satisfaction than women without mentors, and are more likely to hold executive positions. Mentoring is also an important factor for women in developing self-confidence and sustaining ambition.[2] One leader spoke of mentors as part of a "safety net" that women need as they rise up the ranks of leadership, not just for protection, but for reality checks, advice, and counsel. She said: *"Mentors, allies and sponsors are important because they can speak up for you during a contentious meeting, or come to you outside the meeting to fill you in or to help you change or develop strategies or techniques. They can tell you 'Don't let X get to you or make you angry. It's a waste of energy. Focus on Y instead. Y can help you get it done.'"*

Having mentors who bring varied strengths and perspectives to the table is especially profitable to you as a leader or aspiring leader. Different mentors can be helpful to you in different ways. The value of mentors extends from their sending you clients, to explaining firm politics, to offering advice about how to dress. For aspiring leaders, one essential type of mentor is a champion.

A champion is a special kind of mentor who advocates for you and personally invests in your career success by appointing you to, or sponsoring you for, leadership roles. The distinguishing feature of champions is their power. They have the clout to make things happen for you. There is nothing better for your leadership prospects than having a powerful and established senior partner who personally champions your success.

[Section 12:10]

[1]Abbott, I.O., & Boags, R.S. (2003), *Mentoring across differences: a guide to cross-gender and cross-race mentoring*, Minority Corporate Counsel Association.

[2]Higgins, M.C., & Thomas, D.A. (May 2001), Constellations and careers: toward understanding the effects of multiple developmental relationships, *Journal of Organizational Behavior* 22, 223–247.

Because men dominate the leadership of law firms, most of the senior partners who are in positions to help you this way are men. Indeed, the research shows that senior male mentors are more effective than women mentors in advancing women lawyers' careers in terms of promotions, leadership development, and compensation.[3] In a law firm culture where success requires being able to thrive in a masculine environment, a male senior partner who is part of firm leadership can validate your legitimacy as a leader in the eyes of others. His sponsorship signals to the predominantly male leadership that you have what it takes to be a leader. He can also invite you into powerful networks, sponsor you for memberships and leadership in professional organizations, introduce and promote you to clients, put you in charge of client relationships, and send business your way. Having the ear and support of a powerful champion can enable you to avoid problems, get through crises, remove obstacles, and get things done. You need mentors who will champion your efforts, stick their necks out for you, protect you from unfair attacks, and alert you to new opportunities—or even create them for you. If you want to become a leader, make it a priority to find a champion.

Young women lawyers often feel that they should have women mentors with whom they can relate, who will understand what they are going through as women, and who will give them emotional and career support. Women mentors are extremely important. Unfortunately, there are too few of them to provide mentorship to all aspiring women leaders; and there are not enough women leaders with the stature, power, and influence to serve as champions for every promising female leader. Women can overcome this shortage by finding multiple mentors, women and men, for different purposes. While many lawyers believe that having one influential mentor is the key to success, research has found that a diverse, high quality "constellation" of mentors accounts for more successful long-term career outcomes.[4]

Having a constellation of mentors is especially important for women of color. Influential mentors have been strongly associated with minority women's career success, while lack of mentoring is a major factor in their career dissatisfaction and failure to advance. As partners and as leaders, women of color need advisors to explain or interpret the unwritten rules, sponsors to

---

[3]Ramaswami, A, Dreher, G.F., Bretz, R., & Wiethoff, C. (2009), The interactive effects of gender and mentoring on career attainment: making the case for female lawyers, *Journal of Career Development*, issue forthcoming.

[4]Higgins & Thomas (May 2001), Constellations and careers.

ensure they are taken seriously and treated fairly, brokers who steer clients and business their way, and champions who get them appointed to key committees and positions. The women of color who were interviewed for this book gave special credit to mentors and champions for many aspects of their career success. One African-American leader who was appointed to her firm's management committee later learned that the managing partner used his power to override the objections of another partner, a leading rainmaker, who opposed her appointment.

The mentor of another African-American leader, Lisa Gilford of Alston & Bird (and currently President of the National Association of Women Lawyers), was a white male partner, Mark Rochefort. Mark regularly recruited women and minority lawyers to volunteer for various diversity projects. He asked Lisa to coordinate a job fair for minority law students with DuPont, one of the firm's clients, which had made diversity a top priority. Lisa worked hard and did an outstanding job. Mark saw that she was committed to making the client happy, and the client was very pleased with her. Mark became Lisa's champion, making sure that she had more exposure to DuPont, chances to work on DuPont cases, and a personal travel budget to attend DuPont meetings and events. He asked her to talk at partner meetings about what she was doing with DuPont so that other partners could see her leadership prospects. Lisa and Mark came from totally different demographics and backgrounds. They practiced in different areas and never worked together until she had been a partner for several years. However, he gave her a chance to distinguish herself, and she took it, finding a champion in the process.

The experience of the leaders I interviewed confirms the importance and availability of a diverse constellation of mentors and champions throughout your career. Almost every leader mentioned having at least one, and usually several important mentors who offered assistance in a variety of ways. These leaders were highly strategic in identifying possible mentors to whom they reached out and in making use of the opportunities afforded by important partners who took an interest in them. In general, male mentors do not reach out to women as often as they do to men,[5] but that was not a problem for these women. They attracted mentors through their strong performance, commitment to excellence and client service, and eagerness to learn.

Leaders frequently described some of their best mentors as

---

[5]Abbott & Boags (2003), *Mentoring across differences.*

unlikely candidates, partners whose backgrounds, styles, and personalities were completely different from their own. As associates, some of the women worked with partners with whom others did not want to work. Those partners appreciated the women's talent and interest in the practice and became their mentors and champions. They made sure that the women became partners and received the credit they deserved. One woman described her mentor this way:

> I called him my "tormentor" because he was so demanding and frantic. But he showed me what was important. He was a rainmaker, but burned through associates and no one wanted to work with him. He kept after me. He was powerful, but he needed me. I learned by watching him. He was grateful to associates who would work with him. He gave me responsibility and credit. We had no life experiences in common and came from different demographics. But we found mutual value through our work.

The women I interviewed continued to have mentors after they became partners and leaders. Even when they were in significant leadership positions, these women had mentors who helped them in many ways: by sponsoring them for leadership jobs, putting them into positions of high visibility, educating them about the economics and operations of the firm, protecting them from unfair criticism, and inviting them into their personal networks of powerful colleagues. Besides partners who were firm leaders and rainmakers, their mentors included firm executives such as the Chief Operating Officer and Executive Director. These mentors were usually but not always in their firms, and they were predominantly but not always men. A few leaders had powerful women mentors who exerted considerable influence in the firm and on these women's careers. One of the most noteworthy mentor-mentee relationships was between two women, Amy Schulman and Heidi Levine. Their story appears later in this chapter.

Some law firms are beginning to institute leadership development programs for partners. As part of these programs, they often assign senior partners to serve as mentors to junior partners, both women and men, to help them with leadership and business development. These programs are highly beneficial in helping junior partners increase their leadership capabilities and present leadership opportunities that they might not otherwise receive. They often involve "action learning," in which the junior partner is expected to start a designated firm initiative or to solve a real firm problem with the guidance and support of the mentor. The project tests the ability of the new partner and gives her a chance to prove what she can do. Some firms assign mentors (and projects) without input from the junior partner, but most firms will at least consider any ideas you present. If your firm has such a program, try to have input in deciding who your mentor will be. Use the mentoring experience wisely to forge a strong relationship with your mentor and to position yourself as an up-and-coming leader.

Formal programs like these leadership development initiatives are only one source of mentors. There are potential mentors all around you and you can initiate relationships with them on your own. You need to think strategically about the mentors that you want and need and make a determined effort to interest them in helping you. Sometimes you will be lucky and potential mentors will take an interest in you on their own. If that happens, let them know you welcome their help. However, the mentors you need may not reach out to you. One of the reasons that women have trouble finding mentors is that they wait, like Cinderella, for mentors to find them. Women leaders I interviewed agree with the research literature that women do not go after what they want as affirmatively and purposefully as men do. One leader noted that when she became chair of a global firm, *"Men lined up outside my door to be mentored. They felt entitled to it. Women didn't do it."* If you want a mentor, you cannot sit back and hope that Prince Charming will locate you. You have to be proactive.

The most common way that lawyers find mentors is through working together and that was the experience of the leaders who were interviewed. As they worked with partners on client matters, committees, or other projects, the partners were impressed by their talent and drive, saw them as rising stars, and gravitated to them. Sometimes, however, it was the women who took the initiative and reached out to possible mentors. They looked for individuals who had the skills, behaviors, or connections they wanted to acquire and built relationships with them. In the course of building those relationships, they created their own learning and mentoring opportunities. The most important consideration for these women was not gender or race. It was more strategic: how the potential mentor could best help them achieve their particular work or career objectives. By being purposeful in finding mentors, they had multiple mentors from whom they learned and benefited in various ways.

What should you look for in a mentor? It depends on the kind of help you want. Few individual mentors have all the skills, attributes, and inclinations that will help you get where you want to go. Some people can make introductions and open doors for you because they are well connected; some can advise you about firm politics and how to operate within the political culture; others can be advocates and sponsors for positions you want to attain. Once you know what you need, you can identify the people who are best able to help you, determine what would motivate them to invest their time in you, and decide how to approach them.

If you know them well, you might choose to approach them directly. Be specific about the type of assistance you are looking for and what you would like them to do. If you do not know the person, you need to lay the foundation for a relationship. You cannot expect someone to become a mentor unless they know you and believe that you are worthy of their time and effort. Before approaching them, find out about them. Introduce yourself (or be introduced by someone who knows them), and let them get to know you. You might look for an opportunity to work closely with a potential mentor on a client matter, a project for the firm, or a community activity. When a relationship forms, and you think the person would be receptive, you can tell them that you are trying to develop as a leader and would like their assistance in a particular way. You do not even have to use the word "mentor." The relationship, not the label, is what counts.

Mentors may come from unexpected places and are not always obvious candidates. They may not be in your law firm or in the legal profession at all. From a strategic standpoint, all they need is a skill or attribute that you need and a willingness to help you. One partner who left a large firm to start her own practice formed a "personal board of advisors" who served as her mentors. One of those advisors was an insurance agent who helped her hone her business development skills. He taught her the principles of selling, coached her on how to sell her legal services, and was available to answer her questions about dealing with prospective clients. He was not a role model; she did not emulate his style or his interactions with potential clients. However, he taught her the basics that led her to become a successful business generator and gave her the confidence to do it.

Here is what three leaders said about their experience with mentors:

- A partner now in full time executive management: *My mentor recruited me as a summer associate. She wore a purple suit! She was a powerful, nationally known litigator. She helped me network with powerful and influential people in the firm and outside, so I always knew who those people were and they always knew me. My relationship with her gave me instant credibility with them.*

- The managing partner of a large office in a global firm: *I had a wonderful mentor—still do. At first glance, we have nothing in common. I'm from a small town on the prairie. We weren't even working class. I was the first in my family to go to college, much less an Ivy League law school. I was also an athlete and a beauty queen. He is very tall, elegant, and uncoordinated; he went to a fancy prep school and is an intellectual from a long line of lawyers. I thought he was the smartest partner in the firm and he was willing to teach me. That was a huge confidence boost that I needed.*

- A lateral partner: *I recruit mentors. Every organization has its own social mores and protocols that are new to you. Success at your prior firm doesn't mean success here. . . . In the interview process, I try to talk with people I'm comfortable with and make them comfortable with me. I try to get them vested in my success. I want to be someone they will want to take credit for.*

The Value of Mentoring: Amy Schulman and Heidi Levine

Amy Schulman and Heidi Levine have a relationship that epitomizes the positive effects of mentoring for mentors and mentees alike. Amy is currently the General Counsel of Pfizer Corp., but before that, she was a partner at DLA Piper, where she was also the most successful rainmaker in the firm. Amy was so extraordinary as a lawyer, rainmaker, and leader that Harvard Business School developed a case study about her. She was also a mentor to Heidi Levine and to many other women and men on her client teams.

What made Amy such an exceptional mentor? She invested in people so that they worked their hardest and did their best for her. She believed that each individual contributed something of value to the whole, and that by working together, they made each other stronger. She respected, encouraged, and empowered them as professionals, and felt great pride as her team members became successful lawyers and leaders in their own right.

Amy was also generous. She gave credit, including compensation credit, to junior partners. She did this well before she was a major rainmaker, when she had little monetary credit to give away. As she brought in more business, it became easier to be generous. Amy believes that being fair with people economically was one of the reasons her teams did so well. It prevented internal competition and fostered cooperation and support for each other and for clients.

Amy benefited from her mentorship as well. Amy wanted to accomplish a great deal in her practice and career and knew she

needed a strong team to help her. She needed to feel confident
that her clients would receive the best possible service, and she
believed that *"If the team is strong and committed, the work will
benefit. I never worried that anchoring client relationships with
strong younger lawyers would cause problems."* So Amy fostered
teamwork and collaboration. She gave team members respect,
responsibility, and authority; and they, in turn, did their best for
her and her clients. She cultivated a small inner circle of highly
competent lawyers whom she could trust and rely on with no
doubt of their loyalty or dedication. This enabled her to spend
more time on other business pursuits.

One of the lawyers Amy mentored was Heidi Levine. Heidi is
still at DLA Piper and is now a rainmaker herself, as well as a
member of the firm's policy committee, co-chair of the firm's
national women's initiative, and co-chair of the mass tort/products
liability group within the New York Litigation Department. Heidi
credits Amy's support as a mentor for helping her succeed and
for inspiring her to be a mentor to the lawyers who now staff her
client teams.

Heidi recalls many ways, both large and small, in which Amy
brought out the best in her. Amy was willing to share her strategies and insights with Heidi, and she was willing to listen, too;
she was as interested in learning from Heidi as she was in teaching her. They had an egalitarian relationship; they confided in
each other, gave each other feedback, and Heidi felt that she
could speak freely and voice her opinions, including opposition,
without eliciting a negative reaction from Amy.

Amy's conscientious mentoring efforts exemplify the many
small things that a mentor can do to make a big difference in an
associate's development, identity formation, and advancement.
Heidi cited many examples:

- *When we traveled together by plane, Amy upgraded me with
  her points so that we could sit together and talk about strategy, clients, etc. on our way to or from a meeting. It was our
  quiet time to talk.*
- *Amy brought me into meetings and conferences, first to
  observe and later to participate.*
- *When I was an associate, Amy never introduced me to anyone
  as an associate. She always said: "This is my colleague."
  That empowered me.*
- *When we traveled together, we did things together socially,
  for fun, not just for work.*

Amy's and Heidi's mentoring relationship continued as Heidi
became a successful rainmaker and leader. With Amy's encour-

agement, counseling, and sponsorship, Heidi's career progressed steadily. When Amy left for Pfizer, the transition to Heidi as the head of her client team was seamless because Heidi had been functioning in that role for some time. Although she has developed a professional style of her own, Heidi continues to use Amy's collaborative and supportive approach with her own client teams and to serve as a mentor and role model for the lawyers on those teams.

Heidi and Amy remain close. Heidi says that Amy is still her mentor: "I can always call her for advice and she is always there for me, no matter how busy she is." Their relationship has one new twist, however — Amy is now Heidi's client.

§ 12:11   Identify role models

A role model is a person you want to emulate in some way. Unlike mentoring, which is based on a personal relationship, a role model does not have to be someone you know personally or may ever meet. Some mentors are also role models but role models are not necessarily mentors. They might be historical, political, or public figures, like Sandra Day O'Connor, whose example many women find inspirational.

Role models are important for women's leadership development. When women begin to develop their identities as leaders, they eagerly seek role models. Research shows that new leaders who are trying to project a leadership image look for other leaders to emulate. As novices, they think about what leaders are expected to do and engage in behaviors that they hope will lead others to accept them as a leader. As women mature and feel more comfortable being leaders, acting like other leaders declines in importance. They start to expand their ideas about what leaders do and how they behave. They worry less about how others see them or judge their behavior and become more concerned with how to be the best leaders they can be for their followers. As their leadership experience continues to grow, and as their comfort, influence, and impact increase, they eventually become secure and expert in their roles. During this development process, their orientation shifts from finding role models to becoming role models for future leaders.[1]

Most women in senior leadership today had few, if any, women

[Section 12:11]

[1]Ely, R.J., & Rhode, D.L. (2010), Women and leadership: defining the challenges, in N. Nohria & R. Khurana (Eds.), *Handbook of leadership theory and practice*, ch. 14 (Boston: Harvard Business School Press).

role models when they were starting out. Many current leaders were the first women in their firms to become partners or to achieve significant leadership positions. Now there are many women leaders in the profession who can serve as role models to junior women aspiring to leadership. However, young women often have exaggerated expectations, hoping to find women role models who are living the successful, yet balanced lives that younger women want. Senior women whose lives seem to be skewed in favor of work and career success, especially if they are single or have no children, are judged harshly as having "sacrificed too much."

For junior women, it is important to remember that career choices are personal to each woman. They depend on your own personal values, priorities, and circumstances; and you cannot judge what is best for another person based on your values and preferences. All women who have become law firm leaders have learned lessons that younger women can learn from. Rather than reject women who are less than perfect role models, focus on their accomplishments, and look for interests and values you hold in common. If you do not want to emulate a leader's entire style or career, look for aspects that you admire and might want to adopt. Maybe it appalls you that she travels so much that she communicates with her children through a webcam on her laptop, but she also has great presence in the courtroom. How does she do it, and how can you learn to do it? Find out what you can about her courtroom composure that might be of value to you.

As a woman leader, be aware that junior women want you to be their role model. As they try to determine what kind of professional identity they want to have, what kind of leader they want to be, and how to balance all the demands that will face them as leaders, they are observing you and looking for what they can emulate. Be sensitive to the fact that many of them do not want to lead the life you lead—even if their assumptions about you are unfounded. One leader who felt the sting of women's criticism stated: "*Women criticize me, that I work too hard, seek validation from others, have no husband or kids. Women discount the value of my accomplishments. But I have lots of other things in my life.*" She understood where they were coming from but regretted that those younger women scorned her when she had a great deal to offer them.

Many of the leaders I interviewed echoed this leader's sentiments. They appreciate that they made choices other women reject and may not be the best role models for all women. They realize that younger women do not want to be like them and accept the fact that "*you don't have to do it my way.*" These established leaders are also very conscious of being in the spotlight and make a special effort to behave admirably in order to show the world that women can be good leaders. Most importantly, these women want to increase the number of women leaders and are happy to serve as mentors and role models to junior women who are receptive.

§ **12:12** Acquire needed leadership knowledge and skills

In the beginner's mind there are many possibilities; in the expert's mind there are few.
— Shunryu Suzuki

Part of your strategy for becoming a leader is to polish the leadership knowledge and skills that you have and to acquire those that you lack. Some lawyers come to leadership fully prepared; their experience has gradually led them to the leader's chair, and they have picked up the necessary knowledge and skills along the way. Most leaders, however, realize that leadership is an ongoing process of learning and development and they constantly try to become better at it. No matter how much they know, there is always more to learn. One leader explained how she felt going from the Management Committee, where she had served for many years, to the Executive Committee: *"It was a tough transition. I did not have expertise in the issues we dealt with, which were more strategic. I would be asked for my opinion, or would have to vote on things, when I wasn't sure. It was all very intimidating. The ExComm was more about business, so I had to learn more about that."*

Not all of what you need to learn as a leader is substantive. Much of what you do as a leader involves personal and interpersonal dynamics among the firm's partners and employees, but little of what you do as a practicing lawyer gives you the tools to handle such matters effectively. Many leaders find that they lack adequate skills for handling these matters. You have to deal with hiring and firing decisions, negotiate with partners who can't get what they want, knock down high expectations, and cut people's budgets. While handling all those problems, you must balance the tensions between running the business and keeping people happy, especially when many of the people involved are your friends and partners.

There are many ways to prepare for leadership and to enhance your abilities. Once you recognize the skills you want to improve or the knowledge you want to acquire, you can use any one of many resources. Here are some suggestions:

- Reflection. Experience alone does not guarantee that you

will be an effective leader. You have to learn from that experience. This will not always happen automatically. Take time to step back and reflect on what you did, what happened and why, and what lessons you can take away. Otherwise, your experience may be wasted and your learning stunted. It is wise to make reflection a regular habit.

- Observing others. You undoubtedly have opportunities every day to watch leaders as they go about their work. Be observant. Think about what seems to be effective, and try to figure out why it is. Similarly, try to understand why other behaviors are unproductive and how you could do better.

- Ask colleagues. When you lack certain knowledge or understanding, ask people who know, inside your firm and elsewhere. Most people will be very happy to help you.

- Read, read, read. There are countless books on every aspect of leadership. They offer information, insights, and strategies that can be enormously helpful to you; and you can access them at any time. One leader I interviewed who is an avid reader keeps stacks of books on leadership in her office. When she thinks that someone she knows would enjoy or benefit from reading one of them, she gives it to them.

- Consultants. Professionals with expertise in fields relevant to the work that you are doing can be helpful when needed. If the firm is considering a merger, restructuring the compensation system, or planning its first big marketing campaign, working with an expert in the area is important for the firm generally, but for you personally as well. They can share knowledge, insights, and resources that give you the level of understanding necessary to make intelligent decisions on the present issue and others that may come up in the future.

- Internal mentors. Select and work with mentors in your firm who can help you acquire particular skills, knowledge, or experience that you need to be a more effective leader. Some of those mentors might be firm executives who have specialized expertise, like the firm's CFO or chief administrator. For newly appointed or elected leaders, the most logical and relevant source of specialized expertise is the person you are replacing. Leaders assuming significant management roles frequently shadow their predecessor during a transition period that may take many months.

- External mentors. It is a good idea to have mentors outside the firm who can impart their knowledge and wisdom to you. They may come from every aspect of your life. They do not have to be lawyers; they just need to have something that will help you develop as a leader. You can initiate external mentoring relationships informally or through formal mentoring programs conducted by various organizations, including private companies and bar associations. Some of those programs are specifically for women.

- **Coaches.** Working with a coach can help you improve your leadership skills and performance in many ways. Coaches can obtain objective feedback for you by conducting interviews with colleagues about your leadership performance. They can conduct full 360 reviews, also seeking feedback from clients, staff, and others who would have useful insights. Coaches can help you stay focused and motivated as you set and work toward your leadership goals. Some coaches might be retained for a very specialized purpose, such as improving your presentation skills, time management, or handling difficult people.
- **Leadership development programs.** If you will be running a practice group, office, or firm, you are essentially running a business. You need to think like a business leader, not like a lawyer. Firms that realize this are encouraging partners to study business, management, and leadership. Many law firms now conduct their own internal programs or send their lawyers to customized leadership programs conducted for the firm by business schools, law schools, and leadership research and consulting firms. If your firm does not have such a program, there are leadership development programs that you can attend throughout the country. Many of the organizations that customize programs for individual law firms also offer leadership programs that are open to leaders of all law firms. Some law schools, business schools, and consulting companies offer leadership programs specifically for women leaders. One of those programs is the Hastings Leadership Academy for Women, of which I am the Director.[2]
- **Leadership groups.** It is helpful to share your experiences and questions with peers in leadership positions similar to yours. These groups (often called "roundtables") meet together regularly to discuss the challenges and issues that their members face as leaders. The groups are relatively small, with the same participants attending each session. They might be organized and facilitated by a consultant or

---

[Section 12:12]

[2]See http://www.attorneyretention.org/LAW.

third person, or they may be self-directed, with members of
the group alternating responsibility for setting the agenda
and leading the discussion. If there is no such group for your
type of leadership role, find other leaders in your area, and
start your own!

All of these are useful resources that will benefit you as a
leader. However, they are only supplemental to the key learning
strategy for leadership, which is experience. You can study, take
classes, hire advisors, and read books like this one to help you
identify and consider what you need to know and do as a leader,
but at its core, leadership is not an intellectual exercise. The best
way to learn it and be good at it is to do it. Don't wait until you
have studied every aspect and feel that you are fully prepared;
you will never be perfect at it or know all there is to know. Jump
right in and give it a try. If you have any doubts about your
leadership ability, you will not be able to overcome those doubts
unless you actually do what leaders do. If you feel that you need
some seasoning, take on a modest leadership role in the firm or
in bar associations, industry groups, or on boards.

Your client teams are also a source of good leadership
experience. Leading a client team gives you an excellent platform
to demonstrate your talent for leadership. If the team performs
well and functions as a cohesive unit, its efficiency, productivity,
and profitability increase. Leading profitable teams will get you
noticed and perceived favorably by other partners. If team
members get along, morale is good, and the work is interesting,
others will want to work with you, spreading your positive reputation for leadership among associates, paralegals, and staff. As
noted elsewhere, there are differences between being a client
team leader and a firm leader; but many of the skills, attitudes,
and behaviors that you practice with your team will also be useful in larger leadership roles. Plus, you can try out different
leadership styles, approaches, and activities in this familiar and
limited setting, which is relatively safe compared to the bigger
firm or office stage.

Being a good team leader has an additional benefit for you. Client teams form a natural constituency for you if you treat them
well. People's experience with you on these teams will determine
whether, and to what extent, they will support you when you
become a firm leader. Team members see you in action and know
how you perform under pressure. The way you treat them and
make them feel, the standards you set for yourself and them, and
the way you deal with failure, these and other facets of their day-
to-day experience with you give them intimate knowledge of your
potential as a leader. If they believe that you are capable, effec-

tive, fair, and trustworthy, they will trust you to lead them and give you their loyalty and best efforts.

As you move up in the leadership of the firm, these team members will become your followers and supporters. It was noted earlier that achieving leadership is easier when you have support from partners who are influential and powerful. However, it is also important to have people who give you hands-on assistance and do the everyday work that helps you become known as a rising star. You depend on these people for the results that make you shine. They include not just associates and partners, but also legal assistants, secretaries, and other staff and employees who can make your life easier and get things done. When you become a firm leader, your partners may give you the authority to act, but these are the people that you need to handle the daily details and carry out your leadership agenda.

§ 12:13 Practice self-management

"I try to take one day at a time, but sometimes several days attack me at once." — Ashleigh Brilliant

It is difficult for law firm leaders to maintain a sense of balance in their lives because there are so many demands on their time. It is easy to become consumed by work and neglect other aspects of your life, including your social life, family, and emotional and physical health. Whether you are contemplating leadership or are already playing a leadership role in your firm, time is a critical but scarce resource. One of your greatest challenges as a leader will be keeping yourself disciplined and organized enough to attend to all the things you have to do. The only way you can carry out all of your responsibilities is to set clear priorities, plan carefully, stay focused, and delegate as much as you can. People watch you closely. When you are highly organized, people may or may not take note. However, they will definitely notice if you are disorganized, and you will lose credibility and respect if you appear to be scattered or undisciplined.

Planning your schedule should reflect your priorities. Priorities include both the overarching priorities that are grounded in your core values and the shorter-term priorities that determine where you will put your energies during each day. One very busy leader who was asked how she found time to do everything answered: *"That's not the goal. I can't do everything. I do what's important."* It is not easy, especially when you are faced with conflicting demands and have to make tough choices, but it is essential.

No matter how well you plan your day, unexpected events will come up. Some of these events are crises that require immediate attention; some may be noisy but can wait. Many of them involve people who have complaints, needs, or demands and want to see you right away. If you are not careful, these distractions can take a great deal of time and energy, and they can produce considerable stress. If you lose your focus, you will lose control of your priorities, and you will have less time to address them. The more organized you are, the better able you will be to cope with these distractions, and the less stress there will be on you and the people around you. Another way to prevent stress and manage better is to delegate work that you do not have to do yourself.

Women who have families have an extra source of stress and distraction. To manage effectively as a leader in the office, you also have to manage effectively at home. It's a constant juggling act that requires as much planning as your work in the firm. If you do not have the support you need at home, you can become overwhelmed by guilt and conflict. Here, too, good organization will help you maintain your focus and keep you in control.

§ 12:14   Set priorities and plan around them

Leaders constantly face conflicting demands. One of the keys to a leader's success is her determination to be true to her values and use those values to set priorities. Having a clear personal sense of what is important and acceptable to you helps you decide what you will do, when, and for how long. Your values inform your decision about what your priorities are and where to place limits on your work. When your priorities conflict, your core values help keep your options and their consequences in perspective. They make your choices easier. One leader at a 65-lawyer firm decided to forego a very attractive job offer from another law firm. The offer presented a tempting career opportunity but would require her to spend a lot of time away from her family. She explained her decision this way: *"There are some things I do not want to do. For example, I minimize travel. I gave up an opportunity at another firm because it would require travel. I could have built up a huge national practice at that firm, but it would have required 1 to 2 years of non-stop traveling around the country."*

Setting clear priorities and boundaries about where you will direct your time and effort sends important signals to the people around you. Letting people know that you will not be available at certain times each day or each week allows you to set that time aside for things that are important to you, whether it is your family, your health, or your religious beliefs. It lets you manage their expectations about what you will do and when. One law firm partner I know refuses to send or respond to e-mails at night. Co-workers and clients know that she is available in emergencies, but in the normal course of work, they hear from her only during the day.

The way you spend your time also shows the people you lead what is important to you. Because you are a leader of the firm, they view your choices as representing the expectations of the firm. For better or worse, this gives you considerable impact on the firm's culture and work norms. If you work long hours, are efficient and productive, and take a three-week vacation every year, you show that you are hard working but appreciate the personal things that smooth out your life. If you work the same hours but seem to spin your wheels a lot and never take a vacation or time off to be with your family, it suggests that you expect others also to give up personal pursuits for work.

All planning involves making choices, and the choices you make determine how well you manage your time and how much you can get done effectively. You make big choices, such as the kind of law you practice, the firm you join, the city you live in, whether to buy a house or rent, whether to marry and when, your lifestyle, and so on. You also make smaller choices about what you will do each day, what will get your attention, whether you will eat alone in your office or call a colleague or client to join you, and whether to drive to work or take public transportation. Even when you think that your choices are restricted by external forces, such as the partner who threatens to quit unless . . ., or a critical client going out of business, you still make active decisions about where to devote your time and effort. You may shift around priorities to reflect the urgency of a situation, but you are nonetheless making a choice. Likewise, every one of your choices, large or small, has a direct impact on how much time you have for the other items demanding your attention. A leader who took control of her priorities and was very clear about what her choices were put it this way: "*I loved management committee stuff (who knew?), especially the people function. But I also knew that if it took too much away from my family, it would no longer be acceptable and I would walk away. Knowing that was empowering and liberating.*"

In order to attend to all pressing matters and still have time to do the planning, strategizing, and other long-term items on your agenda, you have to do triage. You must prioritize the things that must be done now and those that can wait; those that require a disproportionate amount of time and those that you can get through easily and quickly; and those that will prevent future problems and those that will just put them off for a while. In terms of scheduling, the best way to approach this is to organize tasks according to your priorities, rather than the other way around. Then you can organize your activities according to what is most important to you and keep as much control as possible in your hands.

Steven Covey has a very handy and useful approach to managing work priorities. In *The Seven Habits of Highly Effective People*, he divides matters into four quadrants, as shown below in Table 12.2.[1] The two factors that define an activity are *Importance* and *Urgency*. Importance relates to results: does this matter contribute to my vision, my high priority goals, or the firm's mission and business objectives? Urgency, on the other hand, is about immediacy: how quickly must it be done? Matters that are urgent demand your attention. Because they are "in your face," you may be tempted to take care of them quickly whether they are important or not.

Table 12.2. Setting Priorities		
	URGENT	NOT URGENT
IMPORTANT	I	II
NOT IMPORTANT	III	IV

You will invariably spend a good deal of time in Quadrant I because every leader regularly faces sudden problems and crises. Quadrant I activities deal with damage control. When important things must be taken care of right away, they will grab your attention and your time. You have to do these things, but you don't want to be consumed by crises. To be most effective and efficient, you want to spend more time in Quadrant II, addressing the issues that advance your leadership agenda, such as long-range planning, client relationships, talent development, and communicating with the firm. If you are able to spend more time in Quadrant II, you can prevent many of the emergencies that threaten to keep you in Quadrant I. Quadrant III activities may be loud and glaring but will have little significance in the grand scheme of things. You cannot ignore urgent matters, but they can be a waste of your time. Many of these activities should be

---

[Section 12:14]

[1]Covey, S.R. (1989),*The seven habits of highly effective people* (New York: Simon & Schuster).

delegated to others. For obvious reasons, spend as little time as necessary in Quadrant IV.

Another consideration in your planning is the impact of certain types of activities on your health and well-being. In their study of successful women leaders, McKinsey researchers Joanna Barsh and Susie Cranston stress the importance of placing high priority on activities that energize you.[2] These are activities that you find exciting and creative or at least enjoyable. Spending too much time on activities that sap your strength can lead to burnout. To the extent you can, delegate or outsource the things that you do not enjoy or that drain you, and incorporate as many things as possible into your day that strengthen you, replenish your energy, and keep you going.

To make more time for energy-building activities, you need to eliminate as many energy drains as you can. As noted above, you can choose where to place your effort. You cannot control everything as a leader since much of what you do is in response to the needs of others. However, you can make some choices that give you more energy for the good stuff and require less for the energy drains. This is an area where small changes can have a big impact. Starting small rituals—such as meeting with your assistant first thing every morning to review the day's planned events or organizing your desk before you leave at night so you can get right to work in the morning—can reduce time wasted on trivial and frustrating things. So can identifying the activities that exhaust you and finding ways to get rid of them wherever possible. To do that, try these steps:

- List the regular activities that demand your attention and energy in different aspects of your life (e.g., your practice, leadership, family, friends, community).
- Circle those that deplete your energy.
- Consider how a different choice might reduce or eliminate the energy-depleting activities.
- Determine what is preventing you from making that choice.
- Consider how different choices could give you more time for the activities that energize you.

Scheduling regular time for yourself is one way to replenish your energy. While it may sound paradoxical, taking regular time off may actually make you more effective. Research has shown that taking a set time away from work each week is actually beneficial for professionals and their teams. A four-year study of

---

[2]Barsh, J., & Cranston, S. (2009), *How remarkable women lead* (New York: Crown Business).

high-powered consultants at Boston Consulting Group found that requiring every team member to take a predictable block of time away from work each week led to better communication, greater work efficiency, and overall, better work.[3] Moreover, individuals who participated in the study reported greater job satisfaction, less work-life conflict, and better work habits than those who were not in the study group. The researchers' conclusion was that knowing that people would be absent forced teams to plan work better and communicate more often and forced individuals to be more efficient and focused on their work.

There are many books, classes, and resources on time management. If it is a problem for you, it will be worth your while to invest in them or find a coach. The leaders I interviewed all faced strenuous time demands and managed to stay organized and focused (most of the time). Here is some of their advice:

- *Think more strategically about what you can realistically accomplish. Before diving in consider how long a project will realistically take so that you don't unintentionally bite off more than you can chew.*

- *How do I stay organized? Lists. Project management. They are both important. Also, I live downtown so I have no commute.*

- *Seeking perfection can lead to paralysis and keep women from speaking up or taking risks. Don't wait till it's perfect. Try out draft versions along the way. Tweak as you go.*

- *As a leader you set the agenda. Leadership does not take more time because you can delegate to your team. That frees you up for business development and other activities. I like to run things, I think strategically. I get other people to do the detail work.*

- *When my son was a baby, I took flights the same day rather than stay over so I could be with him at night, even if I was exhausted. It was important to me even if he didn't know or care.*

- *When my kids were young, I pared life down to the essentials. Only home, work, school and kids' stuff. More would have pushed me over the edge. As the kids got older, I added back civic, charitable, and cultural things.*

- *To be a leader you need patience. You need to realize there are trade-offs. You don't get to do everything. I was hugely invested in my job and parenting. Those were my priorities. I*

---

[3]Perlow, L.A., & Porter, J.L. (Oct. 2009), Making time off predictable and required, *Harvard Business Review.*

put other things—like reading, theater, friends—on hold for 10 years while I focused on those two things.

- *My clients have families. They respect my family time—they tell me not to expect to go with them in evenings even if I offer. Many of them have kids too . . . But you have to know, to sense, when you do have to go. If a client supports a cause and asks your firm to buy a table, you'd better be there. They will be, giving their time to it. So should you.*

§ 12:15   Delegate

A critical aspect of personal management is effective delegation. Robert Swaine, a founding partner of Cravath, Swaine & Moore, wrote in 1948 that:

> The art of delegation in the practice of the law is difficult, requiring the nicety of balance which many men with fine minds and excellent judgment are unable to attain . . .. The more nearly he attains the right compromise between [doing all the work himself or turning everything over to an assistant], the greater the amount of effective work a man can turn out, and hence the greater his value to the firm.[1]

Of course, there were few women in practice at the time Swaine made these remarks, but the principle still holds true for men and women alike. When you are a leader, there are many things that you can and should delegate both for your own sake and for the benefit of those around you. Delegate as much as you possibly can. When you lead a client team, your personal involvement and close oversight are warranted because you are responsible to the client for the work product of the team. However, as a team leader, you do not need to do everything yourself. Likewise, as a firm leader, you *should not* do everything yourself. You can be a far more effective and efficient leader if you delegate more to others and give them greater responsibility and autonomy.

When you are a leader, you have to think broadly. Your job as a leader is to achieve the firm's goals *through other people*. The more people who are working with you and behind you toward the firm's goals, the more possibilities there are for success. It is not in the firm's best interests for you to be involved in every project. By delegating responsibilities to others, you can leverage

---

[Section 12:15]

[1]Swaine, R.T. (2007) [1948], *The Cravath firm and its predecessors: 1819–1947*, cited in Henderson, B. (July 2008), *Part II: How most law firms misapply the "Cravath system,"* Legal Profession Blog, http://lawprofessors.type pad.com/legal__profession/2008/07/part-ii-how-mos.html.

your leadership to accomplish more and create better results than any single producer could do.

Men seem to have an easier time delegating. A leader who helped shepherd her firm's merger to fruition made this observation: *"I often feel I have power but don't use it. Most men are better at using power. During the merger, a woman and a man served as department co-chairs. Management would make requests—the woman would respond, prepare the paperwork, etc. The man always delegated it unless it interested him and could get him somewhere."* The work was done either way but the woman spent unnecessary time on it.

Women can become better at delegating once they appreciate that there are many tasks they can easily give up. Sometimes, they hold on anyway because they feel they are obligated to take care of every problem, or they fear criticism if they ask others to do something. If that holds you back, find techniques that make delegation easier. For example, a practice group leader learned from another leader in her firm: *"I learned from the woman who was our previous managing partner. Anytime someone raised an idea or complaint, she turned it back on them and asked 'How would you like to do it?' So I do that now. I let them run with it, even if they're not the best person to do it."*

A great deal of leadership involves administrative and other responsibilities that are tedious, time consuming, and for most lawyers, not very satisfying. Some of these things can be done by others who find it less tedious or even consider it an opportunity to learn and develop new skills. One woman who is a major rainmaker and sits on the policy committee of her global firm used to believe that she had to do everything herself; she felt she could not delegate even administrative tasks, so she didn't. So frazzled by busy work that she almost gave up her leadership goals, she came to the realization that *"If this work can legitimately and ably be done by someone else, why not delegate it? So I did, without remorse or guilt."*

There are many other reasons to delegate. One reason is that you simply do not have the time to do everything yourself. As your workload increases, and certainly when you reach the executive level, you need help managing your work and schedule. Many leaders have assistants who perform this function. One of the leaders I interviewed, the managing partner of a global firm, bills about 1,000 hours annually on client matters and spends another 2,000 hours on management. The demands of her job would take even more time but she is highly organized and delegates what she cannot or need not do. In addition to an assistant, she has a team of lawyers to whom she delegates much of her client work, and she entrusts other matters (e.g., lateral partner hires, ethics questions) to partners better suited to deal with them.

Whenever you are asked to do something, whether work or leadership related, first ask yourself whether it is essential that you be the person to do it. If it is something that another person can handle, pick someone who would do a good job and hand it off. The global managing partner mentioned above is invited to attend many community functions on behalf of her firm. When an invitation comes in, she asks herself: *"How important to the interests and well-being of the firm is the goal to be achieved through my personal appearance? Can another person do it? What will be the impression and reaction if I don't do it?"* Depending on how she answers these questions she either goes or sends someone else in her place.

Some lawyers pride themselves on delegating responsibility to others, but in reality, they stay closely involved. Some hold on because they are not sure how much responsibility the person being asked to do the work is equipped to handle. One managing partner was uncertain about the skill level of certain new practice group leaders especially with respect to financial matters. She had to determine how much authority the group leaders should have to act on their own. She wanted to trust them to act alone but felt that they lacked the skill set to be effective so she kept an eye on what they did. She maintained a delicate balancing act trying to oversee their activities and decisions without being accused of micromanaging them.

It is especially hard to give up control of projects that you have run successfully in the past. After all, you know what it takes to make the project successful and want to be sure that it continues to be done well. Your responsibility as a leader is to find competent people to take it over and to educate the new people in charge so that they know how to do it right. The problem is that some leaders feel the only way to be sure it is done right is to stay involved. However, as a leader, your interference can backfire even if the project is a success because of your effort. When you look over the shoulders of the people who have been given an assignment, you signal that you do not trust them. Leaders who insist on controlling the process and the end product breed distrust and resentment, not gratitude. Leadership is no place for perfectionism or micromanagement. If either is a problem for you, it will be a hard habit to break, but one that is important to overcome.

§ 12:16 Juggling work and family

Doing it all is a learned skill.

—Judge Carolyn Dineen King, United States Court of Appeals, Fifth Circuit

All law firm leaders have lives outside the office (though it may not seem that way), and they struggle with how to balance competing demands from different spheres of life. To devote the necessary time to your job as a leader, you must be able to manage your personal life as well as your work. Women with children have the additional demands that family responsibilities bring. Most women try to find ways to combine career and family, but some women choose one or the other. If you have children, it means talking very honestly with your husband or partner about your respective career priorities and reaching agreement on how you will share household and family responsibilities. However carefully you plan, managing your career and your family is a constant juggling act, and you may frequently feel off-balance and in danger of dropping all the balls that you are trying to keep in the air.

Being able to manage your home life effectively is not just for your benefit but also for the well-being of the people you lead at work. Leadership comes with huge responsibility for others. You need to be able to give your work full attention and energy in order to carry out your duties, make good decisions, and give the people you work with guidance and support. If your home life is a distraction, your work performance will suffer, and you will let down the people in the office who depend on you.

To be a leader and have a family, you will need to create strategies and support systems that allow you to do your work, tend to your family, and preserve your peace of mind. However, you can keep many balls aloft successfully if you choose the balls carefully, stay clear about your priorities and stick to them, and have a plan to manage the things that you can control and back up for coping with the things you cannot.

When figuring out how you can possibly juggle leadership and motherhood, the first critical factor is your husband. As Sharon Meers and Joanna Strober point out in their book, *Getting to 50/ 50*, "The most important career decision you make is whom you marry."[1] Your life will be far easier and more manageable if your husband believes that your career has equal worth to his, enthusiastically supports you, and takes significant responsibility for the home front. Recent studies suggest that "the most stable high-quality marriages are those where men and women share both paid work and domestic work."[2] If you are blessed to have such a husband, you enjoy a great advantage. Most of the married leaders I interviewed said their husbands were equal partners (or close) in caring for children and household. Several had husbands or life partners who stayed home with the children or had the primary responsibility for them. Almost every married woman with children said she could not have risen as high in her firm or career without her husband's participation and support at home.

Unfortunately, not all women lawyers have such supportive husbands, but until men are equal partners on the family front, women's careers will continue to be perceived as less important than their husbands'. Some men do defer to their wives' career advancement, and a growing number of male lawyers are working part-time or dropping out of the workforce to be home with kids, but they represent a tiny number of fathers.[3] In most cases, women lawyers still shoulder the responsibility for home and family even when they work as much as or more than their husbands. There is an underlying assumption that men's primary focus is work, and that even when women share an equal career burden, they will stay in charge at home. In one study of well-educated women who dropped out of the paid workforce, two-thirds of the women cited as reasons for their decision the lack of their husbands' support for home and child care, and the expectation that women should be the ones to cut back on employment when they had children.[4]

One of the reasons that ambitious women struggle so much when they have children is that their careers play second fiddle

---

[Section 12:16]

[1]Meers, S., & Strober, J. (2009), *Getting to 50/50: how working couples can have it all by sharing it all.* (New York: Bantam Books).

[2]Coontz, S. (2009), Sharing the load, *The Shriver Report*, http://www.awomansnation.com/marriage.php.

[3]Chen, V. (Oct. 2009), Paradigm shift: power-lawyer mom, stay-at-home dad, *The American Lawyer.*

[4]Stone, P., & Lovejoy, M. (2004), Fast-track women and the "choice" to stay home, *Annals of the American Academy of Political and Social Science* 596, 62–83, cited in Ely & Rhode (2010), Women and leadership: defining the challenges.

to their husbands.' A study of law firm lawyers conducted by the
MIT Workplace Center found that 74% of male partners described
their spouses as being less committed to their own careers, but
only 57% of female partners described their spouses as being less
committed to their own careers.[5] If a couple decides that one of
them should spend more time at home and less at work, it is
invariably the mother who works less and seeks fewer promotions at the office. This is a reasonable choice if the woman is not
passionate about her career and she and her husband agree
together that his career should take priority. However, many
women's careers lose status by default; they believe that it is
expected of them, or they feel so exhausted by having to do
everything that they give it up.

If your career is important to you, and if you want to become a
leader in your profession, then you have to make that clear to
your husband. Otherwise, he may assume that your career commitment is lukewarm and that he is the one whose career should
come first. When you discuss it, you may find that he underesti-
mates how important your career is to you, or that you overestimate how much time and effort he wants to devote to his. You
may also realize that there are many possibilities that will satisfy
both of you, whatever your respective career goals are. Whatever
you decide, once you are in agreement, you can make suitable arrangements for childcare and home responsibilities. The important thing is that both of you have to be forthcoming about your
career goals and make these decisions together.

Preparing for this conversation will force you to come to terms
with your priorities. Once those are clear to you, you need to reconcile them with your husband's priorities. Each couple needs to
work out their own way to approach what has to be done to
pursue two careers and still keep their home and family life
functioning. The key is for both of you to feel that you have equal
ownership, input, and responsibility. This requires sitting down
together to figure out how you will equitably share home and
family obligations. You have to be ready for the unexpected, e.g.,
who will do what when both of you have to be out of town and a
child gets sick, or when the nanny unexpectedly quits. Developing a plan together reinforces your mutual respect for each other's
careers and outside obligations, acknowledges that you both may
have to make compromises, and lays out some of those compromises in advance.

---

[5]Harrington, M., & Hsi, H. (2007), *Women lawyers and obstacles to leadership: a report of MIT workplace center surveys on comparative career decisions
and attrition rates of women and men in Massachusetts law firms*, MIT
Workplace Center.

As the conversation progresses, you and your husband or partner may have to deal with assumptions about your proper roles as parents and spouses. You may feel that it is your responsibility as a wife to do all the cooking, cleaning, and child care. Your husband might feel that he has to work extremely long hours, earn a large income, and place his career ahead of his family. These assumptions are based on the social roles and expectations that you both have internalized. Trying to conform to them can impose unreasonable pressure on you when your long-held assumptions and your real-life demands come into conflict. To illustrate, let's say you believe that being a good parent means giving your children well-balanced healthy dinners. However, you travel a lot, and your husband serves the kids pizza most nights when you are away. You can deal with this conflict in several ways: stop traveling so much; accept that your husband is doing the best he can and that the children will do just fine; cook wholesome meals and freeze them so he can serve them when you are gone; or hire a cook or home delivery meal service.

If you don't reconcile your assumptions with the constraints that life presents, they can be a continuing source of friction and stress. It is important for you to confront those assumptions and the pressures they impose on you. The key is to put the conflict into perspective. *(How important is it, really? Is it worth stressing over?)* Then try to resolve it in a mutually agreeable way. If you and your husband do not challenge your respective assumptions and resolve the conflict, you will have a hard time fashioning a workable plan for managing your home and family. Unlike the number of hours in a day, your assumptions are not immovable limits but *choices*, and choices can be changed. Choosing to accept new views and attitudes may be hard at first but can ultimately be liberating.

This discussion can provoke deeply felt emotions. As you talk about these things, don't be surprised if you experience some disturbing feelings and disagreements. One or both of you may feel overwhelmed, stressed out, guilty, disrespected, or misunderstood. Some people are tempted to avoid bringing up these feelings but that will cause more distress down the road. These issues need to be addressed openly and dealt with before an unplanned event comes up. That is one of the reasons you want to start having these conversations early and keep them going.

Ideally, this conversation should start before you have children and continue indefinitely, because circumstances and priorities, at home and at work, change over time. If you are discussing

these issues for the first time when you get pregnant, or after
there has been a major change at work or in your home situation,
the added stress may complicate the conversation.

There are many aspects of home and family life that ought to
be included in your discussion. Aside from caring for children and
running your household, you and your husband or partner may
have ailing parents, spiritual needs, community commitments,
and other priorities that require your time and effort. Table 12.3
lists some questions to help you examine your needs at home and
develop systems for dealing with them.

**Table 12.3. Questions for developing a home and family
management plan**

- What are our needs? How are they being met now? Which
  are not being met?
- What future needs should we plan for?
- What is each of us contributing to the family? To the
  household?
- How much time is each of us spending in each category of
  family and household activity? How could that time be re-
  allocated?
- What do we want to keep the same?
- What do we want to change?
- What would each of us like to give up?
- What would each of us like to do more of?
- What would be a better way to do the things we are doing?
- Who else could do some of these things instead of us?

As you consider these questions, you may decide to make some
larger changes than you anticipated. You might decide to take
turns making career a priority, or one or both of you might reduce
your hours or take less demanding jobs. You might decide to
move closer to family members who can provide regular or emergency child care. You might put a priority on finding time for
yourself or to be with your partner. There are all sorts of possibilities once that conversation gets going.

The outcome of your discussions should be a plan. As you go
through the planning process, remember this: whatever you plan
will not be perfect. No matter how well you plan, each of you will
run into occasional conflicts. Things will go out of whack from
time to time. Plan the best you can and be prepared for the
unexpected.

The plan should designate how much of your time and energy
will go into work, family, household chores, and other aspects of

your life. It should allocate responsibilities and address contingencies. It should also identify resources that you can rely on to meet those responsibilities. There are private and public resources that will make it easier for you to carry out your duties at home and at work. You cannot do everything that has to be done, even if you and your husband are both actively involved. So learn what is available and how they can help you. Aside from family and friends, those resources include:

- Nanny and child care services
- Day care centers
- Child care exchanges and cooperatives
- Sick child care companies
- Employer-provided benefits, such as on-site and emergency child care
- Health and family counselors
- Networking and support groups for working parents
- Take-out and food delivery services
- Online vendors for everything
- Cleaning services
- Bartering networks

Familiarity with these resources is especially important for single mothers and mothers of chronically ill or special needs children. Juggling work and family is harder when you are on your own or when your family requires extraordinary attention. It is vital to have a system of family, friends, or caretakers in place to back you up when work and family demands conflict.

You will always be juggling too many balls, and while you may be able to keep them in the air, you will probably never achieve a sense of balance. The greater your ambivalence about the choices you have made the more difficult the juggling process will be. Ambivalence will keep your guilt level high and your commitment—to work, firm, and family—in doubt. You can clear away a great deal of that anxiety and guilt by being clear about your values and priorities. Clarity does not necessarily mean certainty or permanence and you will periodically run into conflicts that make you question your choices. However, feeling centered, knowing that you have made a definite choice based on the things that are most important to you, and communicating your priorities to others will enhance your effectiveness and save you a great deal of unnecessary anguish.

The experience of the leaders I interviewed who were mothers bears this out. Almost every one of them said that she made family her highest priority. These women were often pulled away by work demands but never lost sight of what mattered most. They chose to be lawyers and leaders as well as mothers, and worked hard at managing all three roles. One of the leaders said: *"I have two girls, 13 and 11. My career is my "third girl." I give them all what they need at different stages. I plan my career the way I plan my parenting. It's the only way to do all I want to do."* Another leader explained: *"I carefully choose what I want in my life. If it detracts from billable work or kids, it's because I want to do it. I don't feel guilty about it. When my children were young, I made sure there were no seconds wasted in my day. I put myself in the mindset that I can't do everything so my choices have to be careful. My husband is the same way. He is very engaged and flexible."*

While the majority of the leaders who were married had very helpful mates, several managed without a husband or partner or with a husband who did not share the work at home. Those women had more constraints and fewer options because they bore greater responsibility for both home and family. Some were single mothers at some point in their lives because of divorce, or a husband's death, or because they adopted children without marrying. Some had husbands with extremely demanding schedules who did little to help at home or with the children.

All of the women with children were extremely well-organized and resourceful, and few felt guilty about their demanding work commitments. They were proud of their careers and believed their work to be an integral part of who they are. Whether or not they had family-centered husbands, all who had children had a support structure at work and at home made up of family, friends, or hired assistants to help them deal with the stresses of leadership and the demands of the household. This support network allowed them to attend to their career, work, and leadership responsibilities with relatively little guilt, disorder, or stress.

APPENDIX A

Summary of My Leadership Vision: _____

Ultimate Goals/Objectives:
　1: _____

| | **Time Frame:** |

Interim Goals/Milestones:
　　　a.
　　　b.
　　　c.

　2: _____

| | **Time Frame:** |

Interim Goals/Milestones:
　　　a.
　　　b.
　　　c.

　3: _____

| | **Time Frame:** |

Interim Goals/Milestones:
　　　a.
　　　b.
　　　c.

_____

Additional Considerations:
Time Frame:

People who will help me:

How and when I will enlist their help:

Resources or experiences I will need:

How and when I will obtain these resources/ experiences:

Chapter 13

Personal Power

KeyCiteᴿ**:** Cases and other legal materials listed in KeyCite Scope can be researched through the KeyCite service on Westlawᴿ. Use KeyCite to check citations for form, parallel references, prior and later history, and comprehensive citator information, including citations to other decisions and secondary materials.

---

§ 13:1   Claim your power and your pay

For both men and women the first step in getting power is to become visible to others, and then to put on an impressive show.

—Justice Sandra Day O'Connor

Power and leadership go hand in hand. You cannot be an effective leader of others unless you feel powerful, are perceived as powerful, and act as if you are powerful. Many women view power as corrupting but power is a critical ingredient of leadership. Just as there is no inherent vice in having power there is no virtue in being powerless. If you want to influence change you have to collect power and use it responsibly. You have a great deal of unrecognized and untapped power within you. If you do not accept and make use of your power you will not achieve your full potential as a leader.

Law firms are competitive places, so you must learn how to increase your personal power in order to look out for your own interests. Unless you have an unusually devoted and powerful champion, no one else in the firm is looking out for you. Even in the most collegial firms, partners constantly compete against each other for their share of the pie, whether it is attention, office space, personnel, resources, or money. In that competitive environment, if you do not stand up for yourself, you can easily get lost in the crowd. You must determine what you want and speak up about it so that people know and can help you get it.

You must be especially bold when it comes to clients and money. You will not be influential or powerful if you do not insist on being included in business opportunities and on receiving appropriate credit and compensation for your successes. In order to get the compensation you deserve, you need to understand how the compensation system really works in your firm and how you can make it work for you. You also need to know what you are worth, ask for it, and get it. Many women leaders who are excellent negotiators for their clients find it very hard to negotiate on their own behalf especially when the issue is money.

As the old adage goes, if you don't ask, you won't get; and we know that women don't ask. Whether it is for client responsibility, promotions, credit, or money, well-educated, high-achieving women fall behind because they do not ask for what they want and deserve. In part, this is because women have a lesser sense of entitlement than men do to positions and rewards of leadership. However, it is also because women pay a heavy price when they do speak up. Research shows that women who try to negotiate for more money are penalized by men and women alike when they do.[1] In those circumstances, women's reluctance to stick their necks out is a reasonable response to a potentially harmful situation. As a result of these social risks, women do not engage in the self-promoting behaviors that are critical for becoming and performing as leaders, and they do not negotiate for better advantage. While there are, of course, exceptions, this behavior pattern is one of the most pervasive barriers that women must overcome if they ever hope to move into leadership.[2]

Do not confuse asking for what you want with asking for permission. The former comes from a position of strength; the latter suggests a sense of powerlessness or dependence. For example, a department chair in London described how men in her office felt entitled to an increase in status while women

---

[Section 13:1]

[1]Bowles, H.R., Babcock, L., & Lai, L. (May 2007), Social incentives for gender differences in the propensity to initiate negotiations: sometimes it does hurt to ask, *Organizational Behavior and Human Decision Processes*, 103.1.

[2]Babcock, L., & Laschever, S. (2003), *Women don't ask: negotiation and the gender divide* (Princeton: Princeton University Press).

timidly sought permission for the same thing. She explained that after five or six years in her firm, associates informally become known as "senior associates." *"Men decide when they will use it as a title. They just do it by signing their e-mails or letters 'senior associate.' Women always ask first. One woman 6 1/2 years out asked if it was okay. She saw a more junior man doing it and wondered if she should, too."* If you want something, inform others; don't beg or plead. Professor Cynthia Fuchs Epstein once urged women to claim their power and assert it by remarking: "I don't know how you make change by saying, 'Pretty please, may I have more rights?' and batting your eyelashes."

Studies repeatedly substantiate that men are more likely to ask, demand, and bargain for what they want, while women expect, demand, and accept less:

- Male partners exaggerate their achievements in "brag memos" to compensation committees. ("The client would not have come here but for me.") Women's memos are self-effacing and modest about their accomplishments. ("I couldn't have done it without my team.")
- Male partners treat "no" as the opening of a negotiation and persist until they get more. Women partners accept it as a final answer and make do with less.
- Men ask for substantial bonuses. Women do not specify an amount at all, relying instead on the compensation committee to decide on a fair amount.

The experiences and observations of the leaders I interviewed substantiate these behavior patterns:

- From a managing partner: *Men would line up outside my door to tell me what they wanted, what they expected from me. Women never did.*
- From a department head: *Women are willing to do what they're asked to do rather than give orders. They want to get things done. Women take on the role of doers rather than leaders. They volunteer to be the dishwashers rather than entertaining the guests. As they become more senior, this means they are not perceived as the person who can lead. So they lose the opportunity to be in the front room.*
- From a practice group leader who sets compensation: *Many men have asked me for bonuses and level increases and to be double bumped in the associate ranks and in our partnership track. No woman, save one this year who read the book [Women Don't Ask], has ever asked me for double bumps or anything like that. Women also do not tend to ask to be elevated, though men will make their intentions clear,*

sometimes too clear when they couple their messages with potential consequences. So I balance that to make sure that the fact that men are asking and women are not does not create a misbalance in how men and women advance.

Some women have lower demands because they do not value or promote their contributions as highly as they should, but women are also intimidated by the resistance and criticism they encounter when they are more assertive. Rather than demanding the most or the best and run the risk of being called aggressive, strident, or bitchy, they find safety in lowering their voices and their expectations. One Catalyst survey found that 96% of female executives said it was critical or fairly important "to develop a style with which male managers are comfortable."[3] By trying to avoid disapproval and protect themselves, women lose out on chances and rewards that they deserve.

Women could and should ask for so much more, including credit for the work they do. They should ask for more income, a bigger office, a larger team, an increased marketing budget, just to list a few. Instead of settling for the satisfaction of a job well done, they should take the credit and cash they have earned. Women do not want to be viewed as pushy or ungrateful, so they come up with many reasons for not asserting greater demands: "it was not that important to me," "it does not fit my self-image," "people may disagree with me or dislike me," or "it doesn't matter anyway." However, by failing to ask, they lose out on a lot of benefits that men enjoy, and they make extra work but less money for themselves.

§ 13:2 Advocate for yourself

A woman with a voice is by definition a strong woman. But the search to find that voice can be remarkably difficult.

— Melinda Gates, *The Gates Foundation*

Women struggle with self-advocacy. Self-promotion may be hard for you, but you must do it to protect and advance your interests. If you are called a braggart or prima donna (or worse), it is a small price to pay for controlling the direction of your career. If you do not promote yourself, the consequences can be far worse. You will be underappreciated and overlooked for important business, leadership, and career opportunities. One

---

[3]Catalyst (1996), *Women in corporate leadership: progress and prospects.* By 2004, this number had dropped to 81%, but was still significantly higher than men at 39%. Catalyst (2004), *Women and men in U.S. corporate leadership: same workplace, different realities?*

leader I interviewed explained how hard it was at first for her to self-advocate. She was *"not raised to be a squeaky wheel and had to find a fine line between being noisy enough to get what I want versus a bitch on wheels."* However, she learned that to get where you want to go in the law firm, *"You need to push hard and say look at me!"*

You cannot assume that people know your achievements, expertise, or why you would make a great leader. All the partners in your firm are presumably smart, talented, and successful lawyers, so what distinguishes you from the others? How can you impress that distinction on them so they remember you for a new business lead or a new leadership opening? If you do not let people know your talents, successes, and commitment to the firm, you may never get called when those opportunities come up. Besides, your successes and enthusiasm benefit the firm. Why hide them?

Let decision-makers know as early in your career as possible that you are interested in leadership. Clearly state what you want and why. Otherwise, people may not realize what your ambitions are. When people know exactly what you want and understand why you should have it, they often will give it to you or help you get it. It is never too soon to ask for responsibilities that will let you prove that you have the potential and desire to be a leader. If you are an associate, let your supervisors know and ask them for advice and support. If you have a mentor or work with a partner or coach on a development plan, include leadership aspirations in the discussion of your goals. One young African-American partner told people from her fifth year on that she wanted to be a partner. She was taking a chance by being so candid because she might not have made it, which to her would represent failure. However, she felt that it was important to take that risk. Another leader who wanted to be her firm's managing partner went to the chair of the firm and told him that when the current managing partner stepped down, she wanted his position. For both women, letting their ambitions be known paid off.

If you have your eye on a particular leadership role, let key people know and position yourself for it. Review your firm's written succession planning process and see what you need to do to be considered for the position. If there is no written plan, find out how the selection process works, what unwritten rules apply, and who will be in charge. Talk to the people who will make the selection to find out what they are looking for. Do not assume that decision-makers know your talents, experience, or interest. If you have expertise that is relevant to the job, tell them. Make sure they know what you are good at, what you want, and why you

are the logical choice for the position. If they will not be making
the appointment for a while, remind them from time to time of
your interest. Make it part of your strategy to enlist the support
of other people in the firm who can put in a good word for you
with the decision-makers.

This advice comes with a caveat. Saying openly that you are
interested in firm leadership may backfire. In some firms, anyone
who expresses an interest in leadership, especially a high-level
position, is immediately deemed suspect. Partners see you as
power-hungry or having a personal agenda that you intend to
foist on them. In other firms, it is acceptable, advisable, or even
expected to announce your leadership interest. Consider the
culture of your firm and decide whether it is prudent to pursue a
position openly, or if you need to use a stealth approach, recruiting allies who will help you build support behind the scenes. This
is where being politically astute and connected is especially
important.

Many women undermine their own leadership prospects by
undervaluing their talents and abilities. They have a tendency to
see themselves as less qualified for key leadership positions than
men see themselves. Internal research at Hewlett Packard found
that men applied for available positions when they met 60% of
the qualifications, but women applied only if they met them
100%.[1] Similarly, Lloyds TSB found that although female employees were eight percent more likely than men to meet or
exceed performance expectations, they tended not to apply for
promotions.[2] Never assume that you are not ready for a position
or that decision-makers will not pick you for it. Have more faith
in yourself. Picture yourself in the role and make the case for
why you belong there. Leadership jobs in law firms rarely require
any specific qualifications. While it would be preferable if law
firms expected their leaders to have certain traits, knowledge, or
experience, as we have seen, this is not the case. All the more
reason for you to ask for positions that interest you and which
you think you would enjoy and be good at. If you are not selected
this time, your chances will be better when the position opens up
again.

Do not undersell your abilities, as many women do. When you

[Section 13:2]

[1]Desvaux, G., Devillard-Hoellinger, S., & Meaney, M.C. (Oct. 2008), A
business case for women, *McKinsey Quarterly*.

[2]Desvaux, Devillard-Hoellinger, & Meaney (Oct. 2008), A business case for
women.

speak of your accomplishments and ambitions, be definitive. Do not "soften" your comments or try to minimize your achievements. If you know something, say so; don't preface it with "maybe" or "I think . . ." If you want to acknowledge others who help you, that's fine, but don't give them undue credit or play down your role. If you did something noteworthy, take pride in your achievement and claim it as your own. Alex Tosolini, General Manager of Procter & Gamble in France, once gave this advice to a group of women: "Strive to be arrogant, because you may *just* succeed in coming across as confident."[3]

A variation of self-advocacy is standing up for yourself when you are treated badly. Too often, women put up with unfair treatment and don't fight back. A good example was related by one of the women I interviewed. The chair of a small practice group in her firm received a phone call one day from a management committee member asking how her new co-chair should be introduced to the firm. Until that moment, she had no idea the firm had hired anyone in her department, much less made him co-chair. Her reaction was disbelief, disappointment, and betrayal; but she kept those feelings inside. Rather than get angry and speak up, she took what the firm dished out because she did not want to make a fuss. As a result, she let herself be marginalized in her own group. She proved the point of Hastings Law Professor Joan Williams' admonition that "It's better to be a bitch than a doormat."

Two of the interviewed leaders described situations where they spoke up, and it paid off:

- *I suggested starting a patent group. A partner wanted to bring in laterals to do it and I thought "Why do that, why can't it be me?" I can speak up and brag about business without problems, but it's hard for me to promote myself within the firm. But I did it and I made our patent group happen. It was my idea and my work.*

- *They do not think of me as often as their male colleagues, even when it's my specialty. Three of my partners planned a panel and did not include me. I was furious. The panel was for a business development effort in my area. I went to the men and said, what are you thinking? In the end, I chaired the session. I had to speak up. I can do it more now, as I've become more successful. I'm more comfortable with who I am.*

---

[3]Wittenberg-Cox, A., & Maitland, A. (2008), *Why women mean business: understanding the emergence of our next economic revolution* (John Wiley and Sons), 265.

§ 13:3 Push your way into client opportunities

Most economic fallacies derive from the tendency to assume that there is a fixed pie, that one party can gain only at the expense of another.

— Milton Friedman

One of the most common complaints among women lawyers is being left out of client pitches and other business development activities. It is maddening to women when men exclude them from client events. It is especially irritating when the women are experts in the field being discussed or have pre-existing relationships with the client. You can chalk it up to unconscious gender bias and men being more comfortable with other men. However, a key factor is also the competitive environment within law firms for clients. Men are more likely to recognize the competition and fight for potential clients. If they see women as a threat (and they see anyone competent and engaging enough to attract the client as a threat), they will leave women out of the picture to increase their advantage in landing the client. This is less of a problem in law firms where the compensation system encourages teamwork and credit sharing. However, even there, in today's economic climate where the competition for business is extreme and getting worse all the time, lawyers—especially male lawyers—are fierce rivals when it comes to bringing in business.

As women increase their personal power in law firms, men start to feel threatened. In particular, some men believe that their business interests are at risk when corporate and law firm diversity programs appear to favor women. Whereas some men recognize that greater diversity is a way to increase the whole for the benefit of all and are supportive of women's efforts to become rainmakers, others treat all business development as a zero-sum game and believe that women's advancement will come at their expense.[1] In reaction to this imagined loss, some partners deliberately interfere with women's business development by trying to prevent women from getting the business they originate or by sabotaging women's client relationships or the matters they bring in.

Recent research shows that an increase in the number of women moving into leadership often creates a backlash against

---

[Section 13:3]

[1]Prime, J., & Moss-Racusin, C.A. (2009), *Engaging men in gender initiatives: what change agents need to know*, Catalyst.

women.[2] When men feel that their advantaged status is threatened by the rising number of women leaders, they take steps to protect themselves and hold on to key decision-making positions. They perpetuate and reinforce processes to ensure that they keep the top positions. Consequently, even when women dominate an industry in the middle ranks, "massive favoritism" toward men keeps women out of the highest leadership levels.[3]

The leaders I interviewed gave numerous examples of being excluded from client pitches. Many were willing to give men the benefit of the doubt and assume their exclusion was inadvertent. When they called it to the men's attention, there were apologies and occasionally, invitations to subsequent business and client events. In some cases, however, the exclusion was deliberate. In one egregious case, men who had deliberately excluded women from their pitch team bragged publicly that they were able to get business from a woman corporate counsel, thereby "proving" that they did not need to include women on their team.

Competition for clients is not exclusive to male partners. Women can be fierce competitors, too. Like men, they want to protect their turf. Many women thrive in an eat-what-you-kill environment. They exclude other women from business development activities, frequently out of the same desire as men to get full origination credit or hold the primary relationship with the client. When this happens, it can be more frustrating because women expect women to support each other, especially in this critical activity. However, internal competition will remain a problem, harming all lawyers and the firm as a whole, so long as the rewards of practice are premised on individual rainmaking.

If your firm supports internal competition, either overtly or indirectly through its reward system, you will need to steel yourself against the competition and meet it. You can be tough without being cutthroat, but you will have to promote and protect yourself. Linguistics professor and writer Deborah Tannen warns that failing to assert and protect your power can cause you to lose it: "Wearing the mantle of authority lightly allows it to be more easily pushed from your shoulders."[4]

Whatever system exists in your firm, make sure you are included in client pitches. Let people know not just that you *want*

---

[2]Howard, A., & Wellins, R.S. (2009), *Holding women back: troubling discoveries and best practices for helping women succeed*, Development Dimensions International, Inc.

[3]Howard & Wellins (2009), *Holding women back*.

[4]Tannen, D. (1994), *Talking from 9 to 5: women and men at work* (New York: Avon Books), 185.

to be included, but that you *expect* to be included. One leader stated that a male partner tried to keep her away from a client *"because he feared that the client liked me more. He kept trying to keep me away from the client but I always insisted on being included. Once he purposely neglected to tell me about a meeting with the client. I learned about it and just showed up."* If you believe you belong on a pitch team—say so. If you should be the leader of the pitch team, speak up. If you find out afterward that you were not invited and should have been, call your partners on it. Use a technique appropriate for the circumstance and the people involved. You will want to be more tactful with some people than with others because protecting the relationship with some partners, such as those upon whom you depend for work, is more important than one missed event. However, you still need to let that partner know that you expect to be included next time; otherwise, you may be overlooked again. You have to be vocal and memorable so that the partner will remember you when he or she is planning the next business development activity.

When you are in leadership, you can use your position and authority to prevent the exclusion of other women from business development activities. Several of the leaders I interviewed did just that. Two of the women were in charge of diversity efforts in their firms. They monitored the teams that responded to requests for proposals or met with potential clients. They would call partners whose teams were exclusively white men to bring this fact to their attention; sometimes, they suggested that women should be included. Other women I interviewed were practice group leaders who monitored budgets and plans for business development activities. When they did not see women on client pitch teams, or if the marketing budget for an event was being spent on male-oriented activities such as golf outings, they would contact the lawyers involved to note that fact and suggest that women be included or that other activities be added.

§ 13:4 Ask for clients from retiring partners

Client relationships are the most valuable currency in a law firm. Whenever you can become the partner responsible for a client relationship, you enhance your value to the firm. Aside from the economic benefit to you, controlling lucrative client relationships increases your chances for leadership. Most business development initiatives are directed at bringing in new business, but in most corporate law firms, 80% of new legal work comes from existing clients. One important source of client relationships materializes when partners in the firm retire. Typically, a retiring partner passes along or hands off client relationships to other lawyers in the firm. Today, more than 60% of law firm partners are 55 years of age or older. Although the recession has delayed retirement plans for many of them, we can expect to see an avalanche of baby boomer retirements in the years ahead. Those retirements will create openings for new leadership and a need to transition clients of retiring partners to the next generation of leaders. You want to be in a position to take over some of those clients when the time is right.

Formal planning programs for client transition have been shown effective in helping women advance into leadership by reducing the degree of unconscious bias about performance and leadership and by treating men and women equally.[1] However, few law firms have such programs in place. If your firm does, then learn how it works. If there is no system, suggest that the firm start one. In the meantime, when you are aware of senior partners who might soon be retiring, and they have clients that you want to take charge of, ask the senior partners about their plans for those clients when they retire. Start the conversation with the partners long before they are prepared to leave; the transition process may take many months or even years for large clients. Be very tactful in approaching senior partners. Tell them that when they are ready to start transitioning their clients, you are interested in being considered. Assure them that you are not trying to move in on their clients before they are ready to leave. You simply want to let them know now that you are interested, so that whenever they start to think about nominating a successor, you will be considered as a candidate.

Without a client transition system or constant monitoring of partner retirements, clients will continue to be passed along from one man to another. Retiring partners, who are predominantly white men, are likely to assume that "since the client likes me, the best partner to take over my client is someone like me." They may assume that the client (also likely to be a man) will relate better to a man and may not automatically think of you for the job, even though they know that you work on the client's matters and may have a strong relationship with the client.

If you have earned the status of relationship partner, you may need to protect that status rigorously. If you have any reason to believe that the retiring partner seems inclined to give the client to someone else, you have to assert your right and fight for what's yours. Like you, other partners will want to step into the retiring

---

[Section 13:4]

[1]Howard & Wellins (2009), *Holding women back.*

partner's shoes; you have to protect your interests by proving to the partner that you are the best person for the job. You have to remind that partner that you are recognized by the client, informally if not formally, as being responsible for the client relationship and why that relationship should continue with you.

You may be a natural successor because of your expertise even if your work for the client is limited. You may be the best candidate because you are the leading expert in the firm on the client's industry or the client's future legal needs are expected to require your practice specialty more than those that your firm has provided in the past. If you believe that you should take responsibility for the client relationship, you will have to discuss more fully with the retiring partner why you should be selected over other partners who have closer connections to the client.

Do your homework. Find out what you can about the client's current and future legal needs, the partners now working for the client who might also expect to become the new partner in charge, and what you can expect from those rivals. Be prepared to explain your position, anticipate objections or questions, and have your answers ready. Some of the questions you should consider as you make the case for yourself are:

- Why are you the partner best able to address the client's current and future legal needs?
- How will your experience, capabilities, interests, and strengths benefit the client?
- Why are your knowledge of the client's industry and your expertise in a legal specialty important to the client?
- What outside interests and memberships do you share with the client?
- How can you describe your compatibility with the client?
- How will your taking over the relationship advance the client's desire for diversity?

Regarding the last point, clients increasingly expect their law firms to be more diverse, and many are insisting that women be placed in responsible client relationship roles. If that works to your advantage, use it to build your case.

§ 13:5 Money and credit: get what you deserve

Women (and men, for that matter) have complicated attitudes toward money. Here are a few of the things that the women leaders I interviewed said about money:

- *Power in law firms is all about money. You have to fight for what's yours.*

- *After all, it's a business, it's all about money.*
- *Passion and meaning are more important for me in my work. It's an easy trade-off for money.*
- *Money isn't important to me.*
- *Climbing the ladder is more important to me than money. I like having a sphere of influence. I need external validation of my success.*
- *I work part-time so I can control my schedule. I'm not in it for the money anyway and I have enough. I need time.*

Making large sums of money is a driving force for many lawyers. In general, money is more important to men than to women as either a motivator or a measure of success. In one study of motivation among executives, men highlighted power and money; women executives answered relationships and quality of work, and did not even rate power or money among their top four factors.[1] While men expect to be rewarded handsomely for their efforts, women expect to be treated fairly. They seem to feel embarrassed to *want* money, much less ask for it. The difference in expectations colors their behavior about money. Since the money is less important in women's minds, they accept less and don't fight as hard to get more. That is undoubtedly one reason why men make more money in law practice than women do.

In the largest law firms, fewer than one percent of the top earners are women. There is a significant disparity in compensation between men and women lawyers at every seniority level, with the greatest difference at the highest levels, where women equity partners make 88% of what their male counterparts earn, a difference of about $66,000 annually.[2] The American Bar Foundation has found that in law firms with more than 250 lawyers, women earned a median of $155,000 compared to $200,000 for men, a huge gap. Even accounting for differences in such factors as practice areas and hours worked, a significant portion of this difference is attributable to the effects of gender stereotyping.[3] However, another reason for the income disparity is that women are not direct and forceful enough in asking for more money.

[Section 13:5]

[1]Hewlett, S.A. (2007), *Off-ramps and on-ramps: keeping talented women on the road to success* (Boston: Harvard Business School Press).

[2]The National Association of Women Lawyers [NAWL] (Oct. 2009), *Report of the fourth annual national survey on retention and promotion of women in law firms.*

[3]Redhage, J. (Aug. 2009), Gender gap in legal pay the widest of any profession, *The Daily Journal.*

Making a lot of money may not matter to you personally, but it does matter if you want to be a leader in your law firm. Women do not tend to keep score the way men do. Men measure success by the size of a paycheck, office, team, or budget. They think these things are important; and if you have less than they have, they will see you as less successful, less important, and a pushover for yielding without a fuss. Praise and personal satisfaction are fine and good and may be more important to you, but you should also have the perks that mean the most to your followers, including the highest income you can get. You can turn it down if you choose, but people should know that it is yours to turn down. You should be seen as nothing less than the men's financial equal, not just because it is fair and equitable, but also because you need to do it in order to establish your legitimacy as a leader.

As a matter of fairness, if you are worth as much as they are, you should get as much as they do. It is not the amount of money per se, but your entitlement to reap the full benefits of the investment you have made in your practice and the firm. As a matter of equity, you should be getting as much as your peers with comparable practices. You should know what you are worth and avoid shortchanging yourself or accepting bias-laden excuses. You have special talents and have made valuable contributions to the firm, and they should be acknowledged and rewarded. First, though, you have to recognize your own value. Said one leader: *"I'm a regulatory lawyer. I do mostly counseling. I don't make a big splash, don't do deals, I'm not a rainmaker. I do much of my work for other lawyers' clients. It took me a long time to believe that I'm not a second class lawyer because of that. I didn't think of it in terms of how much these clients need me or the value I bring to them and the firm. My importance is tied to what clients need."*

As a matter of leadership, you should have the things that make leaders look important and powerful. Aside from its utility, money is important as a symbol. Self-effacement (*"Oh, I didn't need it. They were so silly arguing over the size of an office."*) may win you points among your friends, but not from the male partners you are trying to lead. The more you have, the higher you are in the partnership pecking order and the greater your reputation as someone to be reckoned with. The compensation committee may tell you that associates love working with you, you did a great job on a recent project, and you are an excellent firm citizen. However, if you don't get the big bonus, and your male partner down the hall does, your stature will be less than his in your partners' eyes.

Granted, women who take an assertive stance about compensation or credit are in a tough spot. Research shows that women who try to negotiate greater compensation are penalized more than men who do the same thing.[4] If women ask for a lot, they are deemed "difficult" or "overly ambitions," but if they accept less, they are considered "not tough enough" to be a leader. This is a classic double bind. You can't win either way—so choose the way that best protects your interests. Don't let yourself be pushed around. As lawyers, if you zealously believed in a cause, you would not sit back and accept an adverse ruling. You would continue fighting for your cause. You need to believe in yourself as a cause worth fighting for.

How do you do that? You have to know your worth, have facts to support it, and be thoroughly prepared to present your case in a calm and deliberate manner. The more you can substantiate your request, the harder it will be for the firm to deny that you are entitled to it. The worst that can happen is that the decision-makers will say no. They may give you reasons for turning you down, but they will know that they are undervaluing your contributions, and that you can prove it. If they do reject your request, don't take it personally; keep your cool, hold your ground, and treat it as the business transaction that it is.

Being assertive about money and credit is not about being selfish or making inflated claims for more than you deserve. Asking for what you want, need, and can justify is in your best interests personally; but it also enables you to do more for your team. If you are undercompensated, you will have less to offer the women and men who depend on you for work and rewards. However, if you are fairly compensated, you will have enough to be generous to them should you so choose.

Several of the leaders I interviewed routinely share origination and other types of credit with members of their teams. Sharing credit this way is very rare in some firms, and the leaders from those firms were actively discouraged from doing it. Partners told them: *"You should take it all—I would."* However, these women persisted. They cared more about having loyal, high-performing teams than about having the biggest paycheck. One leader said: *"I'm overly generous in giving points (credit) to junior partners. I have an easy time getting my cases staffed; everyone wants to*

---

[4]Bowles, H., & McGinn, K. (2008), Untapped potential in the study of negotiation and gender inequality in organizations, *Academy of Management Annals* 2, 99–132, cited in Ely, R.J., & Rhode, D.L. (2010), Women and leadership: defining the challenges, in N. Nohria & R. Khurana (Eds.), *Handbook of leadership theory and practice* (ch. 14) (Boston: Harvard Business School Press).

work with me. Those partners who are greedy have trouble getting junior partners to staff their cases."

Barbara Kosacz of Cooley Godward Kronish in Palo Alto explained that she tries to be fair with all her partners for a very pragmatic reason: partners need each other to serve their clients—because ultimately, it's all about the clients. Here is how she described her thinking during a program discussing compensation issues:

> *I bring in my own client—hooray! It's mine! Now who will do the work? Who will you need on your team? How will you give them credit? What if the work includes something you don't do? You have more exposure in an area you don't work in—you'll need someone to do it, but you're ultimately responsible to the client. There's more risk and more headaches. Who corrects the relationship with the client if there's an error? How will you deal with credit for that? What if I need another partner on the weekend—I don't want to be negotiating origination credit, haggling over whether they'll come in and help on a deal. I want them to do it because I asked them to, just as I would if they asked me.*

In another example of how women think differently about money than men, one of the leaders I interviewed startled the committee that set compensation by suggesting that she should receive *less* than they decided to give her. She had led a project that generated significant revenues for the firm, and they had decided to increase her compensation by a sizeable amount. She was surprised and pleased by the committee's largesse, but worried that at a time when overall firm revenues were down, it would seem unfair for her to receive so much more than other partners. The committee members, who were all men, were aghast at the request (no one had ever asked for less) but insisted that she had earned it and should accept the full amount.

Women who take the opportunity to negotiate can enlighten the men in charge about their different attitudes toward compensation. One leader made the point that women need to insist that the firm look at things like compensation through a different lens and place greater value on things that are important to women, such as teamwork and fairness. This is one way that women leaders can start to change the culture of law firms. When partners are generous and economically inclusive, the best lawyers want to work with them, and team orientation is strengthened. As more teams share credit, the "eat-what-you-kill" norms of the firm start to bend. The culture that rewards individual contributors who care only about their own clients begins to give way to one where people see clients as "firm clients" and share responsibility for client relationships among a broader base of lawyers.

§ 13:6 Know how the compensation system works

Learn how the compensation system in your firm works. Learn how it really works, not how it is described in policies or by other partners. Most of the time, unwritten rules control, and the difference between description and reality is night and day. No matter what you read or hear, find out what is truly valued, what gets compensated versus what gets praised, and who calls the shots. You need this information so that you can negotiate most effectively. You also need to know whether the leadership activities you intend to pursue will be well rewarded. If they are not highly valued or rewarded, you may change your direction, change your firm, or continue but negotiate harder to get more. When you know how the compensation system works, you can make the decision knowingly. However, finding this information is harder than you would think. Table 13.1 lists some questions to help you.

Law firm compensation systems are very complicated, and the same kind of system may have very different outcomes for lawyers in different firms. Aside from the cultural preferences and peculiarities of each firm, making decisions about partner compensation is an art, not a science, and it is influenced by economic and political considerations. Those who decide have to weigh and balance many competing factors, not the least of which is a finite sum that has to be divided among partners competing with each other to get the biggest share they can. You may not care about the biggest share, but most of your partners do—and they will try to get their share and then some. You need to watch out and protect yourself.

Firms compensate most highly the people they want to keep, and they most want to keep the lawyers whose productivity, profitablility, and value are of greatest benefit to the firm. Firms will tell you that their partner compensation criteria are aligned with the firm's core values, business objectives, and strategic goals. This normally means that the compensation system will reward the performance and behaviors the firm wants to reward because they further the firm's long-term interests. Firms that reward lawyers for referring business internally, for example, foster cross-referrals to their partners, which increases the work and revenues for everyone. However, some firms' actions undercut their stated values and interests. Their compensation systems reward partners only for their own work or invite so much haggling over credit allocation that partners tend to hoard work instead of sharing or referring it.

Table 13.1: How does the compensation system work in your firm?

• Who are the best compensated partners?
    • How would you categorize them demographically (e.g., by seniority, practice area, gender, race)?
    • Why are they awarded the highest compensation? What are their contributions to the firm?
• What compensation do other lawyers at your level receive?
    • How do their practices, clients, activities, and contributions to the firm compare with yours?
    • How do they compare to you and to each other demographically?
• Based on what you learn, what can you tell about what gets rewarded?
    • What makes a lawyer highly compensated in this system?
    • Can you jump ahead, or is it just seniority-based (i.e., lockstep)?
• Do partners understand the compensation system and how it works?
• Do partners understand how compensation decisions are made?
• Are there clear and unbiased criteria for determining compensation?
    • Are those criteria enforced?
    • Are decisions based on other factors? What are those factors?
• Do partners think the compensation system is fair?
    • Do women partners think the compensation system is fair?
• When decision-makers consider how much your compensation will be, how do they know what you have done, are currently doing, and are planning to do?
    • What kind of plan, self-evaluation, or other information, if any, are you expected to submit to them?
    • What kind of additional information can you submit to them?
• What will you ask for in compensation and other rewards?
    • How will you decide?

> - What information do you need? Where will you get it?
> - What will you expect to be asked during your compensation discussion meeting, if there is one?
>   - What should you do to prepare?
> - If the decision about your compensation does not satisfy you, what will you do?
>   - Is there an appeal process? If so, will you use it?
>   - If there is no set process, how will you negotiate for more? With whom will you negotiate?

Law firms also believe themselves to be meritocracies, where people are valued and rewarded purely on the basis of their performance; but the kind of performance they believe meritorious is often questionable. Firms frequently and generously compensate lawyers whose behaviors and activities are contrary to, and may even undermine, the firm's stated values and goals. One common example is where firms assert that one of their core values is collaboration and teamwork, yet partners with dysfunctional teams are rewarded exclusively for their individual contributions.

The dissonance between what firms say they value and what they actually reward usually has a negative impact on women. Law firms want to encourage behavior that they believe will promote their financial security and success: business origination and billings. These are obvious and quantifiable activities, which makes them easy to measure and reward. However, firms do not accord the same value, respect, or rewards to other activities essential to firm success, such as committee work, personnel matters, increasing diversity, and developing and retaining legal talent. It happens that these are areas that firms encourage women to undertake and at which many women excel. However, these activities do not translate easily into dollars, so their value is not as easily measured, and in most law firms, their importance is underrated. Consequently, women who spend a lot of time in such activities are penalized for being good at them because their contributions are not as highly rewarded as, say, billing hours. The same is true for leadership and management activities. Firms have no metrics by which to measure their effectiveness or monetary value, so they are valued less.

The problem is that very few firms articulate competencies or establish procedures for accurately quantifying and measuring the qualities and behaviors that promote their values, business objectives, and strategic goals. Without clear and open criteria, individual partners do not know what it takes to rise to a higher level of compensation nor can the firm ensure that partner evaluations are fair and equitable. Consequently, the systems are prey to bias and political manipulation, and what firms say deserves merit is often at odds with what actually gets rewarded.

Law firms employ many different kinds of systems to decide partner compensation. A few common systems include:

- *Lockstep,* where compensation is based on seniority in the firm
- *Formula-driven systems* based on objective data (e.g., billable hours, realization)
- *Competency-based systems,* in which compensation is based on a set of articulated criteria or competencies that may include any number of factors (e.g., peer reviews, firm citizenship, pro bono work)
- *Business plan-based systems,* where partners submit to the compensation committee personal business plans and self-assessments, then meet with the committee to measure performance against the plan
- *Point systems,* in which a fixed number of total points are apportioned to partners based on certain factors (e.g., business origination, management responsibilities, hours billed), with money distributed to partners based on the number of points they hold
- *Tiered systems* that place partners into tiers or bands with compensation based on the tier/band you are in (and sometimes on your position within the tier)
- *Shares-based ownership systems,* in which partners' equity interests are represented by units based on factors such as seniority and revenues generated, and each unit is given a dollar value based on the revenues to be distributed each year
- *Discretionary systems,* in which one or more partners award compensation according to their discretion.

As you can see, these systems differ in many ways, with varying degrees of flexibility, objectivity, subjectivity, and specificity. Moreover, some systems are short-term while others focus on long-term contributions; some consider only the current year's performance; some use projected contributions for the coming year and others factor in past performance using averages and trends for the preceding one to two years or more. Decision-makers might look only at individual profitability or take into account the profitability of a partner's practice group. They might consider peer reviews, upward reviews, and even 360 reviews that include input from associates, staff, and clients.

Compensation factors also become murky in firms with more than one category of partner. Most law firms are structured as "one tier" or "two tier" partnerships. There is clarity in one-tier partnerships because all partners own equity in the firm and are compensated on the basis of their equity investment. In two-tier partnerships, the majority of partners are equity partners whose capital contributions give them an ownership interest, and whose annual compensation is based on that ownership interest. Non-equity partners, who comprise the second tier, are paid a fixed annual salary and performance-based bonus. However, more than 20% of firms are "mixed tier," in that they have additional categories of partners, including equity partners who contribute capital to the firm but are paid on a fixed-income basis. In those firms, even partners in the firm may not understand how their status relates to compensation.[1]

One of the major factors that influences compensation in most systems, and which is the source of much contention, is how partners receive financial credit for work they do and the business they bring into the firm. The principal activity for which law firms give credit is bringing in new business (origination credit). Some firms give credit only for origination while others have multiple categories. Firms might give credit to partners who manage client relationships when they are different from the originating partner; to partners who "grow the business" by getting new work from existing clients; to those who manage the day-to-day client work; or for other activities that they deem compensable.

The types of credit are often unclear; they may overlap and they are treated differently in different firms. Traditionally, the lawyer who brings in a new client continues to receive origination credit for years, sometimes indefinitely, for all the work done by the firm for that client, whether or not she does any of the work herself. Other lawyers who generate new business from that same client may or may not be entitled to some origination or growth credit. In some firms, only the partner who manages the client relationship receives credit for that work, while in other firms, numerous partners might share credit for managing a single complex case or deal.

Even in the best of systems, disputes arise about how and for what activities these forms of credit are distributed. Origination credit is the cause of much wrangling. It is frequently hard to

---

[Section 13:6]

[1]Report of the Fourth Annual NAWL Survey (Oct. 2009).

determine who should get what when more than one person is
involved in some way in landing a new client. When three people
attend a pitch and all take part, or one person drafts the proposal
but does not go to the pitch meeting, or one of the three makes
the introduction to the client but plays no part in the work to be
done, the amount and allocation of credit are often subject to
dispute. In addition, people may interpret their roles in the process and those of the other lawyers involved quite differently in
terms of who did what, and what it was worth. Table 13.2 lists
questions that will help you learn how origination credit is
determined and allocated in your firm.

Table 13.2. Questions to ask about origination credit
• What form does the credit take? When do you collect? For what period of time?
• How is the credit determined for business from new clients?
• How is it determined for new and expanded business from existing clients?
• Who makes the decision? Using what criteria? At what point in time?
• How common is origination sharing? In your firm, would it be considered collaborative (and is that seen as a good thing or as naïve)?
• When origination is shared, how is the allocation of origination credit determined?
• What is the process?
• What are the criteria?
• Who makes the determination?
• How can the client affect credit decisions?
• Is there an appeals process for an unfavorable outcome regarding credit?

Firms utilize different mechanisms, such as appeals procedures
and ombudspersons, to handle disputes that arise among
partners, or when partners disagree with a committee's compensation decision. Firms prefer, of course, that lawyers work things
out on their own. Pillsbury Winthrop Shaw Pittman, for example,
encourages partners to try to resolve any disagreements by asking three questions about credit sharing on partners' self-
evaluation memos that are submitted to the compensation
committee. The memo forms ask:

• Who have you shared credit with?
• Who has shared credit with you?

• Who has not shared credit fairly?

The last question comes with a caveat: you cannot list a person you believe has been unfair unless you have spoken with him or her about it first.

The level of information given to partners about compensation runs the gamut from full transparency (i.e., all partners can see what every partner makes as well as the bases for their compensation) to none at all (i.e., the "black box" system, in which one person or a small committee decides every partner's compensation and discloses to each partner just his or her compensation amount). Black box compensation systems can succeed only so long as partners have complete trust in the decision makers and believe that they are being treated fairly. Black box systems prevent the dissension and internal competition that often result when partners compare their compensation to others' and try to pick apart the differences. This appeals to many lawyers, and the back box system is used effectively in many outstanding law firms. However, in general, the more transparency there is in a system, the better women are able to understand how it works and what they need to do to be fairly rewarded. In all systems, you need to know who makes the decisions and on what bases they decide.

In any compensation system, partners must believe that the process and outcome are fair to them. Not everyone is motivated by money, but they will be demotivated and upset (or worse) if they believe that the system treats them unfairly, or that they are being underpaid compared to their peers. The problem is that all of these systems can be—and most are—manipulated. Partners trade, share, or redistribute points or credit for political reasons; to benefit another lawyer they favor or depend on; or to keep important lawyers from leaving. Even formula-based systems usually include some wiggle room for factors like contributions to firm management. In any system that considers factors other than purely numerical data like hours and revenues, the nonobjective elements are subject to interpretation and political maneuvering. Likewise, in almost any system, powerful people may be able to influence decisions regarding their protégés or favorite lawyers. In one firm, for example, where compensation is based on a formula plus a discretionary bonus, a new member of the compensation committee was surprised that *"One partner can get a bonus of $40,000 while another only $5,000 just because of who champions them."*

That is also why you need to learn as quickly as possible how compensation is really decided in your firm. One leader described how she learned this the hard way. She was a lateral partner and a highly experienced lawyer but she had spent most of her career in a corporate legal department. No one at her new firm had told her that origination credit was determined when new matters were opened, and that she needed to check new matter memos to see what the determination was. The first time she brought business to the firm, she received no credit for it. The client was an existing firm client, but sent the firm a particular matter solely because of her expertise and effort. She learned much later that she received no origination credit because all of the credit went to the partner who originally brought the client to the firm. She did not fuss about it because she had not checked into it at the time. At a later time, she and a male partner brought in some work together. From her first experience, she knew to look at the new matter memo right away, but she did not know that the partner who opens the file gets to allocate the credit. She discovered that the male partner opened the file and took 100% of the origination credit for himself. This time she did make a fuss. He said it was an oversight and agreed to split the origination credit 50/50. The third time she brought in business, she had a better understanding of the system. She brought in the work with the help of four other lawyers. When she opened the file, she decided the origination credit—and she allocated it among the five lawyers who were involved.

§ 13:7 Know and be able to explain what you are worth

When it comes to asking for credit or money, how much should you ask for? How can you figure out the value of your performance to the law firm? How do you calculate what you are worth? These are not easy questions to answer, but there are some useful guidelines.

The case of one of the interviewed leaders highlights the difficulty of the calculation and presents an effective approach. This highly accomplished lawyer came to the Chicago office of a large law firm after an illustrious career in government and the corporate sector. Although she brought no clients with her, she knew that the firm valued her expertise and connections and believed she could attract new business. However, she was not sure how to place a monetary value on that expertise and potential when negotiating her salary. She sought advice from a large number of people in law firms, corporations, and academia. Based on what she learned, she came up with a compensation figure and a business plan that described what she would accomplish in her first three years and how she would do it. She and the firm came to an agreement and she joined the firm.

She proceeded to carry out her plan very successfully. All the while, she knew what she was earning, but wondered if it was the right amount and how she compared to other firm partners. As she proceeded to build up her practice, other partners in her practice group who were familiar with her success and her compensation arrangement came to her and told her that she should be getting more recognition and money, considering how much she was doing to benefit the firm. They offered to help her and she accepted their advice. They explained to her the factors that contributed to compensation decisions and gave her concrete suggestions, including the kinds of nonmonetary rewards she might ask for that would recognize her achievements and acknowledge her value. They also gave her some critical political advice: they told her that she was talking to the wrong people in the firm and directed her to the key decision-makers and leaders who were in positions to influence her compensation.

Her story illustrates several important points to keep in mind as you negotiate your compensation. First, do your homework and find out what others who are similarly situated are making, both in your firm and in other firms. Note that the agreements you negotiate are not necessarily permanent or final. If it turns out that you undersold yourself at the outset, or your subsequent performance warrants an increase, you should try to make mid-course corrections, as this partner did.

Second, give compensation decision-makers sufficient information about you in your annual business plan or self-evaluation to impress them with your drive, performance, and achievements. The more they appreciate how productive and valuable you are, the more likely they will be to give you what you need to become even more successful. Present as much data as you can to support your request, including what your practice looks like, how it has grown, how you have helped the practices of other partners, and the economic value of your efforts to the firm, as well as your other contributions, accomplishments, and plans. Keep it succinct but highlight the main points. Numbers will get more attention than adjectives. One thing that you might do is to demonstrate your net profitability. If your efficient management has led your teams to reduce costs and produce superior results for clients while maintaining a healthy profit margin, use that data to bolster your value. Another is to state specific business objectives that will enable you to measure the results of future efforts; you can use those objectives the following year to demonstrate how much you accomplished. Most importantly, remember that this document is about you. It is fine to tell the compensation committee how others on your teams assisted, but that should be peripheral. You did the work; give yourself the credit. If you don't, why should they?

Pulling this information together is easier if you track it as you go. Don't wait until the last minute to reconstruct your accomplishments during the year. Keep a record of your achievements on a regular basis. Every time you do something noteworthy—a successful settlement, a speaking engagement, a new client, sending business to another partner—write it down. If you are mentioned in a news article or a client sends you an e-mail praising your superior work, write it down. When you need to submit a business plan, have your annual review, or draft your compensation request, you will have all the data you need at your fingertips. You will be able to be specific and thorough and to provide metrics, which are always useful: how many trials or deals did you lead? How many new clients did you bring in, and how much revenue did they generate? How many associates nominated you for mentor of the year? Whatever data you need, you will have it. As an extra benefit, when you look at it all in one place, you will be amazed and proud to see how productive you have been, which will shore up your sense of what you are worth.

All of this information can be incorporated into your business plan, self-evaluation memo, or a separate submission that supports your compensation request. For women worried about having to promote themselves, the document helps you overcome your concern. Rather than boasting, you are simply presenting a factual record that reflects what you have accomplished and how it has benefited the firm. If you ask for a bonus, you can point out the data that demonstrates why you deserve one. You will not be in the room when others decide your compensation, so give them information that will help them make a decision that favors you because it is based on what you are contributing to the firm's bottom line and to its future. This information will also help you establish a track record. When you are a relatively junior partner, and decision-makers are not familiar with what you do, this document will be especially helpful. As they become familiar with your accomplishments over time, this document serves as a record to reinforce your professional growth and achievements from one year to the next.

A third point raised in the illustration of the lateral partner is to be politically astute. The people whom you most often ask for help may give you decent advice and feedback, but to be sure that you are asserting your compensation request in the most effective way, you need the guidance of powerful insiders who understand how decisions are made. They might be members of the compensation committee, your practice group leader, or other powerful leaders in the firm.

What do you do if you are not satisfied with the firm's decision about your compensation? Do not simply focus on what you will do next year to make more; see if you can get an increase now. If your firm has an appeal process for compensation disputes, consider using it. Approach the people handling the appeal professionally, not emotionally. State your case in a way that persuades them you are right, and they should give you more.

If your firm has no appeal process, find out how and to whom you can voice your dissatisfaction and ask for reconsideration. If you have done a thorough job in making the case for yourself in the initial round, check to see if additional data would bolster your claim, e.g., information about what your peers in other firms are making. Internally, ask mentors and other partners who are in the know for guidance. If information about other partners' compensation is available to you, you can analyze the data about what other partners with similar or parallel practices make. If there are patterns that suggest bias or unfairness you can point them out.

A less confrontational approach might be to pose questions to the decision-makers that will give your position more weight, point out any errors in their thinking, and show that you are reasonable and deserving. Open a conversation that seeks guidance and information; assume that there is no need for hostility. Ask them to explain their decision about your compensation, the factors on which it is based, and whether you are being treated fairly relative to your peers. If you are being paid less than others who are similarly situated, ask why. If it appears that you have little room to renegotiate their decision about this year's compensation, seek information about what you need to do to get an increase next year.

If they have done their homework and made a thoughtful, well-founded decision, they can give you guidance to help you get more in the future. If they cannot explain why, or give you a meaningless response ("Just keep doing what you're doing"), press for more specifics. They should be able to tell you:

- their reasoning in setting your compensation where it is
- what factors they considered
- how you compare to your peers
- what they believe you have done that has been effective
- what they believe you have done that has been ineffective
- how you can get others to appreciate your contributions to the firm

- what the firm values as worthy of being rewarded, and whether your performance reflects those values or not
- how they value your nonbillable activities and the impact of that assessment on their decision
- what kinds of goals you should be reaching for
- if you have met your goals but are not being paid enough, what else you should do
- what it takes to get you to the next compensation level

Partners running a well-managed compensation process should be able to articulate that information for you in a helpful way. If the process is poorly run, and the partners are unresponsive, you may need to use political pressure—or consider other work options. That was the choice of this leader: *When they told me my bonus was the highest of the new partners, I said it's not enough. We reached a stalemate and I waited another year. After the 2nd time I was dissatisfied, I went to the Comp Committee and presented my case. I didn't just make an abstract plea that I'm worth more. I explained the finances and economics of my practice. I told them I need to get what I'm worth.* When she did not get it, she left the firm.

§ 13:8   Ask and negotiate

Too many people let others stand in their way and don't go back for one more try.
—Rosabeth Moss Kanter

To maintain and increase your power, you must always be ready to negotiate. Compensation is not the only thing you will need to bargain for. Assume *everything* is negotiable. Any time that resources are limited or under someone else's control, you may have to negotiate to get what you need to be successful. Studies show that women miss or neglect opportunities to negotiate for things that will benefit them. If you assign a man a project, he will tell you what he needs to get it done. If he is told no, he will keep negotiating until he gets something—or he may beg off the project instead. However, women are expected to work with what they have and get the job done without excuses. A woman partner assigned to the same project may assume that she cannot get more, so she makes do with what she is given. Her team has to work harder because they have less. They are efficient and responsible, so they produce good results. They are also exhausted and frustrated. The next time this partner asks the firm for more resources, the firm will be able to point out how much she produced with less before, so she will fall into a trap of her own making. The negative outcome may also affect her personally.

One woman partner in San Francisco relayed an experience where her failure to recognize the chance to negotiate cost her dearly. As young partners, she and a male colleague did a great deal of work for a large client of one of the firm's senior partners. Under their compensation system, the senior partner received all the origination credit for new matters that the two younger lawyers brought in from that client. So she never thought she could ask, much less negotiate, for credit for the new matters that the client sent directly to her. At some point, she discovered that her male colleague was receiving partial origination credit for the new cases that the client sent to him. When she asked him about it, he was surprised to hear that she had not asked for any credit. He had simply told the senior partner that he wanted a share of the credit, and the senior partner had said OK. It had never crossed the woman's mind that this was possible. She assumed that the rules meant what they said and she accepted that. She learned her lesson the hard way. She did not appreciate the personal power she had to negotiate on her own behalf.

Your opportunities to negotiate go beyond asking for money. When you are offered a leadership position, there are many items you can negotiate, such as your time commitment, the scope of your responsibilities, and the level of staff support you will need. Think about what the job will entail, what you hope to accomplish, and how you want to spend your time. What personnel, budget, and other resources will you need to accomplish what you want? What limits and boundaries will you need in order to make it happen? These resources, staff, and limits are all subject to negotiation.

Some negotiations relate to the scope of your authority as a leader. If you are running a department or practice group you may want the authority to influence partner evaluations and compensation. If you will be chairing a key committee or managing an office, you might want to be sure that you can influence selection of committee members or your leadership team. It may also be important to clarify the scope of your authority vis-a-vis others whose activities or responsibilities might overlap with yours. If you will be running a practice group, you may or may not want total responsibility for long-range planning, strategy, and practice development for your group. Once you decide what you want, ask for everything that you think you will need. It is not a matter of being greedy. To the contrary, the firm wants you to achieve certain results and you want to be sure you have all that you need to make those results possible.

It is important to be persistent in your negotiations. Being turned away once or twice should not discourage you. If you

believe that you deserve more, whether it is more money or resources, or a leadership post, keep bargaining until you are satisfied you have reached the limit of possibilities.

The key is to decide what you want and find a way to ask and
negotiate effectively. It may feel risky, and it may require you to
get outside your comfort zone, but you must do it in order to get
what you are entitled to. Psych yourself up; do not let other
partners intimidate or bully you. As one leader said: *"If you are
feeling sabotaged, you have given away your power. Do not try to
fix it, that's putting energy into the same game. Instead, attend to
what you deserve and want."* Even if you don't get it, you will feel
better about yourself and will show them that you are willing to
push hard for what is important to you.

§ 13:9   See yourself as a leader and act the part

What we think, we become.
—Buddha

Visualize and conduct yourself as the leader you hope to be.
Visualization empowers you—and not just metaphorically.
Neuroscience has shown that you can change your brain functioning, your self-image, and your skills through "mental rehearsals."[1]
When you see yourself as a leader, you are better able to behave
like a leader and be accepted as one. If you are eager to become a
leader from the get-go, you may already have that self-image.
However, some women do not visualize themselves as leaders.
When a leadership opportunity is presented to them, they enter
into it without feeling or conveying the impression to others that
they are, in fact, a leader.

The problem, as we have seen, is that stereotypes make it hard
for women to be perceived as leaders, so you have to work harder
at creating a leadership image. Since you will be judged whatever you do, you might as well have a hand in defining that
image. Seeing yourself as powerful is central to this process.
Envisioning yourself as a leader can give you the feeling that you
are powerful—or could be with just a little effort. It enables you
to advocate for yourself and others from a position of self-
assurance and strength without making excuses for exercising
your authority. You draw a sense of personal power from knowing your own abilities and refusing to let others diminish them.

[Section 13:9]

[1]Allen, S.W., & Schwartz, J.M. (May 2007), Lead your brain instead of
letting it lead you, *The Complete Lawyer.*

When you feel comfortable with your own power, and you act as if being a leader is natural for you, you give off signals to others that you are powerful. Your sense of personal power permeates your gestures, posture, and appearance as well as how you interact and work with people.

Other people's perception of you as a leader is necessary for you to be effective in the role. People treat you differently when they perceive you as powerful. Employees and some partners will act more deferentially or politely to you. Other lawyers, however, try to test your power rather than defer to it. Partners and even associates may question your authority or ignore your instructions. You have to be able to meet those challenges confidently, without defensiveness or fear, and you are better equipped to do that when you accept yourself as a leader.

Seeing yourself as a powerful leader does not mean being condescending, bullying, or autocratic. Many leaders who try to lead through fear or intimidation are perceived to be insecure and petty. While people may obey, they do not respect this type of leader or feel any sense of loyalty to her. To the contrary, the important thing is to be comfortable in your own skin, take confidence in who you are and what you can do, and feel good about yourself as a leader. You may be uncertain about decisions you have to make or actions you have to take, especially at the beginning. That's fine. You can be self-assured without being so sure of yourself that you never have any doubts. The key is to remember that one of your responsibilities as a leader is to promote the interests and develop the talents of others in your firm. When you feel self-assured and focus on helping others rather than justifying yourself, it is easier to be more supportive and to gain the confidence and respect of the people you lead.

To build your image as a potential leader, work hard at endeavors that give you high visibility and a chance to show how good you are. Use sound judgment, cultivate your social capital, and produce good results. Become known as someone who gets things done. Reputations tend to build on themselves and a reputation for having power brings more power.[2] As word spreads that you are leadership material, your reputation will grow, and the shared and widespread view of your leadership will become the "social proof" that makes you a *de facto* leader.[3]

When creating a leadership image, you need to convey cred-

---

[2]Pfeffer, J. (1993), *Managing with power: politics and influence in organizations* (Boston: Harvard Business School Press).

[3]Pfeffer (1993), *Managing with power*, at 208; Cialdini, R.B. (Oct. 2001), Harnessing the science of persuasion, *Harvard Business Review*.

ibility and confidence. To be credible, you have to be seen as competent and professional. There are many ways to produce this impression. This is how one leader I interviewed described the way one of her partners conveys a leadership image: *"She has no problem asserting herself but does it diplomatically. She's impressive because she knows her stuff. She does not simply pose ideas, she offers alternatives. She does not hold back, but only speaks up when she has something to say. She dresses in a non-threatening way too, with softer lines, skirts, less tailored suits, lighter colors, trim looks. Is it calculated to decrease resistance when you first meet her? Maybe, but it works."*

Part of projecting credibility is looking professional. This is a surprisingly hot-button topic for women. Consultants who advise women lawyers on this subject report enormous degrees of resistance from women (mostly associates) who believe that the way they dress or look does not reflect their level of competence or ability and should not be a factor at all. Whether it should or not is beside the point. The real point is that how you look does affect the impression you make on others and how they perceive you. People are constantly observing you and making decisions about you and how they will deal with you based on those observations. When you are a leader, or if you want to become a leader, be mindful of that fact and make sure your voice, bearing, and demeanor convey the image you want them to see. If you are a trial lawyer, you know how important it is to project an image that will enhance your credibility and professionalism with the jury or judge. You do not try to be someone else; people usually recognize and reject phonies. However, you do tailor your appearance and style to the audience. The same is true for leaders. You depend on your credibility and professionalism for your legitimacy and ability to influence others, and you should give your appearance the same level of care. If you want to be perceived and treated as a leader, you have to act and look like one.

So pay attention to making a good impression and creating a positive image. Look professional in a way that engenders confidence in you from clients and colleagues. This does not mean that you need to wear makeup and designer clothes (although you might) nor do you have to wear frumpy clothes like floppy bow ties and severe suits that women lawyers wore in the past. One leader in the Palo Alto office of a national firm is very casual in the office but changes her look for business meetings. She advised: *"You have to make certain compromises to play in a man's world. You need to look professional. I wear lipstick and comb my hair when I meet with clients even if I don't in my own office. Find a level of comfort for yourself without selling your soul.*" The style you choose should reflect who you are and what makes you comfortable. You can highlight your beauty and curves, but avoid clothing that is provocative or distracts from your role; change into those clothes when you are ready to go out partying after work. Instead, wear tasteful clothing that suggests you take confidence and pride in yourself as a leader of other professionals.

You can also use your body and voice to create the image you want. For instance, you can project capability and professionalism by walking briskly and looking busy but not harried. The way you stand, sit, and move reveals how you feel about yourself; how confident you feel; and how prepared you are. If your body and posture appear grounded and stable you can operate from a place of balance and relaxation. Using strong eye contact, standing symmetrically (rather than balanced on one foot), and holding your head still while speaking can all increase your sense of authority. Use your smile, too—not a forced or flirtatious smile, but an expression that makes you seem warm, engaging, and ready to do business.

To be seen as authoritative, you have to be a noticeable presence, a person who "takes up space" in the room. Management consultant Karl Albrecht defines presence as an "inviting demeanor,"[4] a bearing that attracts attention and respect. You have probably seen women and men who walk into a room, and their aura of self-assurance causes others to notice them before they say or do anything. The way they walk and carry themselves, their engaging eyes and facial expression, and their interest in others in the room welcome people to connect with them. Compare them to the woman or man who stands still, with retracted body posture, and downcast eyes or vacant stares that avoid contact. Those people seem to be afraid of connecting.

When you are in a room or even on a conference call with others, especially if you are the only woman, try to make yourself a noticeable presence. Carry yourself with confidence. If you remain in the background, you will have no more impact than a piece of furniture. Speak up early so people know you are there; don't wait until the "right moment," or until someone speaks to you first. Let people know you are present. Do not go on at length if you have nothing important to contribute; but you might ask a question, make a brief comment, or say that you agree with someone else. Make your voice heard.

The way you use your voice can also convey an image. A voice

---

[4]Albrecht, K. (2006), *Social intelligence: the new science of success* (San Francisco: Jossey-Bass), 70.

with strong volume and resonance engenders a sense of authority while a quiet voice that sounds shaky makes you appear insecure. One leader from Atlanta discovered that her Southern accent gave her an advantage. One of her partners, a woman from New Jersey, was criticized for making remarks that others deemed insensitive. The Atlanta partner, who is very direct, realized that her Southern accent and more approachable demeanor softened her messages so that even when they said the same things, she came across as more caring than her Northern partner.

If you want to be sure that you are projecting the image you intend, get feedback from others who have a chance to observe you in different settings. Ask people you trust about how you come across to others, and whether your style, demeanor, presence, and voice are as effective as they could be. You might also benefit from a coach who can give you a more objective and professional opinion as well as specific suggestions for how to improve.

Chapter 14

Interpersonal Dynamics

KeyCite®: Cases and other legal materials listed in KeyCite Scope can be researched through the KeyCite service on Westlaw®. Use KeyCite to check citations for form, parallel references, prior and later history, and comprehensive citator information, including citations to other decisions and secondary materials.

---

§ 14:1   The interpersonal nature of leadership

The most important single ingredient in the formula of success is knowing how to get along with people.

— Theodore Roosevelt

Good leaders have strong people skills. Building and maintaining personal, trust-based relationships is a critical part of your role as a leader. You have to take a genuine interest in the people you lead, build their confidence in you and in themselves, and strengthen their commitment to engage in a common enterprise. With partners in particular, you must invest time and energy to build those relationships one at a time. They need to know that you care about them as individuals and want to help them solve their problems and enhance their careers.

Lawyers and law firms value cognitive intelligence, but in order to handle the interpersonal dynamics of a law firm, leaders also must have high emotional intelligence (EQ). Leaders who are emotionally intelligent know how to foster positive feelings in people whose cooperation and support they need and how to manage people who are embroiled in conflicts, those who make unreasonable demands, and individuals who generally make the leader's work difficult.

Leaders also have to be skilled communicators and use a range of communication techniques. One of the most important is dialogue, through which leaders have meaningful, productive, and strategic conversations with individuals in the firm. In communicating with people, what you say and how you present your message is important, but the ability to listen carefully is indispensable. Attentive listening is the single quality that leaders themselves cite as essential to being effective in the job. In addition, because you lead by influence rather than command, you frequently have to build consensus and use persuasion to win people's support, change their minds, and smooth ruffled feathers. Those skills also come into play after a decision is made or a strategy is agreed upon, for leaders then have to ensure that partners do whatever needs to be done to execute the strategies they adopt.

Much of a leader's time and energy is spent managing interpersonal and intergroup conflicts. Every organization has conflicts and leaders must be able to understand and deal with the emotions behind them. In tough economic times, the usual emotional issues are compounded by painful personnel issues, such as layoffs and compensation cuts. Leaders must be able to manage the constant tensions and clashes and, whenever possible, resolve them. Even when you have to deliver bad news, you have to be the firm's chief optimist at the same time, using your upbeat attitude to allay people's fears and keep them focused on moving ahead together. One unique conflict-management problem for women leaders is that they are often subjected to personal and gender-based attacks. Women leaders need to be able to distinguish between fair criticism and personal insults and to handle each of them appropriately.

§ 14:2 Emotional intelligence

The great gift of human beings is that we have the power of empathy.

— Meryl Streep

Emotional intelligence is a key attribute of effective leaders. Most of what leaders do involves interacting with other people: developing talent, guiding and motivating, communicating, influencing, managing conflict, fostering collaboration and teamwork, building relationships, and leading change efforts. In order to be effective in these activities, especially in the stressful environment of a law firm, you must be able to understand and manage yourself and the people you interact with. That calls for emotional intelligence.

The competencies that comprise emotional intelligence fall into personal and social dimensions (see Table 14.1).[1] Each dimension encompasses awareness and behavioral components. The personal dimension involves self-awareness and self-mastery; the social dimension entails social awareness and interpersonal skills. Emotionally intelligent leaders are able to understand and manage both their own behavior and their interpersonal relations in ways that have a positive impact on others.

Table 14.1.Dimensions of Emotional Intelligence		
	Personal	Social
Awareness	Self-awareness: Knows oneself	Social awareness: Understands others' feelings, social dynamics
Behavior	Self-mastery: Controls feelings and impulses	Interpersonal skills: Has positive impact on others

Researchers estimate that in leadership positions, emotional intelligence accounts for 90% of success. They have found that high IQ and technical abilities are the threshold requirements to obtain leadership jobs. To succeed in those positions, EQ, not IQ, is what counts: "For star performers in all jobs, in every field, emotional competence is twice as important as purely cognitive skills. For success at the highest levels, in leadership positions, emotional competence accounts for virtually the entire advantage."[2] In laws firms especially, where high cognitive intelligence is prized above all and all lawyers are expected to have it, emotional intelligence carries much more weight than IQ in determining who emerges as a leader.[3]

Most lawyers place primary importance on intellectual abilities. Their cognitive and analytical skills are finely trained to solve complex legal problems and negotiate complicated business

---

[Section 14:2]

[1]Adapted from Goleman, D. (1998), *Working with emotional intelligence* (New York: Bantam Books).

[2]Goleman (1998), *Working with emotional intelligence*, 34.

[3]Goleman (1998), *Working with emotional intelligence*, 19.

agreements. Law firms are filled with intelligent individuals who take great pride in their professional success. Yet many of the same lawyers are notoriously difficult to work with and have poor interpersonal skills. They may be successful lawyers but they make terrible leaders.

Lawyers with high emotional intelligence are scarce, especially when it comes to the social aspects of EQ, i.e., the ability to recognize emotions in others, be attuned to others' needs and interests, and respond appropriately. Women have an advantage here because they score significantly higher than men in overall emotional intelligence on three of the four categories.[4] Women have special empathic qualities and show a strong attunement to others' feelings, facial expressions, and thoughts.[5] If emotional intelligence is the primary determinant of leadership we should have far more women leaders.

On the fourth element, self-awareness, men and women score the same.[6] According to Daniel Goleman, who pioneered the concept of EQ, self-awareness is the single most important competency of effective leaders. Individuals who regularly and consistently spend time trying to understand themselves, seek feedback about themselves, and gain insight into their own emotional life have greater success as leaders.[7]

Leadership is stressful. Every day you deal with difficult people and challenging situations, and it is easy to lose control of your emotions. Some of the leaders I interviewed spoke of being verbally humiliated in public by angry partners and having to fight the urge to cry. They spoke of situations where the actions of certain partners made them furious but they resisted the impulse to lash out. In addition to being aware that emotional outbursts might damage their standing as leaders in the eyes of those who were biased against women, they also realized that it would send a damaging message to others about how to behave in such situations.

If you are self-aware, you understand your needs, feelings, moods, and drives, as well as the effect of these emotions on yourself, your performance, and other people. This awareness

---

[4]Su, L.D., & Bradberry, T. (2004), *EQ and gender: women feel smarter*, Talentsmart, https://www.talentsmart.com/media/uploads/pdfs/EQ_and_Gender.pdf.

[5]Pink, D.H. (2006), *A whole new mind* (New York: Riverhead Books), citing the work of Simon Baron-Cohen, a Cambridge University psychologist.

[6]Su & Bradberry (2004), *EQ and gender: women feel smarter*.

[7]Goleman (1998), *Working with emotional intelligence*.

enables you to take greater control over how you act and react to other people. When you understand how your behavior affects others and can influence their behavior, you can be more effective in working with them. You can become more agile interpersonally with a better sense of how to lead and how to respond in a given situation. You do not necessarily suppress your emotions or surrender to them; rather, your awareness gives you the freedom to choose how to respond, which is what self-mastery is about. It is especially helpful when you are under stress—which, as a leader, is often—so that you keep your cool rather than exploding, yelling, or breaking down into tears. When you feel afraid, upset, or angry, you can take a moment to maintain or regain your composure, then control your feelings or channel them constructively. You might still respond in a forceful way, but you do so deliberately, not reactively. Instead of slamming doors or screaming at someone who made a mistake, an angry but emotionally self-aware leader can step back a moment to calm down and decide on an appropriate course of action to deal with both the person and the mistake.

As a leader, your emotions, moods, and personality quirks affect the people around you in significant ways. Whatever you say or do is being watched—and causing reactions—in the people you are trying to lead. If you feel centered and secure, the signals that you send to co-workers will enable them to relax and go about their work even during times of trouble or uncertainty. In contrast, if you are prone to outbursts or have severe mood swings, you keep others on guard, make them wary, and engender suspicion rather than trust.

It can be especially hard to channel your feelings constructively because you often operate in "lawyer mode" and need to quickly switch gears to "leader mode." You have to remember to deal with people in the office differently than the way you might act toward opposing counsel or in front of a jury. Coming on like gangbusters may be effective when you are representing a client in an adversarial setting, but asking questions of co-workers as if you were cross-examining a hostile witness will anger your secretary, intimidate associates and paralegals, and cause you to lose credibility with your partners.

The social dimensions of EQ focus on your ability to understand and engage with other people. When you need people to cooperate with you in order to get things done, you have to be able to get along with them. The foundation for the social dimensions of EQ is empathy: the ability to see through another person's eyes and appreciate how that person experiences different people, events, or situations. With that knowledge, you can manage social encounters. Without empathy, good relationships are impossible.

Empathy is what it takes for you to anticipate, recognize, and serve people's needs. Empathic leaders are able to detect what others want and feel even if those desires and feelings are not expressed verbally. Emotional intelligence sharpens the skills that you need as a leader to comprehend the behavior and motivation of numerous diverse individuals and persuade them to join with you to cooperate for the good of the firm. All the people you lead have their own personal needs, interests, and motivations; many of them have values and opinions that differ from yours and from those of the firm as a whole. You cannot assume that everyone sees things as you do. One practice group leader I interviewed who is a real go-getter recounts that an associate once made her aware of the fact that other women were not as assertive as she was. The associate gave her the book *Women Don't Ask*. When the partner said, "But I do ask," the associate replied, "Exactly, so you need to read about how some women in your group will not."

As a leader, you are asking others to place their trust in you. In order to make your case, you must be able to put yourself in their position and understand how they see things. That is how you can know what will appeal to them, what their interests are, and how their emotions may interfere with the ability to respond the way that you would like them to. When you understand their feelings and interests, you can better frame your proposals and your responses to their reaction. This is imperative for anyone who hopes to influence or persuade others.

Leaders also need to understand people and inspire them to perform at their best. Unless you can get others to do their best, you will not be able to rely on them for high quality performance. This is hard to do if you do not understand or relate well to other people. You cannot assume that what motivates you motivates others; you cannot expect that people will perform at the same high level you do; and you need to deal with all people in the firm, even those you do not like or respect. If you do not learn to understand, develop, and inspire other people, your leadership will fall short.

Integral to the capacity to understand and be empathetic is the ability to listen, as discussed in more detail below. To listen deeply is a very difficult interpersonal skill to master, but successful leaders learn to do it well. In fact, when law firm leaders are asked about essential leadership skills, listening is almost universally cited. Listening is a critical element of one of the most important leadership skills: effective communication.

§ 14:3 Communication is key

When you talk with Mr. Gladstone, you are convinced that he is the cleverest person in the world; when you talk with Mr. Disraeli you think that you are the cleverest person in the world.

—Queen Victoria, speaking of her two most prominent Prime Ministers

Communication is the heart of effective leadership. By definition, leaders are not solitary figures. They depend on individuals and networks of people willing to accomplish an agenda, and the only way that leaders can connect with those people is by communicating. In everything they do, whether the activity is strategic or mundane, good leaders must be able to communicate clearly and productively with the other people involved.

Much of a leader's communication takes place during the daily interactions in which she works with others on firm operations, conflict management, consensus building or any of the myriad tasks involved in the day-to-day management of the firm. But leaders also communicate on a larger stage when they handle firm crises or help people deal with the uncertainty that comes with change or instability. They serve as the firm's representative when they deliver messages about the firm to their internal constituents and as the face of the firm when they speak on its behalf to the public. To fulfill their responsibilities in these larger arenas, leaders have to maintain good communications in their day-to-day interactions with people throughout the firm.

Those daily interactions help leaders to stay in touch with people and keep them apprised of developments that they should know about as they run the firm, office, group, or team. The higher your level in the leadership ranks, the more distant you are from what is happening on the ground, what people see as threatening or disturbing, and what needs they have or anticipate down the road. As a leader, you need free-flowing channels of communication in order to stay informed about what is going on in the firm. It is nice for you to hear about positive developments but critical that people bring you bad news and warn you about problems that are brewing. If rumors are circulating, you need to know about them in order to be able to counter them with the facts. If you are starting an initiative that only your inner circle supports, you need to know if disagreement is widespread. When people know you welcome this kind of information and trust you not to kill the messenger, they are likely to bring it to you early—hopefully, in time for you to turn the situation around. However, if people believe that bad news is unwelcome or that you discourage dissent, by the time that you hear about a problem it may be too late.

Leaders also need to be able to get their messages out to others in the firm in order to keep people informed about what they are doing and planning. Regularly informing people about decisions and developments that affect them personally or the firm as a whole is always good policy. People want this information. They may not read your emails or listen to your presentations, but the fact that the information is available to them signals that you are not hiding anything from them and encourages them to trust you. Especially when the firm is going through significant change, you need to explain the rationale for the change and what the change will mean for them. You need to reassure people if you can, and if the news is bad, you have to prepare them to cope with it. Delivering bad news is never easy and many people may react with anger or distress. When you have to deliver bad news, you will have greater credibility and engender less resentment, if you are open and honest with people. When you do this on a regular basis you will accumulate trust and goodwill.

It is especially important for leaders to communicate frequently and openly during periods of economic turmoil and instability. At times of heightened uncertainty, people are hungry for information about what it will mean for them. When that information is absent, gossip, misinformation, and rumors fill the void. When times are tough, people want to know what the firm will do to support them. When no one tells them, fear, suspicion, and even panic may take over. While it is tempting to avoid facing constituents when the firm is under economic pressure or facing a crisis of some sort, that is exactly when people need to hear from you the most. Your partners and employees deserve honesty. They want to know that you are watching out for them. When you are transparent about how the firm is dealing with a problem, people believe that you are treating them respectfully. You show your confidence in them by acknowledging their right to be informed. When you can explain your strategy and show them that you have the situation under control it builds their confidence in you as a leader. Even though people are worried they can stay engaged in their work without losing morale.

§ 14:4 Dialogue, listening, and questioning

Human conversation is the most ancient and easiest way to cultivate the conditions for change—personal change, community and organizational change.

— Margaret Wheatley

Leaders communicate with people all day long. Whether they engage in serious, business-related conversations or just schmooze in the hallway, they are constantly talking. One firm-wide managing partner said, *"I was hoarse at the end of each day."*

A leader's meaningful workplace communications are based on dialogue, i.e., conversing, thinking, and reflecting together. Dialogue is more than an exchange of information. It involves carefully thinking through what is being said in order to reach a new understanding. Dialogue is the source of innovation and improvement in a group, the basis for effective persuasion and compromise, and a foundation for trust-based relationships. One leader who helped carry out the merger of two large firms said that the management team spoke with almost 300 people in both firms during the course of merger negotiations and implementation. Engaging partners directly in the process made them feel included in designing the merged firm and gave them a greater stake in the firm's future success.

At its core, dialogue requires "a simple but profound capacity to listen."[1] For a leader, attentive listening involves an active effort to understand what the other person says and means and receptivity to the other person's ideas, opinions, and feelings. It creates a safe environment for deep conversations. Because it involves patience, learning, and creation of new understanding, this kind of listening is hard for many lawyers. Trained as advocates, lawyers listen competitively, searching for flaws and vulnerabilities in what others say. Lawyers exchange information all the time, but too often they merely engage in "punctuated monologues," projecting their own opinions, ideas, and arguments rather than listening thoughtfully to what the other person has to say.

Listening is a powerful leadership tool, especially in a law firm. Use it to your advantage. Your partners are probably not good listeners. They would rather present their views and argue their points at great length but they expect you to listen closely to them. Do it. While you may find it tedious it has many salubrious effects:

- People are more likely to listen to you when they believe you are really listening to them. If you listen superficially, they will do the same.
- Leaders who listen attentively empower others by making them feel that they are being heard and taken seriously. It

---

[Section 14:4]

[1]Isaacs, W. (1999), *Dialogue and the art of thinking together* (New York: Doubleday).

shows people that you respect their views and care about what they have to say. For a productive and healthy firm, people must feel that they can express themselves openly and honestly; that the firm values them and welcomes their ideas and contributions; and that you will listen to their ideas without penalty or ridicule.

- Listening helps you make better decisions. It lets people know that you are willing to consider their views, so they offer them to you. It's good to have information that supports your positions, but it is often more important to have information that refutes them. If partners believe that you have an open mind, they will give you their contrary views as well as those that conform to yours. With more complete information, you can make better decisions. In contrast, if partners believe that you are rigid and have your mind made up, they will withhold information that might make a difference in the outcome.

- Listening gives you better quality information. As a leader, you need to know what is happening in the firm and what different people are thinking and experiencing. When you listen attentively, you learn more, and the quality of your information is better. You can pick up cues that suggest that you are not getting the whole story, which leads you to dig deeper and unearth what is not being said. You can also spot hidden assumptions and clarify any ambiguity or confusion right away.

- Listening gives you a sense of which issues are most important to people and demand priority. When you are trying to build consensus, mediate a dispute, or negotiate a compromise, it is necessary to find areas of mutual benefit. Those areas become more apparent when partners talk to you about their needs, concerns, and priorities.

- Listening makes you more effective at getting your proposals accepted. When you hear what partners are thinking and feeling about what you propose, you can determine what the majority will support and how deep and wide the resistance is. Seeing your position from the perspective of others helps remove your blinders and refine your position. If there is major opposition, you can try to defuse it before it reaches a crisis stage.

- Listening helps you to find the most suitable incentives and rewards. To motivate partners, retain them, and support their development, you need to understand what drives them and what is most important to them. They will often mention things to you during conversations that indicate the kind of incentives and rewards that will inspire them.

- Attentive listening enhances your reputation as a leader. People see you as being open to new ideas and diverse points of view. Your reputation as a good listener spreads, which makes people more forthcoming with useful information. As an extra benefit, this frame of mind actually does keep you open to new ideas and new perspectives.

Another benefit of listening is that you can obtain feedback that will help you perform better as a leader. While partners may criticize freely, they are often reluctant to give leaders meaningful feedback about their performance. They rarely tell you to your face what they think. Sometimes, however, they make casual comments that give you insights into how they view your performance or effectiveness. If you are alert and listening carefully, you can pick up on them and put this indirect feedback to good use. For example, in discussions with other firm leaders, one new managing partner with an ambitious change agenda took to heart a passing comment from the partners at a meeting suggesting that she was moving too fast for the rest of the partnership. She acknowledged to herself that he might be right, so she quietly tempered her expectations and modified her plans, tackling various issues gradually rather than all at once.

Paying close attention to what others are telling you is not easy, especially when you have many other things on your mind. Because our brains process information more quickly than others can speak, it is easy to lose concentration and let our minds wander. It is very difficult to find the patience and time required for listening, given the frantic pace of your day, but listening is absolutely essential for effective leadership. Unless you listen attentively, you may misunderstand what others mean and want, and they may miss the true meaning of your message.

Attentive listening is especially important for leaders because so much of what they do takes place during conversations with partners. Law professor Jeswald Salacuse calls these "strategic conversations"[2] because they have a leadership purpose in mind: to change someone's behavior or attitude in a desired way for the benefit of the group or firm. This requires understanding the other person's interests and using techniques to shape those interests in ways that will encourage the desired action. One office managing partner who uses strategic conversations described one use of the method this way: "*Some partners need recognition or need to be included in the brain trust, so I bring them in, talk to them strategically, let them know I think they're important. It*

---

[2]Salacuse, J.W. (2006), *Leading leaders: how to manage smart, talented, rich, and powerful people* (New York: AMACOM), 34.

takes some time, but it's worth it because that way I calm the waters and win their support."

Each strategic conversation is unique, based on the individual, situation, and issues involved. These conversations are competitive because both parties seek to advance their own interests, which may be in conflict, and this requires some desired action by the other. It also makes them highly personal since they involve the participants' personal feelings and thoughts. Strategic conversations depend on choices made by both the leader and the other person, which requires anticipating the other person's possible choices, planning for them, and adapting accordingly. This means that you must be concerned with both the messages that you are giving and those that you are receiving. It also means that you must be skilled at eliciting as much information during the conversation as possible and interpreting it accurately.

The way in which you learn what you need to know in order to develop a strategy that will have the intended effect on the other person is by asking probing questions. In order to address the other person's underlying interests and concerns appropriately, you need to ask questions that will reveal what they are. Partners who may have no hesitation stating their position on an issue may be uncomfortable, unable, or unwilling to articulate the interests behind that position. It is important to ask questions in a way that persuades people to be candid and explain their thoughts. The way you phrase questions is important. Sometimes questions asking "why" can make people defensive. You can avoid this by trying to sound inquisitive or constructive rather than accusatory or challenging. Otherwise you might inhibit the person you are asking instead of getting her or him to open up to you.

When engaging in strategic conversations, listen closely to the responses you get. This requires being emotionally aware and mentally alert, paying attention to both words and nonverbal cues, and placing yourself in the other person's position to try to understand what they say, what they mean, and how they feel. It also means keeping an open mind, hearing people out without judging them, and respecting the other person's point of view when it differs from your own. Part of your objective is to understand the assumptions, experiences, and beliefs that helped form the person's position.

§ 14:5 Expression

Seek first to understand, then to be understood.
—Steven Covey

Communication involves two people: the speaker and the

listener. When you are the one doing the speaking, your concern should be ensuring that your listeners understand you clearly and accurately. This means shifting your focus from *talking* to being *understood*. You want people to understand your meaning not just hear your words. To do this well, you must understand and connect with your audience on their terms and from their perspective, not yours. You cannot assume that what you think is important matters to them or that they think about the subject the way that you do. You also need to think about how others might interpret your comments and how they will respond so that you are prepared to address their reactions. Lawyers tend to be cautious when they speak, choosing their words carefully to convey a precise meaning. As a leader, this is useful. It helps you to communicate the meaning and importance of your message so that listeners correctly comprehend what you say.

This is not an easy task, though, when listeners are busy, distracted, and may have their own agendas—or are preparing to attack yours. You cannot assume that just because you told your partners that they listened to what you said or that because you wrote to them that they read your message. As one leader pointed out, *"Just because we explained it does not mean they heard it."* It is necessary both to ensure that the word gets out to partners promptly (before it appears on Twitter and Above the Law) and to repeat it often, especially for matters of major importance. You may have to reiterate your message many times before it registers. This is especially true when people feel insecure and rumors are flying. As Terry Lundgren, the chairman, president, and CEO of Macy's advises, "The only way to address uncertainty is to communicate and communicate. And when you think you've just about got to everybody, then communicate some more."[1]

In one-on-one discussions, the more you know about the other person, the better you can adapt your style and comments to meet their needs and preferences. If the person is very logical and data-driven, you can emphasize the bottom-line facts; for those who are more intuitive or big-picture thinkers, you may want to present more context. When you know a person's inclinations, you can tailor your comments to emphasize the things they care about. When you talk with partners about a policy change, some people will want to know how it will affect their compensation, while others are more interested in the impact on the firm's

---

[Section 14:5]

[1]Carey, D., Patsalos-Fox, M., & Useem, M. (July 2009), Leadership lessons for hard times, *McKinsey Quarterly*, 5.

people, and still others are worried about how the firm's reputation will be affected. You can discuss all three effects of the policy change but you might start off the conversation differently with each person.

As a leader, you must also learn to express yourself in a tempered and constructive manner. Unlike advocates, leaders are not interested in winning or beating the other side. Their objective is to promote consensus, prevent or clean up misunderstandings, and foster cooperative problem solving. You need to be direct but tactful rather than confrontational. Rational argument, rhetoric, and even bombast have their place when you are negotiating a deal or making a closing argument. However, as a leader, you are dealing with issues involving the emotions and interests of people whom you care about personally or because they are members of the group which you are leading. You want to keep them happy, productive, and contributing to the collective good. One leader who is very involved in associate development sometimes has to talk with associates about their performance problems. She does not believe in soft-pedaling the message and tends to be quite direct. Nonetheless, she says, *"I try to judge with a kind heart,"* because she genuinely cares about them and they know it. This allows her to have tough conversations that would not be as constructive if delivered by other partners.

When presenting to a large audience, there will be many different kinds of listeners with different degrees of receptivity to your message and style. If your communication style does not register with them your message may be lost. They may become distracted by your phrasing or mannerisms rather than focusing on the substance of what you are saying. To connect with an audience, consider both your message and the way in which you present it. When you are clear about the message that you want them to take away from your comments try to find the best way that you can to present it. Choose a style that will be effective not only to get your points across but also to get your listeners to pay attention and follow what you say. Storytelling, audiovisual aids, jokes, and other techniques can be helpful if you do them well. The better you know your audience, the easier it will be to find an approach that works effectively with most of them. You may not reach everyone whose support you would like, but with adequate forethought and preparation, you can capture the attention of a wider group.

Because of gender bias, women leaders need to be especially sensitive about how they communicate to a group. Some leaders have a grand sense of style and presence; listeners become riveted with attention whenever they get up to speak. Most people, however, have to work hard at engaging their listeners. A patent lawyer who chairs her practice group, sits on her firm's executive committee, and co-chairs another firm-wide committee explains that, *"As a leader, I always think of who my audience is. As a female, I know some people will not be receptive to me in this leadership role. If I can at least get them to listen to me with an open mind, I might be able to persuade them, so I need to get their attention right away."*

In order to get their attention, you need to get them interested in your message: Why should your remarks matter to them? Frame the topic and your position in a way that highlights the advantages to them if they decide your way. Your headline and opening comments should address their questions: Why is it in their interests to do what you are proposing? How will it meet their needs or address their concerns? How will it benefit them? If you anticipate a lot of resistance, you might try out your ideas on a few people you trust before presenting them to the larger group.

We know today that decision making begins as an emotional process, not a rational one.[2] But the area of emotion is a double bind for women leaders. It is hard to calibrate the "right" amount of emotion which it is safe to show. People want to believe that you are emotionally committed to the firm and the matters that you deal with on its behalf, but they expect you to do so without being "too emotional." Lawyers are wary of emotion. They are taught to be objective, rational, and distanced from emotional involvement. Many male lawyers are especially uncomfortable around emotional women; they are bothered by women who cry or get angry, upset, or moody. Thus, if you are passionate in supporting your position, some will find your approach moving and persuasive, while others may criticize you as overly emotional or strident. Women leaders cite numerous examples where this double bind hurt women. One leader who sat on her firm's compensation committee described a committee discussion where a male partner who made a passionate appeal for his compensation was called "hot headed" but his position was taken seriously, while a woman partner who made a similar appeal made the male committee members uncomfortable and they discounted her argument. As the sole woman on the committee this leader called their attention to the apparent bias before any harm was done.

To a large extent, the degree of emotion you exhibit depends on your personality and your audience. It is prudent to adjust your

---

[2]Lehrer, J. (2009), *How we decide* (Boston: Houghton Mifflin Harcourt).

tone and demeanor to the emotional state of the group: if they tend to be good natured and jovial, a lighthearted and humorous approach might work well. In fact, humor is a wonderful tool to help you engage even a more reserved audience. Many women leaders are criticized for being too serious and having no sense of humor. If you can use humor effectively, then you should. Not everyone can. Even if you can't tell jokes, smiling frequently and laughing at appropriate times makes you more approachable and the audience more comfortable. Of course, the topic you are discussing should also determine how much emotion to express. When you bring up the new firm vacation policy, a laugh or two might be in order, but if the audience is worried about the firm's declining financial performance, they will expect you to be more serious.

If you want to improve your effectiveness in public speaking or have doubts about the way that you come across to an audience, you might consider attending a training program or engaging a coach who specializes in presentation skills.

Keep in mind that your nonverbal communication also affects your leadership. Leaders are constantly observed, and what you do, the people you talk with, what you wear, how you carry yourself, even your facial expressions, may have an impact far beyond anything you imagine. Everything a leader does is dissected to look for clues and signals. This is especially problematic when tensions are high because of uncertainty in the firm or the marketplace. When people are afraid and confused, they may interpret things in ways that reinforce their fears. A leader described how she learned this lesson. A warm and friendly person, she usually says hello to the people near her office when she arrives in the morning. One morning she arrived at work late, feeling frazzled because she had just had an argument with her teenage daughter. She went directly to her office and shut the door. It happened to be the morning after a partners' meeting where she had given the state of the firm address. Even though the firm was doing fine, people interpreted her unusual behavior as a signal of trouble and soon started a rumor that the firm was having problems.

§ 14:6 Building consensus

Leaders must build consensus among their partners for many decisions, especially those that impact firm strategy and profitability. Consensus is a preferred approach in law firms because it acknowledges partners' status and autonomy. Partners are less likely to support an initiative if the planning process excludes them or ignores their input.

Research shows that women use consensus, team building, group participation, and collaborative problem solving more often than men.[1] These techniques have been found to be more effective leadership styles than the more directive styles used by men, which sometimes hinder effectiveness. Consensus-driven methods embrace people with complementary skills that strengthen the ability to solve problems and serve clients. Social psychologists Alice Eagly and Linda Carli note that using these methods also allows women to project leadership authority while they maneuver around the double bind produced by gender bias. Instead of employing an autocratic, masculine style, women obtain results by bringing others into decision making and leading as "encouraging teachers."[2]

Building consensus among a partnership of lawyers is no small achievement. It requires a clear strategy, a vigorous but tactful approach, and great stamina. The technique involves several steps, all of which are necessary and important:

1. Articulate your objective. Be prepared to explain what you are trying to achieve, the direction you plan to follow, and what you expect the outcome to be.
2. Anticipate possible objections. Think about how you will address them. Be open to hearing objections that you did not anticipate.
3. Figure out who has an interest in the outcome. Not everyone cares about every issue, and some care more than others about particular ones. It is not always clear who expects to be consulted or included in the discussion. You need to know people's sensitivities in general and on the issues in question. Some people will feel left out, and if they are forceful enough, may derail your efforts. This is where a good sense of firm personalities and politics is critical.
4. Identify the power players whose approval is necessary for any project of this kind. They may be among the people who have an interest in the outcome or they may simply expect to be consulted and their approval requested.
5. Identify the people who share your vision and whose support you can count on. Analyze their bases of power and influence and determine how they can help you in the consensus building process.

[Section 14:6]

[1]Eagly, A.H., & Carli, L.L. (Sept. 2007), Women and the labyrinth of leadership, *Harvard Business Review*.

[2]Eagly & Carli (Sept. 2007), Women and the labyrinth of leadership.

6. Talk with stakeholders. Use strategic conversations to ask questions and find out what stakeholders think and why. Do not rely on your assumptions. Acknowledge their interests in the issue. As you listen to them, try to figure out where they are coming from, why they are reacting as they are, and what might allay their concerns. Look for ways to overcome or neutralize their objections before they become entrenched positions.

7. Learn as you go. As you talk with different people and learn their various positions, find ways to explain your position in a careful and persuasive way.

8. Make sure people feel their participation and contributions are valued and give credit to people who facilitate the process. Remember that while you work toward achieving a goal or solving a problem, you also need to minimize any adverse impact on your colleagues.

It is important to get powerful allies on board as early as possible since they can have substantial influence over others, either increasing your support or undercutting the opposition. You want to get other partners' buy-in early, too, before resistance hardens. The more disagreement there is, the longer and trickier the process will be. When resistance takes hold, objecting partners can use the consensus-building process to prevent action. Some partners may deliberately try to thwart your efforts through delay or inaction. Political savvy and persuasive powers are useful to anticipate possible subversion and to recognize and stop it should it occur.

Sometimes and on some issues, despite a leader's best efforts, the partnership cannot reach consensus and she must make a decision. When that occurs, being known as a consensus-builder can actually be a plus for you. Taking time to consult with your partners establishes your credibility and adds to your legitimacy as a decision maker. A leader in Atlanta who is vice-chair of her firm's global corporate department explained it this way:

> Being respected is important—more than being liked—and you earn respect through process and by being fair. The process may differ team to team, but when you are leading a firm of lawyers, it's important to give them a forum where they can have input and feel that you are considering their views. But at some point you have to make a decision. You cannot be too inclusive, because you may never come to an end. If decisions must be made rapidly, you might have no time for consensus, but if you have been fair and they trusted you in the past, you have a stronger base to make quick decisions on.

Many law firms are delegating greater authority to their leaders, allowing them to act without seeking approval from the partnership. The need for nimble leaders with wider authority will continue to increase as firms grow larger and as the need for rapid responses to market and client demands make consensus-building too slow and unwieldy a process. But because law firms are partnerships, consensus building will remain essential for major financial decisions and strategic initiatives.

§ 14:7 Persuasion

Integral to the consensus-building process is the ability to persuade partners to see things your way. Law firm leaders must be experts at persuasion, i.e., using their reputation for integrity, their sense of conviction, and their empathy, as well as reason and logic, to gain acceptance and cooperation from others. Leaders need to convince people to accept new ideas, take responsibility for carrying out projects, and be enthusiastic about efforts that will help the firm progress and succeed. But what if partners do not buy into your ideas, if they resist a new initiative, or if they think a project is fine but give it such low priority that it never happens? How does a leader get partners to do things that they do not want to do, such as implement the practice group's business development strategy, serve as mentors to associates, or provide materials and data for the new knowledge management system? Unlike corporate leaders, who can issue directives and assume others will carry them out, a law firm leader must rely on more subtle techniques to move partners to act.

It is through persuasion that leaders get people to decide or act in the way that the leader wants them to. You are professionally trained to advocate and negotiate, so certain persuasive techniques may come easily to you, but persuasion in the courtroom is not the same as persuading your partners to accept an expensive long-term investment in a new pro bono case or to open a new office in a down economy. As a law firm leader, you need to inspire your partners to advance the good of the group even when it may seem counter to their own interests. Aristotle's *The Art of Rhetoric* sets out the three basic building blocks of persuasion: emotion, reasoning, and credibility. A persuasive appeal uses all three of these elements to connect with the audience, whether a group or an individual.

The default mode that most lawyers use skips over emotion to rational argument based on facts and logic. As a leader of lawyers, however, your ability to persuade depends on more than that; you may present brilliant arguments yet miss the mark completely. You must remember the need to connect with people on an emotional level, too. Some people will be moved by reasoning, but for others, stoking an ego or engaging them in joint problem solving may be more effective. Some will care deeply about a project that will add luster to their legacy, while others have only short-term self-interest at heart. Once you understand what's important to them, you can select a suitable strategy.

When a persuasive leader wants to change someone's mind, she will appeal to the person's wants, needs, and experience, as well as their reason. Her pleas are personal and genuine, expressing her own strong commitment to the subject. Her mastery of the subject and reputation for integrity and honesty make the other person more willing to consider what she proposes. She engenders a sense of common purpose that makes the person feel more receptive to the idea of something new or different. Once someone is receptive to the idea in the abstract, they are more willing to hear the facts and logical reasons that support the desired change. They will then listen to the leader make a case for the proposal by presenting the idea's benefits and advantages and the underlying data and analysis to support them.

There are countless strategies for trying to persuade partners to accept your position. Some of them are listed in Table 14.2.

Table 14.2. Selected Persuasion Strategies
- *Advocacy*: Present reasoned arguments for your position
- *Equity*: Appeal to sense of fairness
- *Greater good*: Do it for the collective good of the firm or a particular group
- *Legacy*: Appeal to long-term self-interest
- *Flattery and ingratiation*: Appeal to ego
- *Consultation*: Let's do this together; what do you suggest?
- *Coalitions*: Build support among an influential group
- *Personal appeal*: Begging; do it for me/another person
- *Social validation*: Other firms are doing it/have done it
- *Peer pressure*: Others in the firm are doing it
- *Exchange*: Trade this for that
- *Third party help*: Involve another person to introduce the issue and smooth the way
- *Pressure*: Warn of consequences

In trying to persuade lawyers, it is important to preserve their sense of autonomy. If your powers of persuasion are effective, you can get them to accept your position voluntarily even though they opposed it initially, or persuade them to go along with you even if they continue to disagree. A leader who excels at persuasion can get partners to see things her way, go along with her, and work toward the same goal while believing that they came to the decision by themselves. Sometimes being effective depends not as much on your position as on your finesse in presenting it. For example, one leader I interviewed explained how she persuaded a male partner to include her in a marketing program. A group of male partners was planning to put on a presentation for a large firm client to show that the firm could handle the client's growing business and legal needs. The practice group leader, a woman, happened to be an expert in the legal area that they were going to highlight, but they had not invited her to participate in the presentation. She learned about the program when one of the men called her and asked if she would write up some background materials for them to use.

Instead of feeling hurt or getting angry, she decided to persuade her male partner to invite her by indirectly making him realize why he needed her to be there. The partner had told her that three of the five lawyers who would be representing the client's legal department at the program would be women, so she asked him, "If three of the client representatives will be women, who do you think should be there from our firm?" He replied, "We should have a woman. Would you come? That would be great." In this brief encounter, she used the three elements of persuasion: She appealed to the male partner's desire for a successful presentation (emotion), made him see the logic of having a woman participate (reason), and had the credentials to be the right woman (credibility).

§ 14:8 Executing strategy

You may have the greatest bunch of individual stars in the world, but if they don't play together, the club won't be worth a dime.

—Babe Ruth

Lawyers do well at strategy creation. They like to research issues, review data, consider alternatives, analyze the pros and cons, and decide on the best way to proceed. The process of creating a strategy is familiar to them, and they are comfortable with it. Where they have difficulty, however, is in execution. As a leader, you need to ensure that everyone (or at least those partners whose agreement and cooperation matter) accepts the strategy, takes responsibility for it, and hardest of all, carries it out. This requires paying close attention to watch the progress being made, identify and anticipate problems, address setbacks, and keep people engaged until completion.

Effective execution means that you must be able to create a plan that translates strategy into specific action steps that move everyone toward the project goals. The plan must identify the individuals responsible for implementing each part and the deadline for performance. Most important, it requires the ability to align all parties so that they are enthusiastically and responsibly pulling their oars in the same direction and to hold them accountable for their performance at the finish line. To accomplish this, you need to understand other people's interests and needs, how much people are willing to do and give, how hard to push, and where compromise will be needed. Like consensus-building, it requires perseverance and great patience.

It also means making sure that everyone knows about the plan, understands what is expected of them, and agrees to do their part. Some people who will not be directly affected but who may be instrumental in its implementation (e.g., because they control needed resources) should also be informed about the plan. You cannot assume that because a plan has been adopted or a decision has been made everyone knows what they need to know and will carry out their obligations. For instance, some practice group leaders seek and receive input from partners about what the group's future direction should be. Then they essentially write the group's strategic plan themselves and circulate the finished product to the group. Some partners in the group may simply ignore the plan, and other partners may make promises but fail to follow through. When that happens, no matter how brilliant the plan is, it will probably not be well executed

It is a good idea to review plans periodically. The review might cover the assumptions underlying the strategy, results to date, or changed circumstances that may require plan revisions. It may disclose unintended biases, misjudgments, staffing mistakes, or leadership weaknesses. If the plan is a poor one, errors were made, or improvements are necessary, you will be able to make corrections before too much damage is done.

§ 14:9 Conflict management

Conflict is natural and unavoidable in any organization, and law firms are no exception. Conflict arises whenever interests collide. In law firms, this collision may be between individuals, groups, or offices, or any combination of them. Sometimes it arises because of competition for resources or clients, e.g., when two partners have clients with conflicting interests and the firm can only keep one of them. Other times conflict is due to lawyers' ego needs, greed, or small-mindedness. One of a leader's most important jobs is to manage that conflict so that it does not get out of hand, impair productivity, or cause serious harm in some other way. Leaders must deal on a daily basis with conflicts both trivial and serious; rarely, they face conflicts that are existential.

Conflict is not necessarily a bad thing. The friction generated by differences can lead to improvements, corrections, and innovations. In that sense, constructive conflict can be healthy. When individuals voice their differences, diverse perspectives can lead to beneficial outcomes. However, conflicts that appear insignificant at first can be dangerous when they veer out of control. They require strong leaders who can curb the tensions and channel them to produce positive energy.

Lawyers deal with conflict all the time; it is in the nature of their work. However, while they can comfortably manage other peoples' conflicts, lawyers generally avoid confronting their own. Whether it is dealing with performance issues or changing the billing structure, most lawyers will deny there is a problem or ignore it until they have no choice but to act. Although problems sometimes do go away with no intervention, more often than not this pattern leaves a lot of office-related conflict unresolved and simmering. These unresolved conflicts, coupled with the constant stress and tension of law practice, frequently result in discord and bad behavior in the office.

Managing conflict well can enhance your overall effectiveness as a leader. It calls upon you to demonstrate your strengths, especially in times of turmoil or crisis or when partners are being especially uncooperative. Lawyers can be extremely demanding and surprisingly petty. They couch disputes in rational terms when the underlying issues are really emotional and they will block all efforts to find a rational solution. This is the time where emotional intelligence really pays off. It helps you handle the frustration, confrontation, and personal attacks that conflict may generate. Being able to maintain your composure and manage conflict constructively will earn you great respect from others.

When conflict occurs within a group you lead or between one group and another, there are many ways to deal with it. You might not be able to resolve the conflict but you should be able to manage and contain it. However it arises and whoever is involved, it is important to appreciate opposing views, look for points of mutual agreement, and express your position in a way that is helpful to finding a solution. It is sometimes helpful to have the individuals or groups involved hear each other out so that they understand the reasons behind their respective positions. One leader I interviewed makes it a point to deal with people in person when there is a serious controversy or conflict. She finds it easier to elicit information and defuse situations face to face than by email or telephone. She can read the other person's body language and carry herself in a way that shows that she is willing to listen. She tries to sit next to the person, which is less adversarial than sitting across the table. Even in less serious conflicts, if she starts by telephone but senses that things are starting to sour, she will try to cut the call short and ask to continue the conversation in person.

Whatever the situation, there are some principles that are helpful in managing conflict:

1. *Clarify the issues in dispute.* What is really the underlying issue? It may not be what the parties are fighting about.
2. *Gather the facts.* Each party interprets the facts through their own filter. It is important for you to find out what really happened.
3. *Identify the stakeholders.* Whose interests are in issue, and who will be affected by possible outcomes?
4. *Assess likely sources of disagreement.* What factors have led the parties to this point? What is preventing them from reaching agreement?
5. *Analyze patterns.* Is this a one-time dispute or are there recurring disputes over the same issues or among the same people? If there is a pattern, what is driving it, and what can be done to resolve it once and for all? What can be done to prevent or short-circuit the problem in the future?
6. *Plan a strategy.* Employ conflict resolution techniques and try to minimize potential pitfalls.

It is important to develop skills and techniques for resolving conflict, preferably with win-win solutions. As a lawyer, you undoubtedly have experience in negotiating, problem solving, and possibly mediation. All of these processes involve techniques for getting past differences and reaching agreement. Leaders who are trained as mediators may be especially adept at employing various conflict resolution techniques. It is valuable to have a repertoire of different methods for different situations and objectives. Some common techniques include those listed in Table 14.3.

Table 14.3. Some Common Conflict Resolution Techniques

Technique	Process	When Useful
Bargaining	Make trade-offs, make concessions, take turns	When compromise may avoid continued conflict
Collaboration	Solve problems together	If you need the other side's support or want to integrate opposing views
Decide	Third-party decision, vote of the group, coin toss	When resolution efforts have stalled, the parties are being stubborn, and you need to force the issue
Accommodate	Concede, give in	When it matters more to them than to you and it allows you to preserve harmony or avoid disruption; also when it may be better for the other person to make mistakes and learn from them
Smooth over differences	Emphasize similarities in positions, shared goals	When parties need to continue to work together
Co-exist	Agree to disagree	When the parties are too far apart and there is no compelling need for a single solution

The leaders I interviewed described many techniques that they used to manage conflict within their groups. Most prefer a direct but tactful approach. One leader described how she handles partners who actively resist decisions or plans. She goes to the person most important in the group and says, *"I want to solve this problem and move ahead. I need your support. I'll talk with you about what's going on, but we need a truce. You must tell me if you want one or not."* Sometimes, leaders bring in other parties who might be able to shed light on the problem or help to resolve it. One managing partner had to deal with a practice group leader who wanted her to fire a senior administrator. As the managing partner, she was the person with the authority to fire the administrator. However, after investigating the situation, the managing partner determined that there was no reason to fire the person, but she wanted to stay on good terms with the practice group leader. She knew that he would be upset with her for refusing to fire the administrator and would likely complain about her to two senior partners in his group. To preempt him, she contacted those two senior partners and told them what her investigation disclosed. She did this to ensure that they had a more complete version of the events and to encourage them to help solve the problem, which they did.

The same managing partner had held high-level leadership positions in two firms and noted the cultural factors that sometimes guided her approaches to conflict management. In the first firm, there was constant bickering and dissension among partners. In that combative environment, partners refused to be reasonable in working out differences. She often had to decide unilaterally and tell partners who did not like it to, "Live with it or leave. It's up to you." In her new firm, partners treat each other as colleagues, not adversaries. If people come to her with a conflict, she encourages them to talk with each other first and try to solve it collaboratively. If they cannot do it themselves then she facilitates the process.

As you direct any conflict management process, it is important to see this as human drama. People may be very sensitive, and small slights can cause lasting hurt. It is important for the process to enable the parties to save face, that is, to preserve their self-esteem and sense of autonomy. As a leader, you have to deal with many people whom you may not like personally, but you must treat everyone with respect and insist that all parties do the same. In most situations, you want everyone to conclude the process on good terms and with relationships intact. Once the disagreement is resolved, you will need their cooperation in order to implement the desired outcome. You will also want their support for other efforts that you lead for the firm in the future.

There are times, however, when resolving the conflict unavoidably damages or destroys relationships. When people disagree over vital strategic or financial issues and there can be no win-win solution, some parties will win, and others will lose. The losers may become bitter and try to sabotage future firm initiatives, which will further test your leadership skills. Most of the time, however, it is in the firm's interest—and in your interest as a leader—to preserve the personal relationships between parties to a dispute.

§ 14:10 Managing poor performers

Leaders must give feedback to partners who are not performing up to the firm's expectations. Failure to act when there is consistent noncompliance with firm policies, standards, or values is a failure to lead. Unlike other firm partners who may try to avoid facing up to an underperformer, leaders must deal with performance problems head on and without delay. A consistently poor performer can poison the work environment. If someone is allowed to work at a consistently low level of performance, to miss financial targets repeatedly, or to behave in violation of the firm's values, co-workers become frustrated, distrustful, and eventually demoralized. People need to believe that the firm holds everyone to the same high standards and that partners are accountable if they fall below those standards.

Moreover, avoiding a conversation about a performance problem is not fair to the partner whose performance is substandard. Partners need to know if they are not meeting expectations and they need guidance about how to correct the situation. Sometimes underperforming partners are aware of the problem but afraid to seek help; they may suffer a great deal of stress because they do not know how to deal with the problem. Talking with you about it may relieve their stress and help them to turn the situation around. A small San Francisco firm had a problem with a partner who was going into a trial with the client more than $300,000 in arrears. The partner knew that he was in trouble, but he and the firm had avoided dealing with it. As the trial date approached, the managing partner sat down with him and told him that this debt had to be addressed with the client before the trial began. The partner worked out a payment schedule with the client that satisfied the firm, and the managing partner concluded that, *"My only regret was that I didn't do it sooner."*

Being honest is important, but sometimes very hard. A practice group leader in a global firm described the experience of having to deliver messages that were sometimes painfully honest: *"I told a very good friend he could not become a partner. I could have said we have too many partners, but that was not the real reason. It would have been unfair. He might hang on longer and think he's a partner candidate here while he could be a great partner at another firm. I wanted him to know the truth. I needed to be honest. It is difficult to give bad news, a skill that I had to learn."*

When a partner's poor performance or behavior needs to change, a leader must have a candid and forthright conversation about the problem. Depending on the nature of the problem, you might want to have a third person participate. When you introduce the problem, state each issue clearly, and give specific factual details. That reduces defensiveness and gives your comments greater weight. Start with the particular situation, behavior, or action, then state why it is troubling and explain what its implications or consequences might be. Lastly, discuss how the partner might remedy the problem.

When delivering this feedback, anticipate how the partner might react. Be prepared for emotional outbursts. If that occurs, try to remain calm and keep the partner calm. Be open to hearing the partner's response and concerns, but remain firm and deliberate about the need for change. Focus on the specific behavior that needs to be altered; do not attack the partner's self-esteem. The purpose of feedback conversations is not to tear people down over what happened before but to preserve their self-confidence so that they can improve in the future.

Sometimes you hear from someone else about a partner's poor performance. If you did not observe the event personally, you need to establish that the feedback you were given is accurate. Then you can explain how you acquired the information and why you are the one delivering the feedback message (e.g., "The client called me to complain about the bill . . ."). Give the person an opportunity the explain the situation from their perspective. Then talk together about an approach to remedy the problem.

Feedback conversations should be designed to help a partner correct a current situation or improve future performance, so while you may raise past problems or events or describe patterns of behavior that have created a bad situation, do not dwell on them. Looking back and harping on something in the past that cannot be changed can be judgmental and demoralizing. Instead, look ahead and discuss how the partner will correct the current problem, prevent it from recurring, and perform differently the next time a similar situation comes up. Leadership expert Marshall Goldsmith has suggested reframing these conversations as "feedforward," which emphasizes learning and future improvement. Instead of leaving recipients upset about a past failure, you can make them feel empowered to perform more successfully as they move ahead.

The most important thing to remember about feedback is that it should be constructive and beneficial. This may seem obvious when the feedback extols good work, but even feedback about poor performance or undesirable behavior should be given with good intentions—to help a person learn and improve. When conveyed in a positive manner it can inspire partners to change for the better.

§ 14:11 Dealing with difficult partners

Lawyers work under great stress; their interpersonal skills are not that good to begin with; and many just make it a point to be difficult. Conflict may arise when you address an individual's misbehavior or bad attitude. These problems are hard to address whether they are routine performance problems or actions rooted in greed, egotism, or meanness. As a leader, you cannot avoid dealing with any of them. As one managing partner noted, *"You don't have the luxury of ignoring people you don't like."*

Partners are difficult in a myriad of ways: they want to be appointed to the management committee, for which they are entirely unsuited; they demand special favors for themselves or their clients or supporters; they fail to carry through on commitments; they act like jerks to people in the office. In some firms, rudeness is a familiar part of daily life. Lawyers abandon the niceties that apply in other social settings, where people are expected to behave with politeness to each other. As a leader, it is your responsibility to ensure that people in the firm behave with civility and courtesy, but the way that you handle the occasional rudeness of law firm life is not the same way that you manage the partner who yells at paralegals. The former often requires a nuanced approach. The latter cannot be tolerated at all; it requires an immediate and forceful intervention.

There are so many ways that tensions can erupt and many different levels of sensitivity in the workforce. Leaders need a range of strategies for dealing with difficult people across a spectrum of behaviors. Here are two examples:

- *A rainmaker wanted to be on the Executive Committee. He is a great lawyer but has the wrong skills for this committee; it would be a big mistake. I talked him out of it. I said I understood he had a legitimate interest in having his voice heard on that committee, but showed him how two other members would represent his interests. Through them, he would have a voice even if he was not a committee member. He came to understand that it was better for the firm for him to use his talents in other ways.*
- *When someone is behaving badly, I ask "What's the reason?" Sometimes it's because the person is under extreme pressure. If they are salvageable, I try to give them options and support to help turn things around. I might offer them coaching, for instance. But if the person is really a bad apple, I need to get rid of them. At least they have to be removed from the inner circle or any positions of authority. I don't let it linger and poison the environment.*

Women leaders are often subjected to offensive behaviors that would never be leveled at a man. For instance, people make accusations intended to patronize women leaders, play up their feelings of guilt or inadequacy, challenge their leadership as too feminine or not feminine enough, give them "feedback" that is deliberately hurtful, openly question their authority, or simply ignore it. All of these challenges seek to diminish your stature or authority and are usually intended to intimidate or embarrass you or to provoke an emotional response.

The best way to handle these situations is to avoid any reaction that would validate the effort to belittle you. Refuse to play your adversaries' game. Instead, stay calm and maintain or take control of the situation. Show your competence and authority. If you have been slighted or insulted, ignore the inappropriate comments, confront them directly but calmly, or try to turn them around and use the speakers' own words against them. Reframe these types of situations so that you are the one defining your role and setting the rules.

A downside of leadership is that you will have to make unpopular decisions that disappoint people or make them angry. Some partners will resent you for being in your role or wielding the authority that you have. One of the most challenging situations that women leaders face is when they become the targets of other lawyers' anger or frustration. Those lawyers may try to undermine you through mockery, by spreading rumors, calling you names, or in some other way. Anger directed against you is especially hard to deal with but it is not always intended to be personal. People may blame you simply because you represent the firm. It is important—though not always easy—to recognize the difference between insults that are personal and those that are thrust at you as a symbol of the firm you lead. Whatever the reason, you have to be prepared to deal with these situations in order to maintain both your peace of mind and your credibility as a leader.

This is especially trying when partners openly berate, humiliate, or sabotage you, especially when the events take place in public. Ideally, it is best to model positive behaviors instead of getting angry, but realistically, your emotions may threaten your control. Sometimes, confronting a difficult person takes more courage than skill. When you are the target of offensive behavior, you have to hold your own and show that the offending person will not intimidate or control you. It is important to deal with the problem as promptly, directly, and constructively as you can. One leader noted that as a litigator, when she is harshly criticized, her first instinct is to fight back. As a leader, she knows that she cannot give in to the urge to counterattack; her first objective is to keep that person productive and part of the group. Instead, she tries to listen, weigh the criticism, and decide whether there is any merit to it. If there is, she takes it to heart and tries to deal with it. If there isn't, she tries to figure out how to penetrate and change the person's mind-set

Another leader, an office managing partner in San Francisco, confronted one of her partners in another city who was spreading rumors about her. Her technique was forthright but tactful. She allowed him to save face but sent him a very clear message.

> Once I heard that a partner in another office was trashing me. When I was planning to visit that office, I made an appointment with him. I told him, "I've heard stories that you have been saying these terrible things about me. I'm sure it can't be true; you wouldn't say something like that, so I wonder where the rumors are coming from. Maybe we can figure out a way to stop them." He didn't confess but blushed completely when I said it. He knew I was on to him and if he continued, there would be consequences.

Not all difficult situations are so benign. The managing partner of a large office in Washington, D.C, described how she dealt with an especially unsettling situation:

> I met with a group of partners in a public bar after work one evening. One of them started yelling at me. He had been docked $10,000 in his compensation. He had a bad year and had $450,000 in write-offs. The firm was going to dock him $40,000, but I pushed it to just $10,000. Even if it's a lot, it's not the end of the world for someone making what he makes, but he started yelling at me, and though I'm no shrinking violet, I became upset. I had a terrible day anyway and was exhausted. I told him very firmly to sit down, that his behavior was unacceptable and unprofessional. He was all arrogance, hubris, did not recognize his own failings. He kept screaming. I spoke to him as if to my children. I felt myself starting to cry so I walked out. I knew the attack was on me, but it wasn't _about_ me. Leaders must make that distinction. As a leader, you have to act differently than another person would in this situation. It's about the organization, not what you need, want, or feel.

There are many tactics and strategies for dealing with troublesome people, and you will need to choose the right one for each situation. Table 14.4 suggests some guidance when you are confronted with a difficult or offensive individual.

Table 14.4. Managing Difficult People

1. *Pick the right time and place.* If you can, set the stage for your discussion. Pick a time and place that will help you feel secure and in control. Depending on the issue and the emotional intensity of the problem, you may want to have a third person present.

2. *Clarify the issue.* What is really going on here? Is there a legitimate complaint or disagreement, or is it something else? It is easy to misinterpret a statement of criticism or opposition as an insult. Do not assume it is personal, and do not make it personal if it isn't.

3. *What is your goal in managing the situation?* Is it to correct a bad situation for others that threatens morale or productivity? Is it to maintain your authority against an effort to undercut you? It may be tempting to try to prove that you are right or they are wrong, or to protect your ego or deflate theirs, but do not let it become personal if it does not need to be.

4. *Plan a strategy.* Prepare if you can. Your strategy should be appropriate for the situation and the desired outcome.

5. *Stick to the issue.* You want to control the agenda, not react to theirs. Deliver a clear message and make sure that it is heard and understood.

6. *Don't accuse.* Use descriptive, not evaluative words or opinions that might sound like a personal attack.

7. *Don't be defensive.* If you are confident of your position, there is no need to be defensive. If you are unsure of your position, especially if they catch you by surprise, do not take their bait. Maintain your equilibrium and conduct yourself as the leader you are.

8. *Keep your emotions in check.* You may be tempted to cry or lash out at the person. It will take great will power, but try not to react spontaneously. If you are feeling swept up by emotions, try to calm down and regain control before speaking or continuing.

9. *Keep your voice steady.* Sometimes when women get upset or excited, they speak more quickly, and their voices get higher. Before you speak, take a deep breath. Then speak slowly and consciously try to keep your voice low and steady.

10. *Give priority to the firm's interests.* As a leader, your object is to preserve the interests and well-being of the firm. Sometimes you have to swallow your urge to clobber someone or show the person up as a fool. However, this is not about you, nor is it about beating an opponent. For the sake of the firm, you need to seek win-win solutions whenever possible.

Chapter 15

Resilience

KeyCite®: Cases and other legal materials listed in KeyCite Scope can be researched through the KeyCite service on Westlaw®. Use KeyCite to check citations for form, parallel references, prior and later history, and comprehensive citator information, including citations to other decisions and secondary materials.

---

§ 15:1   Leaders need to be resilient

If you have made mistakes, even serious ones, there is always another chance for you. What we call failure is not the falling down but the staying down.

— Mary Pickford

To be a law firm leader requires resilience: the ability to deal with stress, tolerate conflict, and cope with the intensity of the job. Resilience enables you to endure extreme hardships and challenges and, most importantly, bounce back. Resilient people tend to be optimistic about the future and confident about themselves; they have the courage to take smart risks and the inner strength and thick skin to cope with tough situations. Because the pressures of leadership can easily wear you down, resilience also requires maintaining your emotional and physical well-being.

Leading any organization is a serious undertaking with a great deal at stake. Your job is to protect the interests and maximize the success of your firm and all of its partners and employees. Some of the leaders I interviewed spoke of an unrelenting sense of responsibility because "*so much depends on what I do.*" One of the leaders I interviewed is a full-time co-managing partner of a large, multi-office firm. She said of her role: *"I have direct responsibility for thousands of people and the welfare of an organization."* Another leader who is the professional development director for a national firm described how she feels about her responsibilities: *"I carry the weight of the world on my shoulders. I worry about the people here. Who's busy, who's not? Who's performing well, who isn't? Can he be salvaged or not? What can be done? My responsibilities for the people here are more significant than my caseload during my whole career at the firm. I know so much, so many things. The burden is harder."*

The job of law firm leadership is hard, the stress is constant, the people can be impossible, and you have little real power to make people do what needs to be done. You will inevitably make mistakes and missteps, and you will be criticized and worse. You will have many sleepless nights, yet you will forge ahead with confidence and optimism because leaders want to build a better firm and know that they can do it. Churchill said, "Success is the ability to move from failure to failure without loss of enthusiasm." He was speaking of resilience.

§ 15:2   Optimism

Optimism makes you more resilient to adversity and able to function more effectively as a leader. Research clearly shows that optimistic people have a lot going for them: they are happier, healthier, more productive, have better personal relationships, succeed more, are better problem solvers, and are less likely to become depressed than pessimistic people.[1] Their confidence inspires teams to action and their mindset is better for making business decisions. Their positive attitude is a virtue for leadership since people must believe that following the leader will lead to a better future. McKinsey researchers have found that positive emotions are a major factor in driving and sustaining successful women leaders.[2]

Optimism and pessimism are ways of thinking about experience. They affect the way you feel and what you do when faced with a situation, especially when something goes wrong.

[Section 15:2]

[1]Sagerstrom, S.C., & Sephton, S.E. (Feb. 2010), Optimistic expectancies and cell-mediated immunity, *Psychological Science*; Reivich, K. (June 2008), The seven ingredients of resilience, CNBC, http://www.cnbc.com/id/25464528/.

[2]Barsh, J., Cranston, S., & Lewis, G. (2009), *How remarkable women lead* (New York: Crown Business).

The classic illustration of the difference between optimism and pessimism is that while looking at the same glass of water, the pessimist sees the glass as half empty while the optimist sees it as half full. The glass and its contents are exactly the same; it is the interpretation that differs.

Optimists are effective leaders because they are able to build commitment and enthusiasm in others. Optimists' positive outlook creates the sense that they can manage challenges and make good things happen for other people. This is especially important when times are tough because you can give hard messages in a positive way. By taking the long view toward a better future, you make people believe that you will lead them to a better place than they are in now. When you believe that you can make a positive difference, you can spread that belief to others. You can give people cause for hope.

Optimistic leaders are not naïve or foolish. They are realistic, and reality is often grim. Having an optimistic outlook does not mean denying reality or always thinking good thoughts. Rather, it means that you can understand and appreciate both the positive and negative aspects of a situation that you or the firm may be in, even—especially—when it is difficult or perilous. In those situations, resilient leaders do not despair or concentrate only on deficiencies and dangers. They look for opportunities and focus on solutions. Optimism allows them to accept the facts of adversity and counter them with constructive action.[3]

It is hard to find optimists in law firms because optimism is not a common trait of lawyers. In a study of personality attributes of people in 104 careers, the research found only one consistent correlation between a particular attribute and career success: the attribute of pessimism was highly and consistently correlated with success among lawyers.[4] Pessimism is evidently a positive personality trait for practicing law. However, pessimism takes a profound toll on lawyers in other aspects of life. Pessimism depletes your energy, can make you feel helpless and stuck in downward spirals, and reduces your resilience.[5]

Tests of personality characteristics bear this out. Lawyers tend to rate extremely low on resilience: 90% of them score below the

---

[3]Barsh, Cranston, & Lewis (2009), *How remarkable women lead.*

[4]Seligman, M.P. (2002), *Authentic happiness: using the new positive psychology to realize your potential for lasting fulfillment* (New York: Free Press).

[5]Seligman (2002), *Authentic happiness.*

50th percentile, with the average score at 30%.[6] According to these tests, people who are low on resilience tend to be defensive, resist taking in feedback, and can be hypersensitive to criticism. In most organizations, these traits would take them out of contention as candidates for leadership. No one wants to follow someone who gives off negative energy and brings people down. With such a high concentration of pessimists in law firms, the pool of resilient leaders is relatively small—and the opportunities for optimists are considerable.

Fortunately, optimism can be learned.[7] If you tend to be pessimistic, you can teach yourself how to think differently about events and what they mean. The same things may happen to you, but instead of assuming the worst, you will see positive implications. Instead of giving up, you will be able to act in a constructive way. According to psychologist Barbara Frederickson, having more positive emotions than negative emotions, in a ratio of at least 3:1, broadens your outlook, increases your satisfaction, and enables you to function at a higher level in work and life.[8] She found that just aspiring to have a more positive outlook can increase your ratio and help you to flourish.

§ 15:3   Self-confidence

Self-confidence is the first requisite to great undertakings.

— Samuel Johnson

To be a resilient leader, you must believe that you are capable of succeeding at what leaders do. You must have self-confidence, which one study has defined as an "internal presumption of competence."[1] It is a belief in yourself and your ability to improve the future for others. It is understanding your strengths and weaknesses and relying on your strengths to guide your thoughts and actions. It is believing that you can effectuate change in the world and can succeed at what you do. An interesting observation during my interviews for this book was the number of women leaders who expressed self-confidence without hesitation. Here are a few of their comments:

---

[6]Richard, L.R. (July 1998), *Herding cats: the lawyer personality revealed*, ABA Journal.

[7]See, e.g., Seligman, M.P. (2006), *Learned optimism: how to change your mind and your life* (New York: Vintage Books).

[8]Fredrickson, B. (2009), *Positivity* (New York: Crown).

[Section 15:3]

[1]Ibarra, H., & Obodaru, O. (Jan. 2009), Women and the vision thing, *Harvard Business Review*.

- *I knew I would be good at this, and I am.*
- *I knew I could lead teams and committees, but wasn't sure I could lead the firm. It didn't take long for me to see that I have what it takes to do this job.*
- *I always assumed I was empowered, never thought I needed to ask. I solve problems on my own initiative.*
- *I always wanted to be a player. I held leadership positions in high school; I like being in charge; I get energized by it. It feels natural to me.*

Being confident that you can perform does not require that you be fully competent in every area the job calls for. Confidence comes from experiencing your strengths in action.[2] Much of what you have to know and do as a leader you learn on the job; the better you do that job, the more confident you become. In this sense, confidence is a product of leadership experience, not a prerequisite for it. If you wait until you believe that you are ready for a position, by the time that it happens, someone else will have the job.

Given the nature of the law firm as an organization, leaders must be confident and direct in order to get things done. However, because you have to lead others who are strong and confident, too, you must also demonstrate humility in order to be considered trustworthy. Finding a way to demonstrate your confidence without coming across as either too modest or too confident can be a challenge for women leaders. As discussed previously (Chapter 2), stereotyping and gender bias make it hard for women to find a way to demonstrate their confidence. If you are too humble, your humility can come across as indecisive and weak. People may interpret it as a lack of capability, temperament, or willingness to do what it takes as a leader. On the other hand, if people believe you are too confident, you may be negatively perceived as pushy or arrogant. Either way, your confidence may be attacked.

Because of the many decisions and actions the job requires, leaders sometimes make missteps or errors. Many women replay events in their minds over and over again, preoccupied with their failures or shortcomings and blaming themselves when anything goes wrong. If you demand perfection in yourself, i.e., if you must feel completely prepared and safe before you step up, you may never become an effective leader. You cannot allow the fear of a

---

[2]Kanter, R.M. (2006), *Confidence: how winning streaks and losing streaks begin and end* (New York: Three Rivers Press).

mistake to stop you from acting or the fact of a mistake to destroy your confidence. Keep some perspective. Leadership involves risks; little is certain, definite, or safe. If you are doing your job as a leader, you will inevitably make some missteps. Learn from them without constantly second-guessing yourself. Learn to accept imperfection, and instead of dwelling on your faults, focus instead on how to rebound from your errors. Choose to be positive and forward-looking. Most mistakes will not be fatal and most setbacks will be temporary. A.G. Lafley, former CEO and Chair of Procter & Gamble, once told an interviewer that you learn more from failure than from success, so "the key is to fail early, fail cheaply, and don't make the same mistake twice."[3]

Effective women leaders do not let self-doubt erode their confidence. They do not give in to the gender bias that others may harbor about women leaders. They keep their goals in mind and keep moving toward them. They focus on doing the job at hand and doing it well. They overcome any self-doubts they may have by producing top results. They are good at what they do, they know it, and it shows. This is not to say that you must eliminate self-doubt entirely but that you confront the doubt and not let it stop you from acting. Similarly, too much certainty can limit your effectiveness. If you believe that your way is the only way because you know better than others, that can also stymie you—and justify the label of arrogance.

As a leader, you must appear confident even when you are not. People need to believe that their leaders are competent and have things under control. One leader I interviewed explained, *"People have to feel confident in you. You need to create a self-image of who you are so you can project that confidence to others."* There may be times, however, when you do not have the experience, skills, or answers that you need to feel completely confident. Admitting uncertainty is fine; admitting helplessness is not. It is hard for people to feel confident in you if you look unsure, frightened, or on the brink of a meltdown, so even when you feel you are on shaky ground, you have to gather enough willpower and strength to make yourself appear self-confident.

This may be challenging when you are a new leader. One of the women I interviewed did not feel fully prepared for the job when she started in her role as practice group leader. She felt like she was in over her head and unsure whether she could do it, but she also felt that she had to appear to be in control. *"How can I let*

---

[3]How Procter & Gamble plans to clean up, *Business Week* (Apr. 2009).

people know how I feel? They need to trust me and have confidence that I know what I'm doing." Rather than give in to self-doubt, she publicly presented herself as confident while she methodically went about learning the things that she needed to know and do.

Similarly, when you are in the center of a storm, it is critical to maintain your composure so that people believe you are in control. It helps to keep your vision and purpose clear in your mind, especially when you face discouragement, rejection, or an uproar in the ranks. Maintaining others' confidence in you is essential if you want to prevent panic, loss of productivity, and partners heading for the exits. By staying centered and focusing on achieving positive outcomes, you will appear calm and reassuring to others—and be able to think more clearly about how to handle the situation.

§ 15:4 Smart risk-taking

Behold the turtle. It makes progress only when it sticks its neck out.

— James Bryant Conan

How much risk can you tolerate? Leadership is about change, and change is always risky, so understanding how you react to risk will help you prepare to deal with the risks you will inevitably face as a leader. Leaders do not always have time to study issues in detail before they have to act. Moreover, some problems are so complicated, murky, or emotional that there are no clear solutions, and any decision could have serious consequences. In these situations, you will have to tolerate ambiguity and move ahead bravely without all the facts. You will need to be confident in your abilities and judgment and rely on that confidence to accept the risk of failure. If the outcome is unsuccessful, you need to be able to recover and move on to face the next decision.

Some women find risk exciting, but most people avoid it. They prefer to continue doing what is familiar and makes them comfortable. They avoid change because they are not sure what it will bring. This is especially true for lawyers, whose training and professional work is directed at avoiding or minimizing risks. On psychological tests, lawyers score much higher on risk aversion than the general population. Lawyers work hard to reduce risk by analyzing situations carefully and making rational, data-driven decisions. In the process, they focus on everything that can go wrong. Thus, when faced with proposals involving change or innovation, they are reluctant to "go first" because untested moves have a heightened risk of failure or adverse outcomes.

Consequently, they prefer to maintain the status quo rather than make any sort of move or change. Leaders, on the other hand, know that "skeptics of change overestimate the safety of the status quo," especially in times of turmoil and uncertainty. After all, leadership is all about change.

Being a leader involves persuading others to trust you to take risks on their behalf, but lawyers' risk aversion also makes it hard for them to trust people, including their leaders. In the practice of law, lawyers frequently witness the effects of betrayal and the worst of human behavior, which reinforces their wariness. Though they authorize you to act on their behalf, they may worry that your actions and decisions might put their financial interests and careers in jeopardy. You can reduce their skepticism by pointing out your past performance, experience, and results. However, you may not be able to put them fully at ease because risk cannot be completely eliminated; it is part of all human relationships, and those relationships cannot succeed without accepting some risk. As one author notes, we must risk being wrong in order to know whether we are right in giving our trust.[1] This creates a tension that you have to learn to live with as a leader.

Risk accompanies every leadership position because as a leader you are out front and all eyes are upon you. You must act, decide, and manage while others watch you and judge. Leaders challenge old, settled ways and experiment with new ideas. They have to be willing to stick their necks out when they believe change is necessary even if it opens them up to the possibility of rejection, embarrassment, or failure. What they do or say may be unpopular or unsuccessful but they cannot treat possible failure as a reason for inaction.

Being unafraid of failure is a tall order for women leaders in law firms. Leadership takes considerable courage. All leaders operate in the spotlight and their partners are unforgiving and have long memories. However, leadership carries a greater degree of risk for women than for men. Because women leaders are still in the minority, they are subjected to closer scrutiny and harsher judgment. Some researchers submit that women in leadership are on "glass cliffs" and in more precarious positions than their

---

[Section 15:4]

[1]Shaw, R.B. (1997), Trust in the balance (San Francisco: Jossey-Bass).

male counterparts.[2] They find that women are more likely to be given leadership roles in firms that are in crisis, which increases their chances of failure and opens them to greater criticism. At the same time, these firms often deny women leaders needed support, resources, and information, making leadership particularly stressful for them. Many women partners avoid such risks by avoiding leadership altogether or taking on management roles that are mostly administrative.

Accepting the need to take chances does not mean that you have to be comfortable with risk or become a gambler. However, since you cannot avoid risk if you are a leader, learn how to manage it wisely. By taking smart risks, you will learn more, achieve more, and enjoy life more. Through experience and with the guidance of trusted advisors, you can learn how to assess risk accurately and develop the wisdom to distinguish reasonable from unreasonable risks. When you take a risk and the outcome is successful, use it to give your skeptical partners evidence that justifies their faith in you. Even if you err, you can learn from the failure and try to use it to strengthen your standing as a leader. Show partners your humility, ability to laugh at yourself, and capacity to accept a loss and move on. Try to turn the failure around, reframe it, and emphasize any positive lessons and outcomes. Sometimes, circumstances vindicate your risk-taking, turning what looks like a loss into a clear win. This is how that happened to one leader I interviewed:

In a meeting to decide new partners, I spoke out against someone. People were surprised. It was risky, especially because the senior partner supported the person. The person was elevated, but something happened soon after, and he had to leave. Then I was seen as courageous and correct, having stood up for the firm's standards. This reinforced partners' view of me as not just outspoken, but a person with good judgment.

§ 15:5   Inner strength

I was always looking outside myself for strength and confidence, but it comes from within. It is there all the time.
— Anna Freud

Given the challenges that come with leading lawyers, resilient leaders must have the inner strength to confront their own and others' legitimate fears and anxieties and move forward in spite of them. For many leaders, the hardest part of the job is dealing

---

[2]Ashby, J., Ryan, M.K., & Haslam, S.A. (2007), Legal work and the glass cliff: evidence that women are preferentially selected to lead problematic cases, *William and Mary Journal of Women and the Law* 13(3).

with the emotional and interpersonal issues that confront them. By temperament and training, lawyers try to be rational and dispassionate, to keep their distance, but as a leader, you cannot escape these emotionally draining issues. You have to deal with partners with performance problems, distraught partners going through traumatic events in their personal lives, personnel with drug or alcohol abuse, or other discomforting problems. You learn things about people you work with that are dark and depressing.

Much of what you learn and do as a leader happens behind the scenes where no one sees it, and a lot of it cannot be shared with anyone else. You might negotiate with an angry former client to prevent a malpractice suit against a wayward partner or arrange rehab and counseling for an alcoholic administrator. In doing these things, you protect the reputation of the firm and you save the partnership thousands of dollars, but for reasons of privacy, these issues must be handled without disclosure. In many cases, your achievements may never be known to your partners, so you will not receive credit for your good work. One former managing partner said, *"Much of my work was confidential. You cannot brag that you just saved the firm from a malpractice suit."* If you are the kind of person who needs to talk about your accomplishments or if you need constant approval from others, this is not a job for you. You must have the inner strength to do your work and follow your mandate even when people take you for granted or fail to appreciate what you are doing for them.

§ 15:6   Thick skin

Do what you feel in your heart to be right—for you'll be criticized anyway. You'll be damned if you do, and damned if you don't.

— Eleanor Roosevelt

Law firms can be pretty rough and tumble in the best of circumstances, and the stress of law practice can bring out the worst in partners. When they do not agree with the firm's decisions or actions, they may behave badly. As noted earlier, partners may blame or ridicule leaders without reason or justification or make them scapegoats for decisions that the firm has made even if the leader lobbied against the decision. When you are the face of the firm or committee, you are identified with the actions it takes; even your friends sometimes fail to separate you as a person from you as a member of management. You also learn very quickly as a leader that there are no secrets among partners, especially if they involve you. People may promise to keep things confidential, but somehow word gets out. In these and any number of other situations, you may feel under siege. To remain resilient, you must develop a thick skin.

One of the difficult things that many women have to cope with is how relationships with partners change when they become leaders. You might work together and talk with each other casually as partners, but as one leader noted, after you become a leader, especially at a senior level: *"When partners want to talk with you, each one has an agenda."* Another leader found that she had a hard time getting people to give her honest information: *"Everyone tells me what they want me to hear or what they think I want to hear."*

Even more difficult for some of the leaders I interviewed was the realization that the actions they took as leaders sometimes caused fractures in personal relationships with other partners. Sometimes leaders make decisions that are unpopular or controversial; sometimes they speak up for unpopular causes or speak out against favored ones. Partners who disagree or whose interests are harmed may become angry, upset, or defiant. While leaders should be concerned about acting wisely, they cannot worry about their popularity; they have to do what they think is right. One leader explained the tension this way: *"You have to stay aligned with the department or firm's strategy and interests even when many of the people in the department are your friends and what you decide will be problems for them. It's hard to juggle personal relations and business interests."* In extreme cases, you may lose friends because of your obligations to the firm as a leader. Indeed, a few of the leaders I interviewed spoke of friendships ending because of difficult decisions they had to make as leaders. They regretted the lost friendships but accepted them because their decisions were correct for the greater good of the firm. One young leader said, *"There's a lot you need to block out in order to succeed. I know, for example, that not all people will like me. You need to set your mind to accept that."*

Sometimes women leaders take workplace comments and disagreements too personally. When partners' anger flares up over firm policies or decisions, it is important to distinguish between comments made in the heat of the moment over the business dispute and offensive comments that are directed toward you personally. When you take those comments to heart as personal insults, they can undermine your confidence and your ability to do your job. Regardless of the issue, some women start to wonder if the constant bickering and criticism is their fault, not the other person's problem. One of the interviewed leaders said that she struggled with this issue and noted that other women had similar difficulties: *"The guys will disagree strongly and then go out for a beer, but women seem to internalize the issues and the disagreement, which limits their effectiveness."* Another leader, who sits on the capital committee of a global consulting firm, routinely confronts rude comments and attitudes from male committee members. She explained, *"I hold a very important position worthy of great respect. It is fast-paced and high-stress. When another partner says to me, 'That's a stupid idea,' or 'Don't be stupid,' women take it personally. We wonder, is it stupid? The problem, of course, is the partner's lack of civility, but our reaction is personal."*

Resilient leaders deal with blame and criticism by maintaining a clear perspective and learning not to take everything personally. When they start to entertain self-doubts because of comments made over a business issue, they recognize their emotional reactions and try to separate the business dispute from the personal relationship. They do not let the emotional turmoil they feel prevent them from coping with the situation and moving forward. One of the keys is maintaining a clear sense of purpose. They think to themselves: *"This problem is not about me; I won't make it personal; I am acting for the collective good of the firm even if certain individuals do not see that."*

Leaders who are women of color develop special coping mechanisms to help them stay resilient. One Latina leader said she finds that some younger women of color automatically presume insensitive comments or rude behaviors toward them are due to racial hostility. She found it helpful not to have such a "quick trigger" because many people are just thoughtless, not racist. The advice she gives to young women of color is, *"Conduct yourself as the best, most confident lawyer. Don't make race the agenda. Don't hide it, be proud of it, just don't wear it on your sleeve. Don't think people are waiting for you to fail. It adds pressure to your psyche that you don't need."*

It is not just other people who are hard on women leaders. Women leaders put a lot of pressure on themselves to be perfect, fully prepared, and error-free. Even when they are asked to be leaders because they are the most qualified and capable individuals, many women doubt their readiness and worry that they are not up to the task. Many women think that they have to have all the facts and answers at their fingertips. As lawyers, this is how they do a good job for their clients, and as leaders of lawyers they strive to do the same in order to establish credibility and earn the respect of their partners. As a leader, it is healthy and wise to prepare thoroughly, but some women overanalyze and overprepare; they have difficulty with spontaneity and often miss new ideas that come up because they are so focused on the details they know. Effective leaders know how to improvise when necessary. There are times when you do not have all the facts you need or know all that you should. At those times, it is fine to admit that you are not sure of a point, but you do not have to avoid addressing a subject because you do not know every detail. You should appear confident, use what you do know, rely on your experience and intuition, and do the best you can.

§ 15:7 Emotional support

A critical mechanism for helping leaders stay resilient is emotional support. Law firm leadership can be emotionally draining, and women leaders tend to experience more emotional ups and downs more often and more intensely than most men do.[1] Many of the things partners say and do have the potential to exhaust you and erode your self-confidence and self-esteem. They also can make you feel isolated. Combined with job pressure and intense scrutiny, feelings of isolation and exclusion can have profound mental health consequences for women leaders.[2] The level of isolation can be akin to physical pain.[3] The higher the leadership position the greater the likelihood of stress and isolation.

Emotional support from others can promote your emotional healing and increase your resilience. Numerous studies have shown that social ties are a source of strength and have significant benefits for mental and physical health. A UCLA study found that when women are under stress, they seek social contact. Stress triggers an innate "tend and befriend" response in women, unlike the "fight or flight" response in men exposed to stressful situations. Stress releases the hormone oxytocin, which is enhanced by estrogen. The combination "buffers the fight or flight response and encourages [women] to tend children and gather with other women instead." This behavior counters stress and produces a calming effect.

The leaders I interviewed placed great importance on maintaining strong social connections with family and friends, colleagues in the firm, and people outside the firm. They seek trusted individuals with whom they can share their joys and successes as

---

[Section 15:7]

[1]Barsh, J., Cranston, S., & Craske, R.A. (Sept. 2008), Centered leadership: how talented women thrive, *McKinsey Quarterly*.

[2]Howard, A., & Wellins, R.S. (2009), Holding women back: troubling discoveries and best practices for helping female leaders succeed, Development Dimensions International, Inc.

[3]Rock, D. (Aug. 2009), Managing with the brain in mind, *strategy + business*, no. 56.

leaders as well as the difficulties and frustrations they face. They need people who will listen to them when they are angry or upset, cheer them on, and give their egos an occasional boost. They also seek people who remind them that being a leader is only one part of who they are; there are other important aspects of their identity. In most cases, these people are husbands, life partners, close friends, and family members. They remind the leaders of what is important in life and help them maintain a sense of perspective. Women leaders also find solace in community, charitable, religious, and other activities that address important personal values, allow them to separate from work for a while, and round out their lives.

Many women leaders rely on networks of friends. One leader described the value of her networks this way: "*I have tough days when I wonder, why am I doing this? I try to keep the bigger picture in mind. My colleagues and I support each other. I have networks in and out of the firm where I hear the same stories happening in all firms and practices. I take some comfort in that.*" Having networks of women friends in other firms or other professions is common among women leaders. These groups get together to discuss common problems and how to deal with them, to offer encouragement and good cheer, or just to play and have fun.

Making time for fun and relaxation and maintaining a sense of humor are critically important for staying resilient. The beneficial effects of humor are well established. Fabio Sala, who studied the use of humor by executives, discovered that an ability to use humor is a marker for high emotional intelligence. He also found that skillfully used humor "reduces hostility, deflects criticism, relieves tension, improves morale, and helps communicate difficult messages."[4] In addition to keeping your constituents happy and making your work go smoothly, one managing partner emphasized that for a leader to maintain a healthy state of mind, it is important to be able to laugh, especially at yourself.

Some of the leaders I interviewed had confidantes in their firm, while others had mentors or coaches outside the firm who took on the role of trusted confidante. Having someone you can confide in is especially helpful if that person is or has been in a similar leadership position. Another leader who understands the challenges and frustrations that you face and the emotional ups and downs that accompany them can give you comfort and support your self-confidence. They can offer practical insights and advice about how to deal with problems because they went through similar experiences themselves.

---

[4]Sala, F. (Sept. 2003), Laughing all the way to the bank, *Harvard Business Review*.

Emotional support is essential for women of color who face the special challenges and stresses of being minority women in mainstream leadership. The importance of having a confidante has heightened significance for them. Women of color need to be able to confide in someone who has been through the experience of being an outsider in a leadership role and knows what it feels like. Because there are so few of them in most law firms, many women of color form networks across firm lines. Several of the leaders I interviewed built networks with other minority women to help find affirmation and emotional support. These networks help them alleviate the pressures of the workplace and maintain a positive sense of self. One leader, the only African American woman in her office, has *"a tight circle of friends who are all going through the same things. We are women of color at high levels in different law firms, companies, and government agencies. We get together to let off steam."*

§ 15:8 Physical stamina

Physical stamina is a critical aspect of resilience that is often overlooked by busy leaders. Leadership is physically hard work. In addition to long hours, exhausting travel, and social demands, leadership involves dealing with constant problems, unexpected crises, and making hard decisions involving the business of the firm and the lives of its people. The emotional stress combined with the physical demands can deplete your energy. If you are not physically strong it is hard to carry out your leadership responsibilities.

Women who are both leaders and mothers bear a double burden that leaves them drained in especially challenging ways. Many women come home from work only to have a "second shift" at home. Of women executives, 92% still manage all household tasks such as meal preparation and child care. Having significant responsibilities on both fronts can leave them constantly exhausted.[1]

Resilient leaders understand that they are in a marathon, not a sprint, and that they must take care of their health in order to make it to the finish line. One leader said, *"I conserve my energy. I don't have enough energy to fight every battle."* Especially when you are under a lot of stress, it is important to "balance your energy flow" in order to stay focused and prevent burnout or

---

[Section 15:8]

[1]Barash, Cranston, & Lewis (2009), *How remarkable women lead.*

defeat.[2] This means giving priority to activities that energize you, at work and at home, avoiding those that sap your strength, and maintaining your health and fitness. Looking fit and healthy can give you greater self-confidence and public credibility. Regular medical check-ups and attention to fitness are very important. Unfortunately, many women ignore their own health while taking care of everyone else at work and at home.

Many of the leaders I interviewed made exercise a priority and had a regular routine. They try to maintain good nutrition. They recognize the importance of sleep, although many of them seem to operate with remarkably little sleep. Those who need quiet time to replenish their energy use a wide variety of techniques: sitting alone in a quiet room, going to a spa, or taking a hike in the mountains. Others prefer to take part in sports and social pursuits or talk things through with other people as a way to clear their heads and recharge their batteries.

---

[2]Barash, Cranston, & Lewis (2009), *How remarkable women lead.*

Chapter 16

Empowerment

KeyCite[R]: Cases and other legal materials listed in KeyCite Scope can be researched through the KeyCite service on Westlaw[R]. Use KeyCite to check citations for form, parallel references, prior and later history, and comprehensive citator information, including citations to other decisions and secondary materials.

---

§ 16:1   Empower other women leaders

If your actions inspire others to dream more, learn more, do more and become more, you are a leader.

—John Quincy Adams

Women leaders can play a decisive role in accelerating the movement of other women into law firm leadership. They can empower women who, with encouragement, guidance, and support, will also become leaders. Empowering others means helping them appreciate and release their personal talents and potential. One of a leader's most important responsibilities is to ensure that the firm has the talent it needs to serve its clients, carry out its strategy, and both succeed and endure in an extremely competitive marketplace. Leaders must make sure that potential new leaders are identified, nurtured, and prepared for leadership and that women are among those future leaders. When you are a leader, you have countless opportunities to reach around and give a nudge or extend a hand to other women. You have a platform to advocate for women and the wherewithal to create a work climate where women can thrive.

As a leader, you can take steps to break down barriers and change perceptions by reframing the discussion and emphasizing the need to change the male-centered norms of law firms, not the women who work in them. You can be a vital and vigorous champion for women, encouraging them to unleash their ambitions and insisting that the firm acknowledge them. You can focus on eliminating bias, redefining models of effective leadership and career success, and helping women learn to embrace their power and deploy it to create a better law firm. Leading by your example, you can be a compelling mentor and role model. One leader who tries to do this explained that, *"As a model, I try to change the perception of women in law, power, and partnership. I'm kind to people and also focused on business. I smile and try to be approachable, and I'm also a successful rainmaker."*

The benefit of your advocacy on behalf of other women accrues to you as well as to the women you help. Being effective in your efforts will expand and improve your firm's pool of leadership talent which will make you a more respected and successful leader. Moreover, knowing that you played a role in empowering other women can be a source of personal strength and gratification.

Marie Wilson, author and founder of the White House Project, has said that in order to be taken seriously, women "must be seen as commanding and powerful."[1] Today, many women lawyers are successful and powerful and perceived that way, but for the most part, their successes are still seen as individual—and therefore extraordinary—accomplishments. A number of women have broken barriers but law firm norms remain the same and continue to deter many more women who want to reach the top. What is needed is "a critical mass of diverse women [in] leadership alongside men."[2] When we reach critical mass, i.e., when at least one-third of law firm leaders are women, individual women leaders will no longer be exceptional, and the word "leader" will naturally evoke images of women as well as of men. As a leader in your law firm, you can use your example, authority, and influence to empower other women lawyers to join you in leadership and move toward this desired state.

[Section 16:1]

[1]Wilson, M.C. (2007), *Closing the leadership gap: why women can and must help run the world* (New York: Penguin Books).

[2]*The White House Project report: benchmarking women's leadership* (Nov. 2009), http://benchmarks.thewhitehouseproject.org..

Many firms are trying to remedy the absence of women from firm leadership by appointing a woman or two to their highest governing committees. However, having one or two women partners on the executive committee is not sufficient. When there are only a few women in positions of power, they can easily be ignored or marginalized. Only when women leaders are too numerous and powerful to ignore will their identities as women become less salient. Until then, colleagues are more likely to judge them as women leaders rather than on the basis of their abilities and performance simply as leaders. Moreover, without a critical mass of women in power, bias will persist. Firms will make accommodations to women (mostly those with children) but will not initiate the fundamental cultural and institutional changes needed to create a more humane and equitable workplace for women and men.

To develop future leaders, you must help women find the confidence and experience they need to develop their leadership strengths. In addition to assigning women high profile projects or opportunities, you can make leadership possibilities available to more women by eliminating impediments that otherwise keep women out of the running, such as exclusion from leadership positions and client relationships and the hidden bias inherent in evaluation and compensation systems. You can spearhead change efforts, although in most law firms you will be limited in what you can do on your own. You will need to join with allies and other leaders in the firm who share your commitment to change. Women's initiatives can also be instrumental in helping you to promote women and to create a better workplace for all lawyers.

§ 16:2 Reframe the conversation

Somewhere out there in this audience may even be someone who will one day follow my footsteps, and preside over the White House as the president's spouse. I wish him well!
—Barbara Bush

As a leader, you can help shape changes in attitudes, policies, and practices by reframing the discussion so that people think about leadership, work, and careers in new and different ways. Most law firm efforts to promote women's advancement try to help women fit into the current law firm model without changing the model, but it is the model that needs to change. Women need to understand the rules of the workplace, written and unwritten, to reach high positions; but women also need to rewrite the rules. Among other things, they need to create and legitimize more diverse concepts of career success and push firms to move away from hours-focused compensation. The recent recession has forced firms to question long-held assumptions, and some firms are beginning to try new approaches. These nascent developments are moving in the right direction and they need to be nourished and pressed forward.

One of the first things that must be done is to redefine mental models of leadership. Social and economic factors have started to change our definitions of good leadership. "Feminine" behaviors and skills that were previously unappreciated, such as building collaborative relationships and nurturing talent, are now being recognized as sources of strategic advantage. However, the change is not happening quickly enough in law firms. Current law firm leadership models remain rooted in masculine notions of how leaders look, act, and lead.

There are many ways that we can alter these images, beginning with the very words we use when discussing them. We can reprogram our thinking about leadership by consciously imagining women when we speak of leaders. Forty years ago, feminists attacked the way that people used pronouns, insisting that "he" be replaced by "he or she" "s/he," or some other term because using only masculine pronouns suggested women were irrelevant. As cumbersome as it often was for writers and speakers, stressing the importance of inclusion made a difference in the way people think about women. From then on, women could no longer be ignored in public discourse; they had to be acknowledged and included. In this book, all references to leaders are to women unless they are specifically designated as referring to male leaders. This presupposes a world where the term "woman leader" is redundant and the only time a gender qualifier for "leader" is needed is when the sex of the individual is relevant to the discussion.

We need to envision successful leaders as more diverse in all respects. With a new, more open mindset, the measure of a leader's style will be effectiveness, not whether it is feminine or masculine. Devaluing labels will be eliminated. Lawyers who work reduced hours will be described as lawyers, period, without the part-time marker. When diverse leadership styles are expected, not just tolerated, all lawyers will benefit. In that sense, deconstructing stereotypes and biases is a creative process. By liberating leaders from preconceived gender roles and behaviors, women and men will begin to see new solutions and try new approaches. By focusing on more objective and relevant characteristics the range of accepted behaviors will expand for everyone.

Reframing the norms regarding lawyers' career paths is also

necessary. Career paths that follow anything other than a full-time, uninterrupted, upward track are now spoken of as "alternatives." By being labeled this way, anyone who does not fit the norm is implicitly abnormal—with all the negative connotations of that word. We need to change our expectations of what constitutes a normal career path to account for women's nonlinear life experience. Instead of envisioning a straight line, we can redefine a normal career path as one that is continuous but has periodic detours, bumps, and dips.

Women leaders must also urge women lawyers to reframe their attitudes toward leadership. Women need to think positively about their aspirations and abilities to become law firm leaders. As a leader yourself, you can promote a more upbeat mindset by emphasizing why law firm leadership and power are worthy, desirable, and attainable goals for women. Throughout this book there are references to the negative self-talk that women often engage in: *I cannot be a rainmaker; I cannot be a leader and a mother; I cannot ask for more than they give me.* This negative state of mind should be reframed to stress the positives: *I can be a rainmaker by . . ., I can be a leader and a mother if . . ., I can ask for more because I deserve more.* Instead of accepting timidity, women should reimagine themselves as powerful and view power as exhilarating, liberating, and a positive force that allows them to craft their lives and careers in the way that they choose. Whether they want to better their financial status or make a positive difference in the firm, personal power is what gives them the voice, platform, and influence to make it happen.

Changing the language and metaphors used to discuss women, leadership, and career success is integral to the reframing process. The power of metaphor can be seen in companies that are successfully devising new approaches to professionals' work and careers. When an image changes shape in our minds, we can take an entirely new approach to the issue. Historically, the most common metaphor for career paths has been a ladder: it is linear, and you can climb up, step down, or fall off. Consulting giant Deloitte has reformulated the image to that of a career lattice in which people may move up, down, diagonally or laterally from time to time without having to drop off. Deloitte has done this by implementing and publicizing a career customization program which affords flexibility in professionals' schedule, workload, level of responsibility, and pace of career progression.[1]

The outdated paradigm of the ideal worker as the only legitimate career model for lawyers is finally starting to budge, in large part because the labels for the underlying issues have started to change. For years, women have been arguing that this model places unfair burdens on women and prevents many capable and motivated women from succeeding because it forces them to choose between work and family. Until recently law firms trivialized work-life conflicts and discounted their importance because they were thought to be of concern only to women, and, therefore, merely "women's issues." The perceptible shift in this area is occurring because "women's" issues are no longer limited to women; instead they have become business issues that affect the work and lives of all lawyers. Now that men increasingly demand more flexible schedules and career tracks, firms are starting to view the issues as universal concerns for men and women alike.

The Families and Work Institute has been studying national attitudes toward gender in the workforce for more than three decades. Their 2008 study[2] found that fathers now spend considerably more time and take more responsibility for child care and household work than at any time in the past. It has become far more socially acceptable for men not just to be more involved in child care, cooking, and cleaning, but to talk about it openly. As men do more at home, they are beginning to feel greater work-life conflict. Other research has found that Baby Boomer women and men share the work-life views and demands of GenYs regarding workplace flexibility, indicating that the change is even more widespread and stretches across generations.[3]

Issues that were once marginalized as women's issues are now gaining traction because their wider importance is becoming acknowledged. While women's responsibilities for childbearing and caregiving make their need more apparent and intense, men today want the same flexibility and support. In response, many firms are adopting policies that provide greater flexibility, such

---

[Section 16:2]

[1]Benko, C., & Weisberg, A. (2007), *Mass career customization: aligning the workplace with today's nontraditional workforce* (Boston: Harvard Business School Press).

[2]Galinsky, E., Aumann, K., & Bond, J. (2009), *Times are changing: gender and generation at work and at home*, Families and Work Institute.

[3]Hewlett, S.A., Sherbin, L., & Sumberg, K. (July/Aug. 2009), *How GenY and Boomers will reshape your agenda*, Harvard Business Review, 121–126.

as reduced hours, telecommuting, extended leaves, and gradual return to work following parenting leave. As a leader, you can take steps to keep the momentum going generally and to start these changes in your firm if they have not yet been introduced there.

§ 16:3 Advocate for women

There is a special place in hell reserved for women who don't help other women.

— Madeleine Albright

Given the absence of women from law firm leadership, it is imperative that women leaders act as advocates, mentors, and champions for other women both personally and through the policies and actions they undertake on behalf of the firm. While there have been incremental improvements over the last three decades, the fundamental institutional and cultural barriers to women's leadership remain entrenched. There is no reason to be optimistic that the people running the vast majority of law firms today will take the initiative to make the necessary changes. For years, they have known the data, business case, and best practices for retaining and advancing women. They have also known the high cost of losing talented women and the clamor of clients for greater diversity. Yet none of these things has ignited the sense of urgency necessary for serious change to take place.

We are beyond the point of waiting for law firms to change. Meaningful progress will occur only when women demand it and lead it. Until women recognize and assert the power which they possess, there will be nothing but modest, ineffectual change. Women will continue to be perceived as less qualified and motivated than men for leadership, and existing law firm culture, policies, and practices will continue to deny women leadership success. Making fundamental changes to perceptions, business models, and institutionalized bias will require steady, unwavering pressure by large numbers of women. Women who are successful and powerful need to make their own voices heard and also support and protect the women whose careers are too young or vulnerable to take the lead. Women leaders should act without hesitation, asking for forgiveness if necessary but not for permission.

The more women who attain leadership, the more women are likely to follow them there. We know that women who work in organizations with higher numbers of women at the top are better paid and more likely to reach leadership positions.[1] This happens when firms have favorable cultures and practices; women are able to reach high positions and then help the women beneath them rise up the leadership ranks. The very presence of a significant number of women leaders in powerful law firm positions positively affects the conditions that younger women need to succeed.[2] Women in law firms with higher proportions of women leaders have more role models and female mentors and are able to develop professional identities and styles that are authentic for them and not mired in or hindered by gender stereotypes.

Many women lawyers focus on individual strategies for advancement. It is their own career advancement, not advancing women as a group, that drives them to succeed. They concentrate on increasing their book of business for their own financial security not the financial benefit of the firm. This attitude makes sense for a young woman on the way up, and as a leader, you should make it a point to help each woman achieve her goals, but a leader must also take a broader view. Leaders have to place the good of the firm at the forefront of their minds and actions. The ability of your firm to compete, succeed, and endure makes it imperative that all women who come there find the inspiration, encouragement, and support they need to become the best possible lawyers, partners, and leaders. The effort may depend on individuals but the environment must welcome and support all women. A leader in Washington, D.C. who sits on the executive committee of her international firm explained how senior women view their obligation to other women in her firm: *"Senior women need to share with younger women and support them even though we would prefer to just do our work and go home. Women need recognition, support, pats on the back, especially as you get more senior, because you hear that less and less, so we try to let other women know that we recognize them and give them verbal rewards. We try to build their confidence."*

There are countless ways that you can personally advocate for and support women in your everyday interactions, e.g., inviting a woman to join you for a business development event, sponsoring her for a leadership position, introducing her to an influential partner in another office as someone he or she "should know," or

---

[Section 16:3]

[1]Bell, L.A. (July 2005), Women-led firms and the gender gap in top executive jobs, *IZA Discussion Paper No. 1689.*

[2]Ely, R.J., & Rhode, D.L. (2010), Women and leadership: defining the challenges, in N. Nohria and R. Khurana (Eds.), *Handbook of leadership theory and practice* (Boston: Harvard Business School Press), ch. 14.

writing a note to the compensation committee praising the work she did for a client or for you. Small gestures can make a big difference. Recall that in the case study of Amy Schulman and Heidi Levine, Heidi said that when she was an associate, Amy never introduced her to clients as an associate but rather as "my colleague." It did not change the fact that she was junior to the partner, but psychologically, it made a big impact on her. Clients thought of her as a lawyer first, not an associate. The lack of status distinctions also made Heidi feel more confident and empowered her to take more initiative on client teams than she might have done otherwise.

Advocating for women gives your firm a competitive edge. By empowering all women in the firm to see themselves as potential leaders you expand the number and diversity of firm leaders and rainmakers. As a woman leader, you can recognize and promote new approaches to leadership and business development that men might not appreciate. You can watch out and advocate for women who have strengths that other partners might overlook, such as a woman who is highly regarded by her clients but is not widely known because she is a single mother and does not participate in firm social events. You can endorse innovative business development activities that are more enjoyable and feasible for many women than conventional approaches like sporting events and golf dates.

In business development especially, the results are what should count. When leaders acknowledge that new and different business development approaches are legitimate and effective, women feel free to develop their own unique styles. If women generate business in nontraditional ways, the new approaches become accepted and eventually, mainstream. Women can become better positioned to bring in business as their skills develop, their networks expand, and their confidence grows. When young women see that women with varied styles, personalities, and family situations can and do succeed in their firm, being a leader there seems more desirable, and as more women become rainmakers, the potential power of all women increases.

One example of a woman-oriented approach to networking and business development is Mother Attorneys Mentoring Association of Seattle (MAMAS). MAMAS is a group of lawyers who are also mothers. Its purpose is to "empower attorney mothers and encourage them to succeed while celebrating their roles as attorneys and mothers."[3] Members come from all sectors of the legal profession; they socialize, network, share experiences, learn from, and refer business to each other—and they bring their kids along. Begun in Seattle in 2006, MAMAS has expanded to several other cities. This is not the type of activity that most male lawyers would consider a source of business and career enhancement but it works for the women who participate.

Another way that leaders can support women is by monitoring and remedying situations where bias might be interfering with women's advancement. One leader who works in firm management full-time uses her position as a member of her firm's management committee to ensure that women and minority lawyers are included in business opportunities. She is the management committee's liaison for business development programs, which include the women's initiative, diversity program, and the client transition process. In her role as liaison, she receives reports about all major new business proposals, and she always asks the initiating partners, "Who constitutes the team?" By simply asking that question and discussing the response, she is able to raise awareness about the need to include women and minorities on business development teams. Similarly, when senior partners are transitioning business to younger lawyers, she works with the transitioning partners to identify and select candidates. This gives her power to influence what senior partners think, how the process works, and who is selected to take over client relationships.

Your advocacy efforts as a leader will depend on the status of your firm and the conditions for women there. Your personal priorities and the political climate in the firm will also influence where you expend your energy and exert your power. There may be a general consensus among the women in your firm about the particular issues that should be on your agenda, but unanimity is unlikely, and there may, in fact, be serious disagreements. Make it a point to understand the issues that unite and divide different groups of women in the firm so that you can maneuver adroitly and try to resolve the conflicts.

The status of women in the firm may have an impact on the priorities that you set. If women are becoming partners and leaders in higher numbers every year, then you may be ahead of the game and should expand and build on current successes. However, a firm with few or declining numbers of women partners and leaders may need to implement a comprehensive

---

[3]http://www.mamaseattle.org.

strategy to create a more hospitable workplace for women. Regardless of the firm, one area that should be a priority for all leaders is eliminating all forms of bias from your firm. Few law firms today would argue against the necessity for greater diversity, and none can accept a workplace where discrimination is accepted.

§ 16:4 Make elimination of bias a priority

One of the difficulties in dealing with bias today is that most of the time it is invisible. Most lawyers do not discriminate deliberately or maliciously; in fact, they may not even realize that they do it. Moreover, gender bias is not necessarily *against* women; it is frequently preferential, i.e., favoring men. This means that while women are not purposely denied work, business, and mentoring, they enjoy fewer opportunities for them when partners tend to favor interacting with men. As a leader, it is up to you to bring hidden biases into the open so that they can be rooted out and eliminated. Some law firms have made considerable progress, and many women now report that they have not experienced bias at work and do not feel disadvantaged because of their gender. But gender bias still exerts a powerful force that adversely impacts most women in some way, and leaders must be prepared to deal with it when they see it in their firm.

Your first target should be to eliminate the stereotype of women as powerless and the management systems that would keep them that way. Eradicating gender bias from your law firm requires attacking on two fronts: the institutional bias inherent in systems and processes that govern work and career advancement, and the everyday encounters where comments and behaviors reflect stereotyping and bias. At the institutional level, flawed or absent systems and processes can unwittingly allow bias to flourish. Table 16.1 lists several law firm systems that should be examined for bias.

One area where subtle bias is pervasive is performance evaluation systems. Even systems that appear to be objective may harbor hidden biases that result in women receiving lower scores than their on-the-job performance would justify.[1] The cumulative effect of small amounts of gender bias can over time create significant disadvantages for women. When women get lower perfor-

---

[Section 16:4]

[1]ABA Commission on Women in the Profession (2008), *Fair measure: toward effective attorney evaluations* (2d Ed.), American Bar Association.

mance ratings, they receive lower quality work assignments, less client contact, and less mentoring. This translates into lower compensation and curtailed progress toward partnership. As a result, many women become discouraged and leave their firms.

Table 16.1: Systems to Examine for Evidence of Bias

- Recruitment and hiring
- Compensation systems
- Work assignments
- Performance evaluations
- Merit-based promotion systems
- Employment benefits (e.g., health care coverage for same-sex partners)
- Parenting policies (e.g., fairness to men and same-sex parents)
- Part-time and flexible work policies
- Client transitions
- Leadership succession

On a personal level, leaders can exert influence to tackle the unconscious bias they encounter in their daily interactions with co-workers. The way to address the demonstration of bias depends on the circumstances, including the people involved, where it takes place, the gravity of its impact, and what you feel comfortable doing and saying. Your approach should be situational because there are no hard and fast rules. For example, a common complaint is that men take credit for a woman's ideas and suggestions. If you see this happen to another woman, you might say to the man, "I'm so glad that you agree with the idea that Lisa presented a few minutes ago." One leader I interviewed said that she sees this occur so often that she amuses herself by turning it into a game: *"I call it silly male tricks. I try to find silly female tricks to combat them. For example, when a woman presents an idea and is ignored and a man who presents the same idea is considered brilliant, if I'm the senior woman lawyer in the room, I do what I can to empower the woman. I might say, 'Thanks, John, for repeating Mary's suggestion.'"*

Sometimes a man may take credit for your ideas. Your immediate impulse might be to confront him and claim the credit that you are due. However, as a leader, this might not be the optimum approach. It may be better for you to stay in the background or allow the idea to be attributed to someone else. If your objective is to promote acceptance of the idea, getting personal credit may not really matter as much as winning support. In this scenario, a better tactic might be to build on what the man has now set forth as his idea: "I'm so glad to hear that suggestion, Tom. Let's take it further. Here's what the next step should be."

As a leader, you need to be versatile, with a broad spectrum of techniques to combat gender bias when you see it occur. You want to preserve your credibility and command of situations even as you are trying to change prevailing assumptions and expectations. Here are some points to keep in mind:

- Assume that the person does not intend to be biased or unfair. Do not assume gender bias when the person may simply be ignorant or rude. Unfortunately, there are many clueless lawyers. They treat everyone badly, not just women. In what other profession could a defendant law firm win a case brought by a black associate alleging racial discrimination with the argument that they treat all associates badly, not just minorities?[2]
- Call them on it directly. If a person's conduct suggests deliberate bias, call them on it. Cite what you observe, explain the bias, and further explain why it is unacceptable and harmful. Do not worry about being too outspoken. You must call attention to it even at the risk of being seen as "overly sensitive" or as if you are the problem. For example, one woman had to correct her managing partner's sarcastic reference to maternity leave as a "pregnancy vacation." If the bias you observe is inadvertent or the speaker's purpose is benign, it still needs to be addressed, but you can acknowledge the speaker's innocent intent.
- Use humor to make a point. Humor can be a very effective way to counter bias or make a point about it without coming across as overbearing. If you are comfortable using humor, you can kid someone and point out that a comment was inappropriate. Be careful not to be sarcastic; a little lighthearted embarrassment can be effective, but humiliating someone can cause anger and backlash.
- Investigate. If you see a pattern that may reflect gender bias, investigate and gather facts to support your suspicions. For instance, to see whether bias may be affecting women's compensation, one leader suggested reviewing the percentage of women at the top and bottom of the compensation levels every year. You want to examine the entire distribution of partners, not just averages, to look for any patterns that suggest bias in the system.

---

[2]Barrett, P.M. (2000), *The good black* (New York: Plume).

- <u>Counteract bias preventively</u>. Prepare less experienced women to recognize and handle situations where they might encounter bias. Consider whether you can do anything to preempt foreseeable problems. For instance, a relationship partner knew that a client was difficult to deal with and was sometimes especially hard on women. When a new woman partner joined the client team, the relationship partner emailed the client in advance, introducing and praising this new team member. It created a good impression on the client and eased the woman's way into the team.
- <u>Reframe the situation and turn it around</u>. When someone makes a blatantly stereotypical statement, hold up a mirror to show them their bias: "Just last week, before you knew she was pregnant, you told me how brilliant she is. Are you suggesting that her pregnancy has destroyed her ability to think?"
- <u>Describe women using business terms.</u> When describing a woman lawyer, do not use language that reinforces feminine stereotypes. A woman may be a lovely person and enjoyable to work with, but emphasize her business and professional traits: refer to her as an effective negotiator, winning trial lawyer, highly respected leader, or tough-minded risk-taker.
- <u>Be aware of your own stereotypical thinking</u>. Although many women lawyers recognize the influence of gender stereotypes in men, they often fail to see the extent to which they hold similar beliefs about women, including themselves.

§ 16:5 Develop future leaders—especially women

Be the change you wish to see in the world.
—Gandhi

One of the key characteristics and responsibilities of successful leaders is a commitment to help the people in their firms succeed. Leaders must cultivate the potential of other lawyers to ensure that the firm has the legal talent necessary to carry out its work now and in the future. To do that, you have to be able to recruit, develop, and inspire a diverse group of highly talented professionals and give them support, interesting work, and opportunities to flourish. From that group of outstanding lawyers, you must also develop the firm's future leaders. This involves recognizing and helping others see their leadership potential, encouraging them to take steps to pursue it, and creating opportunities for them to express it. Determining the kind of talent your firm needs today and in the future is challenge enough; finding ways to attract, engage, and retain the people you need is even harder. Law firms have been remarkably unsuccessful in doing this, especially when it comes to women. Firms' failure to embrace diverse populations and create inclusive cultures has led to a persistent shortage of women partners and leaders.

In a highly competitive, constantly changing marketplace, talented and high performing lawyers are a law firm's chief source of competitive advantage. Increasing the number of women leaders is especially important because research shows that companies that consistently promote women to positions of power and leadership have greater financial success across a variety of measures.[1] A leader who can engage smart lawyers, keep them motivated, and command their loyalty and respect when they could choose to go elsewhere should be highly prized by law firms—but rarely is. Most law firms venerate rainmakers instead. In their book, *Aligning the Stars*, authors Jay Lorsch and Thomas Tierney stress that "over time starmaking is more important than rainmaking and that, in fact, the latter is entirely dependent on the former."[2] What they mean by starmaking is the firm's ability to attract, develop, and keep the lawyers who build enduring client relationships, consistently perform to their highest potential, put the firm first, and implement its strategic imperatives. These are the people others emulate and follow; they are the lawyers who will lead the firm in the future. Since women make up half of all of the new lawyers every year, starmakers who can inspire women to become leaders are indeed law firm treasures.

§ 16:6 Promote succession planning

Firms have many ways to identify and influence the selection and grooming of future leaders. The most important mechanism is a succession planning process that sets out leadership needs, competencies, and criteria, and uses them to identify and groom the best qualified people. Succession planning can help a firm recruit and prepare the next generation so that when a current leader retires, steps down, or leaves (especially if the withdrawal is unexpected), there is a smooth and seamless transition to new leadership. When new leaders can step right in, disruption is minimized, lawyers' performance and morale remain high, and

---

[Section 16:5]

[1]Harrington, B., & Ladge, J.L. (2009), Got talent? It isn't hard to find, *The Shriver Report*, http://www.awomansnation.com/business.php.

[2]Lorsch, J.W., & Tierney, T.J. (2002), *Aligning the stars* (Boston: Harvard Business School Press), 77.

clients remain confident about the firm's services, governance, and continuity.

Formal succession plans identify current and future leadership needs, as well as assess lawyers' probable ability to address those leadership needs. Succession planning involves:

- Articulating the core competencies necessary to be an effective leader in your firm,
- Identifying lawyers who
  - Possess these competencies,
  - Have demonstrated leadership attributes in their past performance, and
  - Are motivated to lead,
- Providing the training, mentoring, coaching, and experience needed to turn partners into top-notch law firm leaders.

Systematic succession planning is especially important for women lawyers, but few law firms do it. If designed properly, succession planning increases the selection and development opportunities for highly qualified women leaders who might otherwise go unnoticed. Without succession planning, leadership appointments tend to be subjective and political. Because women are not automatically perceived as leaders the way that men are, nor are they as well connected in the firm power structure, this hurts women's chances to become leaders. If your firm does not have a process in place to plan for leadership succession you can urge the firm to initiate one. Table 16.2 lists some of the questions to address as you get started.

The criteria you use to determine attributes, competencies, potential, and readiness for promotion to leadership must be based on objective factors. Otherwise, gender bias about performance and leadership potential can creep into the system. It is important to monitor how the criteria are applied and the overall selection process to ward off any inadvertent or unconscious bias in the execution of a succession plan.

In developing criteria, do not focus entirely on the competencies of leadership today. As markets expand and shift, client expectations change, and technology transforms the practice of law, consider the competencies that partners will need to adapt, innovate and lead your firm in the future.

If your firm resists having a leadership succession plan, you can still find ways to develop new leaders by cultivating and mentoring lawyers who show promise as leaders, using your authority to appoint people to committees and leadership posts, and allocating rewards and resources to encourage leadership conduct. These processes are more subjective than using leadership competencies and criteria, but as a conscientious leader, you can try to make them as fair and unbiased as possible. You should foster leadership talent in any lawyer who demonstrates it, not just in women, but you should make sure that women are among those who are tapped.

Table 16.2. Questions to consider when starting a succession planning process

- When and in what areas or positions will the firm need new leaders?
- How will we identify leadership talent and potential?
- What knowledge, experience, skills, and personal attributes will leaders need to have in order to fulfill the firm's long-term strategy?
- What foreseeable future challenges will leaders have to deal with?
- How should our leaders reinforce the firm's brand internally and publicly?
- How will we explain and communicate our expectations to leaders?
- How will we develop leaders among the people we have in the firm?
- How will we ensure that new leaders have appropriate role models and mentors?
- How will we ensure that the process of leadership selection and preparation is fair and inclusive?
- What resources and how much money are we prepared to invest in the people who show leadership potential?
- What incentives will we provide for possible leaders?
- What factors will impact the success and failure of our efforts?

---

§ 16:7 Identify and nurture leaders

There is nothing in a caterpillar that tells you it's going to be a butterfly.

— R. Buckminster Fuller

Law firms are filled with lawyers who possess diverse skills and talents, many of which could make them good leaders. Always be watchful for those who seem to be drawn to leadership and perform effectively in the role. Some lawyers are recognized as leadership material through formal assessments and evaluations or on the basis of past performance. Keep your eyes open for a lawyer who consistently exhibits the drive and behavior that suggest that she could become a leader, such as taking initiative, questioning the status quo, or going beyond what is explicitly asked or expected of her. Additionally, look for lawyers who are highly admired by clients, whether through their ability to bring in new clients or the strength of their ongoing relationships with their own and other partners' clients. Nurture lawyers who demonstrate those qualities and encourage them to fulfill their leadership potential. Point out or assign them experiences that will help prepare them for ever higher levels of leadership and suggest that they be proactive about seeking other new positions and responsibilities.

When assessing a lawyer's potential for leadership, watch the way that she functions and interacts with others, how she operates under stress, and the way she handles crises. Most lawyers can quickly learn the content needed for leadership roles; what matters more is how they will deal with the many different challenges that come up in the job. A lawyer may be brilliant and effective for her clients but when in charge of committees, projects, or teams, she turns people off, gets lost in details, avoids dealing with unpleasant staff issues, or manages her teams very poorly. Her leadership potential is less than the lawyer who is able to create and sustain a common sense of purpose in her teams, communicates well, deals promptly with conflicts and underperformance issues, runs meetings efficiently, and creates a sense that everyone on the team matters.

Additionally, because someone has the talent and ability to be a leader does not mean that they want to be or even realize that they could be. Part of starmaking is being able to recognize latent leadership attributes in lawyers and inspire those lawyers to become leaders. In particular, watch for women of color, single mothers, and other lawyers who face extra obstacles that may make them less apparent as future leaders. A leader once told me that she seeks the "hidden talent" in lawyers. She finds many lawyers who have smart, practical ideas and are capable of taking on more "starring" roles but who have traditionally kept a lower profile. She helps them bring their ideas forward and put them into effect and makes sure that they receive recognition and credit for it.

When you identify someone who shows promise, let her know. Depending on whether or not she envisions herself as a leader, she may be excited or surprised by your observation. In either case, your encouragement can instill confidence and optimism in her, inspiring a vision of her future as a leader where she might not otherwise see it. You can have a great deal of influence when you take an interest in a potential leader's career, help her understand why leadership is worth pursuing, and serve as a mentor. You might suggest activities that will enhance her practice, expand her leadership skills, give her greater visibility, improve her business development efforts, or take any steps that will increase her prospects for leadership. Preparing lawyers for leadership in this way is particularly significant for women because they are mentored and groomed far less often than men are.

Letting someone know that you are priming her for leadership can be enormously empowering. A partner currently in the London office of a global firm had that experience. She had spent her first four years of practice in another firm where no women were in leadership, very few were partners, and women were constantly being passed over for good work. When she decided to leave, she looked carefully at the culture of the firms where she interviewed. She chose her present firm because during her interviews she learned that they were looking for senior associates to prepare for leadership. They gave her a clear message that *"they were willing to consider me as an individual"* and that they would not hold her back in any way because she was a woman. When she arrived, they were true to their word. *"Two senior partners in the department guided me. They explained the politics of the organization. They were completely open. When I asked why they were doing these things, they said they wanted me to be a bridge between partners and associates, so they were priming me to be able to do it. When a male associate came to the firm a few months later, they treated us absolutely equally. They said they would treat us the same, and they did. They invited us to partner meetings. We attended and participated in the meetings as associates. We learned how the firm worked, why they decided what they did . . . We both became partners at the same time."* She is now the relationship partner for one of the firm's major clients.

Prepare future leaders. Once leaders are identified, you need to help them develop the competencies they need to be successful in the job and acquire the experience that will let them put their abilities to good use. Developing talent is more important in a law firm than in a corporate setting because the quality of its lawyers is so fundamental to the firm's ability to succeed and endure. At the leadership level, talent development is essential.

As discussed in Chapter 7, few lawyers who are asked to be firm leaders have the preparatory training or experience for the job. Even if they manage their client teams well, the skills, temperament, and competencies to lead a major unit of the firm or the firm as a whole are more complex and often require a dif-

ferent way of looking at leadership. Finding ways to develop and
enhance lawyers' leadership attributes is critical because you
cannot afford to have future leaders who are not fully up to the
task of leading the firm. Many larger law firms now have leadership development initiatives to prepare emerging law firm leaders, but even small firms can employ methods like stretch assignments, action learning, formal training, mentoring, coaching, and
other leadership development techniques to prepare their future
leaders.

Delegate. Chapter 12 discussed the importance of delegating
work to others in order to keep your own time and work under
control. Delegation is also a practical way to empower potential
leaders. When leaders empower people, they inspire them to exert their best efforts toward a coherent purpose. Leaders derive
significant benefits from delegation because it enables them to
leverage the talent of others in the firm. Leaders cannot do
everything or respond to everyone's needs and problems. They
have to believe that they can rely on others around them. When
you give others a chance to show leadership you increase their
confidence and enhance their credentials. When they produce
good results, the confidence that you show in them spreads to
others in the firm. You and your leadership team can accomplish
far more than you could ever do alone. On the other hand, if you
do not empower others to act or if you focus on others' inadequacies as a reason not to delegate, you undermine people's
confidence and weaken the group.

Leaders can make others feel confident about their own leadership abilities by presenting them with challenges and relying on
them to do a good job. You can ask associates who demonstrate a
knack for leadership to join high profile committees or take
responsibility for portions of major firm projects. You can ask
partners to spearhead new initiatives, shepherd the planning or
implementation of high visibility projects, lead key firm committees, or represent the firm in public arenas. These are not everyday tasks; rather, they put individuals in the spotlight and let
them run the show. You give them the authority to act and make
decisions and expect them to take responsibility for the results. If
you stay in the picture at all, it is only to offer guidance, feedback,
and support along the way.

When people know that you are giving them an extraordinary
assignment and trust them to take charge of it, they usually
want to perform up to your expectations and prove that you were
correct to place your trust in them. When they perform well, it
builds their confidence, and for individuals who may have been
undecided about leadership, it may entice them to seek more. Of

course, it may prove that they are not cut out for leadership which is also an important lesson.

As a leader, you often have to rely on partners who hold other leadership positions to carry out certain responsibilities. Sometimes you may believe a partner is not up to the task. You need to find a way to balance your desire and duty to make sure that the work is done right with the partner's need for autonomy. You have to walk a fine line between coaching and interfering. The managing partner of an intellectual property firm described how she handled this kind of dilemma:

Many of our lawyers are also scientists and engineers. It is hard to find partners who have the people skills required and the interest to be practice group leaders . . . I try to find a balance between giving them feedback, guidance, and support and trying not to tell them what to do. For example, a midlevel associate was not working out and the practice group finally decided to let him go. I asked the practice group leader how he planned to tell him. He said that three partners were going to take the associate to lunch and tell him in the restaurant. I asked him to consider what issues that plan might pose, how the associate might react, other ways they might approach the associate with this message, etc. I coached him to consider a different way.

Give supportive feedback. Sometimes emerging leaders are a little rough around the edges. They may need to develop or hone certain leadership skills, change some ungainly habits, or exhibit different behaviors. By talking with them about their performance, leaders can give them feedback based on what they observe, make them aware of their deficiencies, and offer suggestions for improvement.

Good leaders know how to deliver feedback so that it has a positive impact with a minimum of discomfort for themselves and the aspiring leader. Positive feedback is especially valuable for emerging leaders who may feel insecure. It is empowering for them to know not just that they did well but that you noticed and approved. When you deliver your message generalized praise is not sufficient. The most important point is to deliver a clear, constructive, and action-oriented feedback message. Be sure to highlight specific actions, behaviors, or work product and point out why they are valued. Suppose that you just left a contentious meeting with a client where you thought a partner handled the situation very well. You might say something like this: "The way you handled the client's outburst at the meeting was very effective. By staying calm and letting him vent before you explained your reasoning, you showed him that you were listening and taking his fears seriously. Then you explained that what you were proposing took those fears into account. Did you notice how he relaxed after that and became more willing to hear you out?"

Appoint women to leadership roles. When you have the authority to make appointments to committees or leadership positions it gives you extensive power over current and future firm leadership. You are able to appoint lawyers whom you trust and upon whom you can rely, who are capable and share your commitment to the firm and the issues at hand. In addition, you can ensure that women are appointed to significant positions. Making strategic appointments also expands your span of influence. Your decisions give the people you appoint the opportunity to become more prominent and influential, to pursue an issue they care about, or to serve in springboard positions where they will become ready for higher leadership posts. Lawyers who appreciate the chances that you give them will be grateful to you for your confidence in them. However, some lawyers may at first decline your offer. If you persuade them to do it anyway, in order to hone their leadership skills, further their career, and help the firm, they may find that leadership suits them just fine. If they do well, you will add one more recruit to the firm's leadership talent pool. Those who decide not to do it will still be flattered that you asked.

Reward leadership behavior. A law firm's reward system has tremendous influence over partners' behavior. In order to be effective, the reward system must identify the behaviors desired in leaders and reward them. The way that you allocate the rewards that you control can improve the firm's ability to recruit and inspire future leaders. The most critical part of any reward system is compensation. Depending upon your position, you may have some input into determining a partner's compensation, but most leaders have little individual ability to control compensation processes or decisions. What you can control are sought-after, nonmonetary rewards and distinctions such as client and business opportunities, speaking engagements, high visibility special projects, and public accolades. These acknowledgments can have a powerful impact on lawyers' careers, especially if they are trying to build their practices or their credentials as leaders. In using these rewards to highlight the leadership of women in your firm you can increase the chances that women will have opportunities to prove themselves and enhance their reputation as leaders.

Support leadership by allocating resources. You can encourage leadership behaviors by distributing or withholding the resources you control, such as staff, marketing budgets, or technology. You can choose to give staffing priority to a partner who promotes learning, efficiency, and loyalty in her teams. Alternatively, you can refuse staffing requests from autocratic partners who mistreat the people on their teams or who consistently omit women from business opportunities. In doing this, it is a good idea to let the autocratic partner know why you are doing it and to offer coaching or other assistance to help that partner improve. The idea is not to be punitive (unless the partner has been warned repeatedly), but to identify and support positive leadership conduct.

§ 16:8   Be a mentor to women and men

The greatest good you can do for another is not just share your riches, but reveal to them their own.
— Benjamin Disraeli

By serving as a mentor, you can be highly influential in helping women realize the power that they possess and acquire the confidence to use it. Mentoring is a highly effective vehicle for career advancement and all leaders should be mentors to women and men in their firm. As discussed in Chapter 12, having a mentor is especially important for women who aspire to leadership. In addition to promoting women's professional and business development mentors can help women identify their aspirations and support them as they try to realize their goals.

It is also important for women leaders to mentor men. Increasing men's awareness of gender issues and making them comfortable with strong women in leadership roles is an important way to engage men in efforts to promote gender equity in the law firm. A 2009 Catalyst study showed that men who had women mentors were more aware of gender bias than men who did not.[1] The study concluded that respected women play an important role in educating men about gender bias by supporting these men while at the same time challenging them to think more critically about gender relations in the workplace. For the same reason, women leaders should encourage their male colleagues to mentor promising women. In addition to providing invaluable and needed support to young women leaders, the men who are leading your firm need to learn women's perspectives about work and careers in order to be effective leaders.

Unfortunately, many junior women neglect to take advantage

[Section 16:8]

[1]Prime, J., & Moss-Racusin, C.A. (2009), *Engaging men in gender initiatives: what change agents need to know*, Catalyst.

of the mentors available to them. In some cases, they are intimidated about approaching women leaders even when they are specifically invited to do so. They worry about imposing on the leaders' time or bringing up concerns that leaders might see as trivial. This underscores the need for women leaders to reach out to junior women, either to be their mentor or to encourage them to seek others.

§ 16:9   Use women's initiatives to advance women and promote change

Women's initiatives are important mechanisms for advancing women's interests in the firm. When strategically focused, well designed, and carefully executed, women's initiatives have been shown to produce tangible, measurable benefits not just for women but for the entire firm.[1] Simple forms of women's initiatives existed in law firms more than 30 years ago. Women started them originally for mutual support when they were a distinct minority in their firms. The women in an office would meet from time to time to discuss their experiences, voice their frustrations, and share strategies and techniques to overcome feelings of isolation or exclusion. They occasionally held educational or social events to which women clients and prospective clients were invited. Women helped each other and promoted their mutual interests by campaigning for maternity, part-time, and other family-friendly policies. Today women's initiatives have grown into elaborate programs primarily oriented toward business development and other matters of strategic importance for women's careers. In a 2008 survey by the National Association of Women Lawyers, virtually all participating law firms reported having a women's initiative.[2]

Women's initiatives are valuable to women in many ways:

- They can help women learn business development, leadership, and other skills.
- They create a sense of community, belonging, and mutual support that make women feel connected to each other and to the firm.

[Section 16:9]

[1]The Women's Initiative [WIN] of Deloitte LLP (2009), *Talented. Empowered. Leaders. We are the women of Deloitte*; For an example of one law firm's experience, see Rimer, K., & McNair, C. (Sept.-Nov. 2009), Setting the standard, *Women Legal Magazine*.

[2]The National Association of Women Lawyers [NAWL] (Nov. 2008), *Report of the third annual national survey on retention and promotion of women in law firms*.

- They provide a platform and support network for women to showcase their leadership abilities and increase their sphere of influence.
- They can be a source of mentors and role models who exemplify and validate the rewards of partnership and leadership in the firm.
- They help women overcome a sense of isolation and reassure them that their concerns are legitimate.

Most importantly, women's initiatives can lead to cultural and institutional changes that make the work environment more conducive to the success of women lawyers.

The subjects and activities that come within the purview of women's initiatives vary from firm to firm. Most women's initiatives focus on giving women the tools they need to succeed in a professional world run by and for men. These initiatives typically concentrate on training and coaching women in business development. They spend at least some time on increasing women's individual networking and rainmaking abilities so that more women can become rainmakers and earn the clout that comes with a book of business. They also host periodic women-oriented educational programs, retreats, or social events. They sponsor programs directed at helping women develop confidence, business networks, and support. Some women's initiatives are adding leadership development programs for women as well. All of these features are extremely valuable—so long as they are seen as building on women's strengths, not curing deficiencies.

A smaller number of women's initiatives are comprehensive efforts to eliminate the institutional barriers to women's advancement, yet these initiatives have far more significant impact because they go the heart of the problem. After all, so long as law firm systems, culture, and biases remain unchanged, it will be hard for women to become rainmakers and leaders regardless of their widespread contacts and polished business development skills. Instead of ascending to positions of power in the firm, women will continue to leave law firms and go where they can express their talents in a more appreciative environment.

Comprehensive women's initiatives provide women with necessary business tools and also undertake systemic change. The overarching goal of these initiatives is to transform the firm so that women will be able to advance more readily and fairly to positions of power and leadership. They may also feature business development programming, but rather than focus exclusively on strategies that strengthen women individually, they undertake activities that will benefit everyone by changing institutional norms and practices. Some of these activities include:

- Benchmarking the progress of women into partnership and leadership,
- Lobbying for policy changes,
- Educating everyone about gender bias,
- Supporting greater flexibility in work arrangements,
- Ensuring fairness and transparency in the firm's work allocation, evaluation, and compensation systems,
- Monitoring women's access to career-enhancing work, clients, and business opportunities,
- Developing new approaches to how client work is done and rewarded,
- Pressing for the election of women to significant leadership positions.

Women's initiatives usually start with great fanfare, but unfortunately, many of them fizzle out after a while. There are many reasons for the demise, e.g., enthusiasm wanes, new leaders do not step up, or members disagree over the initiative's purpose and goals. However, some women's initiatives are fruitful, far-reaching, and sustainable. They flourish because they have seven key elements:

- A clearly articulated business purpose
- Well-defined objectives
- A coherent strategy for achieving their objectives
- Strong backing from firm leadership
- Active engagement from women at all experience levels
- Ongoing administrative and financial support
- Outcome measures

Asserting a strong and clear business case for a women's initiative and explaining what it hopes to accomplish makes it clear to everyone why the initiative is needed and how it will benefit the firm. The process of clarifying the initiative's purpose and setting objectives must be approached strategically. Women's initiatives often mistake events for strategy. A calendar of events is not the same as a strategic business plan. A women's initiative must have well-thought out and articulated goals that are explicitly aligned with the firm's overall business objectives. To develop those goals, it is important to assess existing obstacles and needs in order to determine which areas to address, the relative urgency of the problems identified, and the best ways to proceed. It must also have a coherent plan for achieving its objectives with a timeline and responsible individuals for every part of the plan.

Part of the women's initiative's planning strategy should

include securing support from women and men throughout the firm and especially from firm leaders. The clearest, most powerful show of support comes from making retention and advancement of women part of the firm's strategic plan. At the very least, strong, visible, and genuine leadership support is essential for a successful women's initiative. The people making the case to the firm should include influential men. They are the ones who will be able to convince other men to support the initiative. If they cannot or will not do it, then there may not be sufficient support in the firm for the initiative to have an impact. Because men represent the power structure, initiatives that lack support from at least some powerful male partners can produce only limited outcomes.

The Catalyst study *Engaging Men in Gender Initiatives* explored why some men support women in leadership roles and others do not. They found that men who do not support gender initiatives believe that women's gains will come at their expense.[3] Law firm compensation systems and cultures that incite competition among partners fortify this kind of zero-sum thinking and generate opposition to activities that might benefit women. However, many men realize that increasing the number of successful women partners and leaders can increase the overall success and profitability of the firm for all partners. These are the male leaders whose support you need to enlist, both for their individual contributions to the initiative, and for their ability to influence and turn around the zero-sum thinkers. At White & Case, a women's initiative was started and led by a male partner with three daughters who wanted to create a better workplace for women from which they could someday benefit. This generated national publicity for the firm and gave the initiative high visibility and importance internally.[4]

Women at all levels must be actively engaged in the initiative. Senior women must be ardently committed to the initiative's success to show younger women that they care and to give the effort legitimacy. Junior women have to be personally vested in the initiative's success because it is, after all, primarily for their benefit as they move toward partnership and leadership. A substantial number of women must be actively involved so there are sufficient workers and leaders to sustain the initiative and to achieve its goals over time. Widespread participation also ensures that the initiative addresses the needs of women in different practices, offices, and career stages.

---

[3]Prime & Moss-Racusin (2009), *Engaging men in gender initiatives.*

[4]Pulitzer, L., & Davis, W. (Feb. 2007), More than just talk, New York Law Journal Magazine.

Women's initiatives sometimes run into resistance, not just from men but also from women. Not all women support these initiatives, and some who do support them in theory do not want to lead them or get personally involved. There are many sources of friction:

- Some women worry that there will be a backlash to them personally and to women in general if they call attention to women's needs, concerns, or differences. One practice group leader and major rainmaker in a prominent New York firm said, *"I wouldn't touch women's issues. It's the kiss of death around here. I support them, but I won't be the leader."*

- Many women reject anything that singles women out or suggests that women need "special" or "different" treatment. They feel that it implies that women are less capable than men. Their attitude is, *"I want to be seen as a great lawyer, not as a great woman lawyer."*

- Some women want the initiative to emphasize work-life issues, and others emphatically do not.

- Women who have not had negative experiences due to gender bias contend that there is no need for such initiatives, that women's initiatives are for older women, or that they counter the goals of diversity and inclusion by dividing women and men. One office managing partner in Los Angeles who felt that way eventually changed her mind. She had been a skeptic most of her career and had never participated in women's activities. When she started to move up in firm leadership and heard that 100 women in her firm belonged to the women's affinity group, she learned more about it and became a supporter. *"I had underestimated how great it could be for so many things that would help women in the firm."*

As a leader, you should use your influence to generate support for the women's initiative from women throughout the firm. You should also be an avid supporter yourself, and if other women partners have reservations about the initiative, you should persuade them to back the effort. Without the vocal and visible support of senior women leaders, it is hard for other women in the firm to maintain enthusiasm for an initiative. Moreover, when senior women oppose the initiative or withhold their support, it creates chasms where women need bridges. Instead, urge all women to support the initiative so that women can use their collective power to give themselves tools for success and produce meaningful, lasting change for the good of the firm.

Women's initiatives are time and labor intensive, and they can be expensive as well. A meaningful initiative should have a healthy budget. In addition to providing the money and time required to enact its objectives, a hefty budget gives the initiative legitimacy and signals that the firm takes it seriously. Administrative support and engagement are required to keep the effort going without relying on a few women lawyers to do everything. Marketing support is also important to help promote the initiative to internal and external audiences.

To prove the value of the initiative and establish accountability, the vision and goals of the initiative should be stated in a way that allows success to be measured. Outcomes should be quantified to the extent possible. Partners individually and the firm as a whole should be evaluated on their efforts and held accountable for results. This can be done in many ways. Some firms incorporate initiative goals into business plans, then measure and publish results in annual reports. Others have outside advisory boards made up of clients, business, and civic leaders who monitor the initiative's progress.

§ 16:10 Creating an uplifting future

The future belongs to those who believe in the beauty of their dreams.

— Eleanor Roosevelt

Women have been a latent force in the legal profession for three decades, but women in leadership are still pioneers, blazing trails to a better future for all lawyers. For women who have been long-time advocates for change, the failure to make significant inroads at the top of the power structure is profoundly frustrating but there is finally some cause for optimism. Women are in a better position today than ever before. Although the percentages are small, thousands of women are law firm partners. They have a voice in their firms if they are willing to raise it. Today's younger women lawyers are more willing to talk about their career ambitions and feel less ambivalent about seeking and wielding authority. What all these women need is strong support, steady encouragement, and fair chances.

There are also many promising law firm trends: the collaborative leadership styles that women favor are gaining acceptance; traditional ideas about gender roles are giving way to more fluid and equitable views; gender bias is decreasing; and many firms are implementing flexible work arrangements and career tracks. Women leaders can do a great deal to keep the momentum for change moving forward in a positive direction. It is possible to envision an uplifting future where women who practice in law firms can achieve their leadership ambitions, lead meaningful personal lives, and fulfill their dreams of career success.

Olivier Marchal, managing director of Bain & Co. in France, once remarked, "In improving gender balance women may hold the keys, but men still control the locks." Women do indeed hold the keys to the future of law firms. If men fail to open the power structure fully to women, women must find another way in—or be willing to knock down the door. Either way, women must claim their rightful places as partners and leaders. They must be ready to challenge and change current models and norms to make them equitable and hospitable for women.

Smart men will open the door wide and welcome women into leadership. In terms of numbers and talent, most law firms cannot survive today without women. Women possess critical leadership skills and a diverse array of leadership styles that are vital for 21st century law firms. This will make women leaders even more essential to law firms in the years ahead.

But as long as doors to leadership remain locked, women must support each other in the struggle to break through and reach the top. As one leader exhorted, *"Women, we are in this together."* When women flex their collective muscles their power to bring about change will be awesome indeed.

Index